Accounting Standards... in brief

FIRST EDITION

Oppermann

Booysen

Oberholster

Binnekade

JUTA
AND COMPANY LTD

Accounting Standards… in brief

First edition 2008

© Juta & Company Ltd
PO Box 24309
Lansdowne 7779
Cape Town, South Africa

ISBN 978 0 7021 7699 9

Project manager: Seshni Moodley
Editor: Ian Parsons
Cover design: Eugene Badenhorst

Printed and bound in South Africa by Paarl Print

Accounting Standards... in brief

The first edition of *Accounting Standards... in brief* presents accounting standards and interpretations issued by the South African Institute of Chartered Accountants in a summarised format.

Incorporated into this text are the changes brought about by new accounting standards, issued as a consequence of the South African Institute of Chartered Accountants' Improvement of Accounting Standards Project.

This publication may be used in conjunction with the well-known and established question book, *Accounting Standards*.

Accounting Standards... in brief is intended to satisfy the specific requirements of learners not studying to become chartered accountants. Learners aiming to become chartered accountants are encouraged to use the original source text, namely the accounting standards and interpretations thereof.

Authors

C.S. BINNEKADE
MCom (Pret), CA (SA), Associate Professor, UNISA

S.F. BOOYSEN
DCom (Acc) (Pret), CA (SA)

S. GRIESEL
MCom (Acc) (RAU), CA (SA), Associate Professor, UNISA

M. HATTINGH
BCom (Hons) (Acc) (Pret), CA (SA), Senior Lecturer, UP

E. HUMAN
BCom (Law) (Pret), BCom (Hons) (KZN), CA (SA), Senior Lecturer, UJ

Z.R. KOPPESCHAAR
MCom (Acc) (Pret), CA (SA), Associate Professor, UNISA

S. LAMPRECHT
BCom (UFS), BAcc (Hons) (Stell), CA (SA), Senior Lecturer, US

K.B. LEITH
BAcc (Natal), CA (SA), Senior Lecturer, UP

J.G.I. OBERHOLSTER
MCom (RAU), CA (SA), Associate Professor, UP

H.R.B. OPPERMANN
BCom (Hons) (Acc) (Pret), CA (SA)

D. PRETORIUS
BCompt (Hons) (UNISA), CA (SA), Senior Lecturer, UNISA

E. RAUBENHEIMER
BCom (Hons) (Acc) (Pret), CA (SA), Senior Lecturer, UFS

J. ROSSOUW
MAcc, CA (SA), Associate Professor, UFS

D. SCHEEPERS
MCom (Pret), CA (SA), Professor, UNISA

H.H. SMITH
BCom (Hons) (Stell), CA (SA), Lecturer, US

H. STRYDOM
BCompt (Hons) (UNISA), CA (SA), Senior Lecturer, UNISA

T. TOMES
BCom (Hons) (Acc) (Pret), CA (SA), Senior Lecuter, UP

E.R. VENTER
MCom (Tax) (Pret), CA (SA), Senior Lecturer, UP

R. VON WELL
BCom (Hons) (Acc) (Pret), CA (SA), Senior Lecturer, UNISA

Preface

This publication is meant to introduce learners to the requirements of Accounting Standards and Interpretations issued by the South African Institute of Chartered Accountants.

Terminology and concepts implemented in revised statements issued by SAICA during its improvement project, are applied. With this project virtually completed, a smaller number of statements will change each year and for this reason, revisions to this publication will hopefully become less extensive in future.

The late release of the revised IAS 1 (AC 101) (it was issued only in July 2007) made it impossible to consequentially amend all other standards in this work. However, the chapter on IAS 1 (AC 101) was revised in total and may be used as a guideline in respect of the latest formats and presentation of financial statements. In addition, it was endeavoured to keep summaries in line with the questions currently appearing in the sister publication, *Accounting Standards*.

We would like to extend a word of gratitude to the publishers for their willingness to participate in a contribution to the accounting field and also to Natasha J.v. Rensburg, who has done the typesetting with great care and also contributed substantially to the organisation of the project.

The Authors
November 2007

Contents in Chronological Order

Note the following

1. Tax rates and allowances are not necessarily those currently applicable but are chosen for convenience and illustration of accounting principles.
2. Statements issued up to the end of July 2007 were taken into consideration, where practicable.
3. All references are in respect of either the statements (standards), interpretations and circulars of SAICA, as well as the Income Tax Act. In the chapters dealing with a specific topic, the international IAS and IFRS numbers related to that topic were used.
4. Any suggestions or comments may be addressed to:

Prof Johan Oberholster
Department of Accounting
University of Pretoria
PRETORIA
0002

Contents: Standards Arranged by Theme

INCOME STATEMENT

GROUPS

OTHER

Framework

Framework for the Preparation and Presentation of Financial Statements

❑ **SUMMARY**

Background
The accounting framework

BACKGROUND

Accounting standards may be defined as authoritative and generally accepted practical guidelines for the recording and measuring of financial information in the annual financial statements. These statements attempt to enhance the usefulness of the information for economic decision-making purposes.

The main criticism of accounting standards prior to the issue of the Accounting Framework was the fact that they were prepared without reference to an acceptable theoretical framework. To counter this criticism and to maintain the initiative in the setting of standards in the private sector, the accounting profession in the USA embarked on intensive research into the development of a conceptual framework. The first programme was launched in the USA in 1973 and resulted in the development of a conceptual framework. This was followed internationally by the issue, during July 1989, of a document by the International Accounting Standards Committee (IASC) titled *Framework for the Preparation and Presentation of Financial Statements*. This document was reviewed in 2006.

THE ACCOUNTING FRAMEWORK

1. Objectives of the framework

The following are, inter alia, the objectives of the framework:
- to assist in the development of future International Accounting Standards and International Financial Reporting Standards, as well as the review thereof;
- to provide a basis for reducing the number of alternative accounting treatments and in so doing facilitate the harmonisation of accounting standards, regulations and procedures;
- to assist national accounting standard setting bodies in the development of national standards;
- to assist the preparers of annual financial statements in applying International Financial Reporting Standards and in addressing topics that have yet to form the subject of an International Financial Reporting Standard;
- to assist auditors in forming an opinion as to whether financial statements comply with IASs and IFRSs;
- to assist users of annual financial statements to interpret the information contained therein; and
- to provide interested parties with information about how IASB approaches the formulation of International Financial Reporting Standards.

2. The objective of financial statements

The broad objective to be observed in preparing financial statements can be formulated as follows: "… to provide information about the financial position, performance and changes in financial position (cash flows) of an entity that is useful to a wide range of users in making economic decisions."

The financial position of an entity is impacted on via the control exercised over economic resources, the financial structure, liquidity and solvency as well as the capacity of the entity to adapt to the changes in the field of business in which it operates.

Information regarding the performance (profitability) of an entity is required in order to evaluate changes in economic resources that it is likely to control in the future.

Information related to the changes in the financial position (cash flows) of an entity is useful in order to evaluate the investing, financing, and operating activities during the reporting period.

3. Underlying assumptions of financial statements

There are two broad basic assumptions that underlie the preparation of financial statements, namely:
- The accrual basis. In accordance with this basis, the effects of transactions and other events are recognised when they occur (and not as cash is received or paid) and they are recorded in the accounting periods and reported in the financial statements of the periods to which they relate.
- The going concern concept. It is assumed that the entity will continue to operate in the foreseeable future.

4. Qualitative characteristics of financial statements

Qualitative characteristics represent the attributes that make the information provided in financial statements useful to users. The four core qualitative characteristics are:
- understandability;
- relevance;
- reliability; and
- comparability.

Information provided in financial statements should be readily **understandable** by users. These users are assumed to have a reasonable knowledge of business and economic activities and accounting as well as a willingness to study the information with reasonable diligence.

Information is **relevant** when it influences the economic decisions of users by helping them evaluate past, present and future events or confirming, or correcting, their past evaluations. The relevance of information is affected by its nature and materiality. Information is deemed material if its omission or misstatement could influence the economic decisions made by users on the basis of the financial statements.

Information is **reliable** when it is free from material error and bias and users can depend upon it to represent faithfully that which it either purports to represent or could reasonably be expected to represent. The reliability of information is influenced by the following considerations:
- faithful representation;
- substance over form;
- neutrality;
- prudence; and
- completeness.

Users must be in a position to **compare** the financial statements of an entity over time in order to identify trends in its financial position and performance. Users must also be in a position to compare different entities' financial statements to evaluate their relative position, performance and changes in financial position. The following would enhance the comparability of financial statements:
- consistency of accounting treatment of like transactions and other events;
- disclosure of accounting policies applied by the entity;
- disclosure of changes in accounting policies and the effects thereof; and
- presentation of comparative information for the preceding periods (comparative amounts).

The following constraints on relevance and reliability of information are identified:
- timeliness of information;
- balance between the benefit of and cost associated with information supplied; and
- balance (trade-off) between qualitative characteristics (the achievement of the main objective of financial statements is the overriding consideration should a conflict between qualitative characteristics arise).

Financial statements are frequently described as providing a true and fair view of, or as presenting fairly, the financial position, performance and changes in financial position of an entity. The application of the principal qualitative characteristics and of appropriate accounting standards normally produces such financial statements.

5. Elements of financial statements

Financial statements provide a view of the financial effects of transactions and other events by grouping them into broad classes according to their economic characteristics. These broad classes are known as the elements of financial statements.

Elements directly related to the measurement of financial position are:
- Assets. These are "resources controlled by the entity as a result of past events and from which future economic benefits are expected to flow to the entity."
- Liabilities. These are "present obligations of an entity arising from past events, the settlement of which is expected to result in an outflow from the entity of resources embodying economic benefits."
- Equity (Owners' interest). This is "the residual interest in the assets of the entity after deducting all of its liabilities."

Elements directly related to the measurement of the profitability of an undertaking are:
- Income: "increases in economic benefits during an accounting period in the form of inflows or enhancements of assets, or decreases of liabilities which result in an increase in equity (other than increases resulting from contributions by owners)."
- Expenses: "decreases in economic benefits during an accounting period in the form of outflows or depletions of assets, or incurrences of liabilities which result in decreases in equity (other than decreases because of distributions to owners)."

The definition of income takes account of both revenue and gains.

The revaluation or restatement of assets and liabilities gives rise to increases or decreases in equity. While these increases or decreases meet the definition of income and expenses, they are not included in the income statement under certain concepts of capital maintenance. Instead, these are included in equity as capital maintenance adjustments or revaluation surpluses.

6. Recognition of the elements of financial statements

An item that meets the definition of an element (discussed earlier) should be recognised if:
- it is probable that future economic benefits associated with the item will flow to or from the entity; and
- the cost or value of the item can be measured with reliability.

7. Measurement of the elements of financial statements

The measurement of elements of financial statements is done in a number of different ways. These include the following:
- historical cost;
- current cost;
- realisable (settlement) value; and
- present value.

8. Capital and maintenance of capital

- Financial capital: Capital is synonymous with the net assets (equity) of the entity. It is defined in terms of nominal monetary units. Profit represents the increase in the nominal monetary capital over the period.
- Physical capital: Capital is regarded as the operating capability. It is defined in terms of the productive capacity. Profit represents the increase in productive capacity over the period.

PROPOSED APPROACH TO ANSWERING QUESTIONS ON THE ACCOUNTING FRAMEWORK

The issue is to decide whether an item is an:
- asset or expense (for example, Cost to plant a crop, Development costs); or
- liability or income (for example, Deposit received).

Bear in mind that most, if not all, transactions will influence two elements in the financial statements owing to the nature of the double entry system. We are not looking at the obvious leg but at the less obvious leg. For example money borrowed to purchase goods will obviously be a liability, but will the goods be an asset or an expense?

Approach to solving this kind of problem:

1. Classify the item according to the criteria in the Accounting Framework .47 – .81 (that is, asset/liability/income/expense). Pay special attention to the definitions in the Framework .49 and .70.

2. Take note of Framework .50 and decide in terms of Framework .82 – .88 as well as Framework .89 – .98 whether the item should be recognised in the financial statement, considering:
   - probability of future economic benefits; and
   - reliability of measurement.
3. Apply the qualitative characteristics and underlying assumptions to determine whether the item should be disclosed, how it should be disclosed and at what amount, for example;
   - materiality (whether);
   - substance over form (how); and
   - prudence (amount).
4. Take note of the important distinction between recognition and disclosure.

IASs, IFRSs, SIC (AC 400) and AC 500

Preface to International Financial Reporting Standards and Interpretations Thereof

❏ **SUMMARY**

Background
Objectives of the IASB
Scope and authority of IFRSs
Due process
Timing and application of IFRSs
Preface to IFRSs
Interpretations of statements of GAAP relating only to South Africa – AC 500 series

BACKGROUND

The responsibility of the IASB (International Accounting Standards Board) is to approve International Financial Reporting Standards (IFRSs), related documents, exposure drafts and discussion documents.

The responsibility of the International Financial Reporting Interpretations Committee (IFRIC) is to prepare interpretations on financial reporting issues not addressed in detail by the IASB. The interpretations are done in the context of the Framework and are approved by the IASB.

OBJECTIVES OF THE IASB

The objectives of the IASB are to:
- develop global accounting standards (high quality, understandable and enforceable) to help users to make economic decisions;
- to advocate the use and diligent application of their standards; and
- to facilitate national standard setting bodies in bringing about convergence of national accounting standards and IFRS.

SCOPE AND AUTHORITY OF IFRSs

IFRSs provide guidance on the accounting treatment of transactions and events that are contained in general purpose financial statements of all profit-orientated entities. Although not designed for this purpose, it may also be appropriate for not-for-profit entities in the private sector, public sector or government.

A complete set of financial statements comprise:
- a balance sheet;
- an income statement;
- a statement of changes in equity (or equivalent);
- a cash flow statement;
- accounting polices; and
- related notes.

Interim reports in terms of IAS 34 (AC 127) require less information as set out in IAS 34 on Interim Financial Reporting.

The IASB may permit different accounting treatments for certain transactions or events. Provided a permitted treatment is used, the financial statements will be prepared in accordance with IFRSs. Over time, these options in respect of accounting treatment will be revisited by the IASB with a view to reducing the available choices.

Interpretations of IFRSs as prepared by IFRIC and approved by the IASB provide authoritative guidance on issues that are likely to receive divergent or unacceptable treatment in instances where such guidance is not present.

Scope limitations of IFRSs are set out in the individual standards.

DUE PROCESS

The due process followed in the development of IFRSs and IFRICs are set out in .18 (IFRSs) and .19 (IFRICs).

TIMING AND APPLICATION OF IFRSs

The effective dates of IFRSs are set out in the relevant documents. New or revised IFRSs contain transitional arrangements to be applied at initial implementation.

Exposure drafts are prepared and issued to obtain comment and may be substantially revised. For this reason the requirements of any existing IFRS that may be affected by new proposals in an exposure draft, will be in force until the effective date of the replacing IFRS.

The preface in respect of South African Interpretations now follows.

INTERPRETATIONS OF STATEMENTS OF GAAP RELATING ONLY TO SOUTH AFRICA – AC 500 SERIES

- Interpretations of Statements of GAAP relating to RSA specifically, provide authoritative guidance to preparers, auditors and users of financial statements and in so doing facilitate the standardisation of accounting treatments.
- Interpretations relating to RSA specifically, have the same authority as Statements of Generally Accepted Accounting Practice (GAAP) and other Interpretations of Statements of GAAP and provide guidance on individual aspects contained in relevant statements, as well as matters where unsatisfactory or conflicting issues have arisen.
- If the financial statements of an entity purport to be presented in compliance with Statements of GAAP, they should also comply with South African Interpretations of Statements of GAAP.

IAS 1 *(AC 101)* & SIC 29 *(AC 429)*

Presentation of Financial Statements

❑ **SUMMARY**

Background
Structure and content
Illustrative example: Statement of financial position
Illustrative example: Statement of comprehensive income (expenses by function)
Illustrative example: Statement of comprehensive income (expenses by nature)
Illustrative example: Statement of changes in equity
Annexure: Accounting policies
SIC 29: Disclosure – service concession arrangements
Circular 8/99: Compliance with Section 286 (3) and paragraph 5 of Schedule 4 of the Companies Act, 1973 (as amended), and Statements of Generally Accepted Accounting Practice

BACKGROUND

1. Objective and scope of the statement

The objective of this standard is to prescribe the basis for presentation of general purpose financial statements. These financial statements need to be comparable to those of the entity in previous periods as well as those of other entities. To achieve this objective, this standard sets out:
- overall considerations for presentation of financial statements;
- guidelines for their structure;
- minimum content requirements;
- guidance on compliance with Statements of Generally Accepted Accounting Practice; and
- guidance on departures from Statements of Generally Accepted Accounting Practice.

2. Purpose of financial statements

General purpose financial statements shall provide information about the financial position, performance and cash flows of the entity that is useful for economic decision-making by users of these statements.

3. Components of financial statements

- Statement of financial position.
- Statement of comprehensive income.
- Statement of changes in equity.
- Statement of cash flows.
- Accounting policies and explanatory notes.

Entities are encouraged to also furnish the following:
- a financial review by management, including aspects such as:
  - performance factors;
  - policy for investment to maintain and enhance performance;
  - dividend policy;
  - sources of funding and targeted ratio of liabilities to equity;
  - resources the value of which is not reflected in financial statements; and
- supplementary statements, such as:
  - value-added statements; and
  - environmental reports.

4. Overall considerations

Fair presentation: The financial position, financial performance and cash flows of an entity shall be fairly presented in the financial statements. The appropriate application of Statements of Generally Accepted Accounting Practice with additional disclosure will virtually always achieve a fair presentation.

Compliance: If financial statements comply with Statements of Generally Accepted Accounting Practice that fact shall be disclosed. This fact may not be disclosed unless the financial statements comply with all the requirements.

Inappropriate accounting treatments are not rectified by disclosure of such treatments.

In the rare circumstances when management concludes that departure from a requirement in a Statement of Generally Accepted Accounting Practice is necessary to achieve fair presentation, an entity shall disclose:
- that management has concluded that fair presentation is achieved;
- that it has complied in all material respects with applicable Statements of Generally Accepted Accounting Practice and Interpretations except that it has departed from a particular statement in order to achieve fair presentation;
- the standard or interpretation from which the entity has departed;
- the nature of the departure, including the treatment that the standard or interpretation would normally require;
- the reason why that treatment would be misleading in the circumstances and the treatment adopted; and

- the financial impact of the departure on the entity's profit or loss, assets, liabilities, equity and cash flows.

Going concern: Management shall make an assessment of an entity's ability to continue as a going concern. Financial statements shall be prepared on a going concern basis unless management either intends to liquidate the entity or to cease trading

Uncertainties relating to events or conditions, which may cast significant doubt upon the entity's ability to continue as a going concern, shall be disclosed.

The entity shall disclose the fact that the financial statements are not prepared on a going concern basis, together with the basis used and the reason why the entity is not considered to be a going concern.

Accrual basis: Financial statements must be prepared under the accrual basis except for cash flow information.

Consistency of presentation: Items in the financial statements shall be presented and classified consistently from one period to the next unless:
- a significant change in the nature of operations or a review of its financial statement presentation demonstrates that the change will result in a more appropriate presentation; or
- a change in presentation is required by a standard or interpretation.

Materiality and aggregation: The presentation of condensed information on the face of financial statements or in the notes is based on the following guidance:
- Each material class of similar items shall be shown separately.
- Immaterial items of similar nature and function must be aggregated.

Offsetting: Items shall not be offset, except in the following circumstances:
- Assets and liabilities may be offset when required or permitted by a standard or interpretation.
- Income and expenses shall be offset when, and only when:
  - an accounting standard requires or permits it; or
  - gains and losses arise from the same or similar transactions, provided events are not material.

Comparative information: Unless a standard or interpretation permits or requires otherwise, comparative information is required in respect of the previous period for:
- all numerical information; and
- narrative and descriptive information when relevant to an understanding of the financial statements.

When the presentation or classification of items in the financial statements is amended:
- comparative amounts shall be reclassified, unless it is impracticable; and
- the nature, amount and reason for reclassification shall be disclosed. When it is impracticable to reclassify comparatives, an entity shall disclose the reason and the nature of the changes that would have been made if the amounts have been reclassified.

STRUCTURE AND CONTENT

1. Identification and reporting period

- Financial statements shall be clearly identified and distinguished from other information in the same published document.
- Each component shall be clearly identified.
- The following information shall be prominently displayed:
  - name of reporting entity and any change in this regard since the previous reporting date;
  - whether the entity's own or group statements are presented;
  - reporting date or period covered;
  - presentation currency, as defined in IAS 21 (AC 112); and
  - level of rounding used in amounts presented.

- Financial statements shall be presented at least annually. When the reporting date changes, an entity shall disclose:
  - reason for a period other than one year being used; and
  - the fact that comparative amounts are not entirely comparable.

2. Statement of financial position

Information is provided about the financial position in the statement of financial position.

Current/non-current distinction

Each entity shall present current and non-current assets and current and non-current liabilities as separate classifications on the face of the statement of financial position. In the case where an entity chooses not to make this classification but use liquidity to present its assets and liabilities (thus being more reliable and relevant), assets and liabilities shall be presented broadly in order of their liquidity.

Whichever method of presentation is adopted, an entity shall disclose separately amounts of assets and liabilities expected to be recovered or settled within and after 12 months from the reporting date.

Current assets

Current assets include:
- assets expected to be realised in, or held for sale or consumption in, the normal operating cycle;
- assets held primarily for trading;
- assets expected to be realised within 12 months after the reporting date; or
- cash or cash equivalents not restricted in use.

All other assets are non-current assets.

Current liabilities

Current liabilities include:
- liabilities expected to be settled in the normal operating cycle;
- liabilities held primarily for the purpose of being traded;
- liabilities due to be settled within 12 months after the reporting date; or
- liabilities where the entity does not have an unconditional right to defer settlement for at least 12 months after reporting date.

All other liabilities shall be classified as non-current liabilities.

Long-term financial liabilities to be settled within 12 months after reporting date are classified as current even if:
- the original term > 12 months; and
- agreement to refinance or to reschedule payments on a long-term basis is completed after reporting date, but before the financial statements are authorised for issue. If the latter happens before reporting date, liability can still be carried as non-current.

The amount of above-mentioned liability together with supporting information shall be disclosed in notes using the disclosures for non-adjusting events.

Minimum information to be presented on the face of the statement of financial position

Line items shall present the following amounts:
- Property, plant and equipment
- Investment property
- Intangible assets
- Financial assets (excluding *)
- Investments accounted for using the equity method*
- Assets classified as held for sale in accordance with IFRS 5 (AC 142)
- Liabilities included in disposal groups classified as held for sale in accordance with IFRS 5 (AC 142).

- Biological assets
- Inventories
- Trade and other receivables*
- Cash and cash equivalents*
- Trade and other payables#
- Tax liabilities (current and deferred)
- Tax assets (current and deferred)
- Provisions#
- Financial liabilities (excluding #)
- Minority interests, within equity
- Reserves and issued capital attributable to equity holders of the parent

Additional items may be required by other statements of Generally Accepted Accounting Practice such as assets and liabilities held for sale.

Other information presented either on the face of the statement of financial position or in the notes

- Appropriate further sub-classifications of line items in the statement of financial position
- For each class of share capital:
  - number of shares authorised;
  - number of shares issued and fully paid;
  - number of shares issued and not fully paid;
  - par value per share or that shares have no par value;
  - reconciliation of number of shares at beginning and end of the year;
  - rights, preferences and restrictions;
  - restrictions on distribution of dividends and repayment of capital;
  - shares in the entity held by the entity itself, subsidiaries or associates; and
  - shares reserved for issuance under options and sales contracts, including terms and amounts
- Nature and purpose of each reserve (this basically rules out using a general reserve)

Additional statement of financial position required

When a change in accounting policy or prior period error is adjusted for retrospectively, an additional statement of financial position should be presented as at the beginning of the earliest comparative period (that is, an opening statement).

3.   Statement of comprehensive income

Information is provided about financial performance and all items of income or expense shall appear in the statement of comprehensive income unless a standard or interpretation requires otherwise.

Extraordinary items shall not be presented for any type of income or expense either in the statement of comprehensive income or the notes.

Minimum information to be presented on the face of the statement of comprehensive income

- Revenue
- Finance costs
- Share of profits/losses of associates and joint ventures equity accounted for
- Tax expense
- Profit or loss
- Other components of comprehensive income classified by nature
- Share of other comprehensive income of associates and joint ventures which was equity accounted for
- Total comprehensive income
- A single amount comprising the total of the post-tax profit or loss of discontinued operations and the post-tax profit or loss recognised when measuring an asset or disposal group held for sale to the lower of fair value less costs to sell and its carrying amount

The following items will be disclosed on the face of the statement of comprehensive income as allocations of profit or loss, but not as part of the body of the statement of comprehensive income:
- profit or loss attributable to minorities and owners of the parent; and
- total comprehensive income attributable to minorities and owners of the parent.

Additional items may be required by other Statements of Generally Accepted Accounting Practice or Interpretations or could be necessary to understand the entity's financial performance.

Other information presented either on the face of the statement of comprehensive income or in the notes

- Analysis of expenses based on the nature of expenses or their function within the entity, whichever provides more reliable and relevant information.
- If classified by function, disclose in addition:
  - depreciation;
  - amortisation expense; and
  - employee benefit expense.
- When material income or expense items occur, their nature and amount shall be disclosed separately.

4. Statement of changes in equity

Changes in an entity's equity between two reporting dates reflect the increase or decrease in its net assets or wealth during the period.

Minimum information to be presented on the face of the statement of changes in equity

- Total comprehensive income for the period, allocated to owners of the parent as well as minorities
- Transactions with owners, showing separately contributions by and distributions to owners
- Cumulative effects of changes in accounting policy for each component of equity
- Cumulative effects of correction of errors for each component of equity
- Dividends as well as amounts per share recognised as distributions to equity holders (this can also be disclosed in the notes)
- Reconciliation of the balance of each component of equity at the beginning and end of the period, disclosing each change

5. Statement of cash flows

IAS 7 (AC 118) sets out these requirements.

6. Notes

Structure

The notes to the financial statements shall provide information about:
- the basis of preparation and the specific relevant accounting policies selected and applied (refer to the Appendix to this chapter);
- aspects required by Statements of GAAP that are not presented elsewhere in the financial statements; and
- additional aspects which are not presented on the face of the financial statements, but that are required for fair presentation.

The notes should be presented in a systematic manner. Items shall be cross-referenced from the face of the financial statements to the notes.

Disclosure of accounting policies

An entity shall disclose the following in the summary of significant accounting polices:
- measurement bases used in preparing the financial statements;
- other accounting policies used that are relevant to the understanding of financial statements; and
- the judgements management has made in the process of applying the entity's accounting policies that have the most significant effect on amounts recognised in the financial statements.

Other disclosures

- The amount of dividends proposed or declared after the reporting date, but before the financial statements were authorised for issue
- Amount of cumulative preference dividends not recognised
- Key assumptions concerning the future and other key sources of estimation uncertainty that have a significant risk of causing material adjustments to assets and liabilities within the year
- In respect of affected assets and liabilities above: their nature; and their carrying amount at reporting date
- Domicile of the entity
- Legal form of the entity
- Country of incorporation of the entity
- Address of registered office or principal place of business, when it is different
- Nature of operations and principal activities
- Name of the parent and ultimate parent of the group
- An entity shall disclose sufficient information to enable users of financial statements to evaluate the objectives, policies and processes used by the entity for managing capital.

Illustrative example: XYZ GROUP
STATEMENT OF FINANCIAL POSITION AS AT 31 DECEMBER 20.2

	20.2 R'000	20.1 R'000
ASSETS		
Non-current assets	X	X
Property, plant and equipment	X	X
Goodwill	X	X
Other intangible assets	X	X
Investments in associates	X	X
Available-for-sale financial assets	X	X
Current assets	X	X
Inventories	X	X
Trade and other receivables	X	X
Other current assets	X	X
Cash and cash equivalents	X	X
Total assets	X	X
EQUITY AND LIABILITIES		
Total equity	X	X
Equity attributable to owners of the parent	X	X
Share capital	X	X
Retained earnings (1)	X	X
Other components of equity	X	X
Minority interest (1)	X	X
Total liabilities	X	X
Non-current liabilities	X	X
Long-term borrowings	X	X
Deferred tax	X	X
Long-term provisions	X	X

	20.2 R'000	20.1 R'000
Current liabilities	X	X
Trade and other payables	X	X
Short-term borrowings	X	X
Current portion of long-term borrowings	X	X
Current tax payable	X	X
Short-term provisions	X	X
Total equity and liabilities	X	X

(1) Note that minority interest forms part of equity.

XYZ GROUP
STATEMENT OF COMPREHENSIVE INCOME FOR THE YEAR ENDED 31 DECEMBER 20.2

(Illustrating the classification of expenses by function)

	20.2 R'000	20.1 R'000
Revenue	X	X
Cost of sales	(X)	(X)
Gross profit	X	X
Other income	X	X
Distribution costs	(X)	(X)
Administrative expenses	(X)	(X)
Other expenses	(X)	(X)
Finance costs	(X)	(X)
Share of profit of associates	X	X
Profit before tax	X	X
Income tax expense	(X)	(X)
Profit for the year from continuing operations	X	X
Loss for the year from discontinued operations	(X)	(X)
Profit for the year	X	X
Other comprehensive income		
Exchange differences on translating foreign operations	X	X
Available-for-sale financial assets	X	X
Cash flow hedges	X	X
Gains on property revaluation	X	X
Actuarial gains/(losses) on defined benefit pension plans	X	X
Share of other comprehensive income of associates	(X)	(X)
Income tax relating to components of other comprehensive income	(X)	(X)
Other comprehensive income for the year, net of tax	X	X
Total comprehensive income for the year	X	X
Profit attributable to:		
Owners of the parent	X	X
Minority interest	X	X
	X	X
Total comprehensive income attributable to:		
Owners of the parent	X	X
Minority interest	X	X
	X	X
Earnings per share (in currency units):		
Basic and diluted	X	X

In the above example, components of other comprehensive income are disclosed on a pre-tax basis. The combined tax effect is then reflected as a single line item following these components. It is allowed to alternatively present each of these components net of tax.

Irrespective of whether the components of other comprehensive income are disclosed before or after tax, IAS 1 requires disclosure of the tax effect of each individual component, either on the face of the statement of comprehensive income or in the notes. Disclosure in the notes will be as follows:

XYZ Group – Notes

15. Tax effects relating to each component of other comprehensive income

	20.2			20.1		
	Before-tax amount	Tax (expense) benefit	Net-of-tax amount	Before-tax amount	Tax (expense) benefit	Net-of-tax amount
Exchange differences on translating foreign operations	X	(X)	X	X	(X)	X
Available-for-sale financial assets	(X)	X	(X)	X	(X)	X
Cash flow hedges	(X)	X	(X)	(X)	X	(X)
Gains on property revaluation	X	(X)	X	X	(X)	X
Actuarial gains/(losses) on defined benefit pension plans	(X)	X	(X)	X	(X)	X
Share of other comprehensive income of associates	X	-	X	(X)	-	(X)
Other comprehensive income	(X)	X	(X)	X	(X)	X

XYZ GROUP
STATEMENT OF COMPREHENSIVE INCOME FOR THE YEAR ENDED 31 DECEMBER 20.2

(Illustrating the classification of expenses by nature)

	20.2 R'000	20.1 R'000
Revenue	X	X
Other income	X	X
Changes in inventories of finished goods and work in progress	(X)	X
Work performed by the entity and capitalised	X	X
Raw material and consumables used	(X)	(X)
Employee benefit expense (2)	(X)	(X)
Depreciation expense (2)	(X)	(X)
Amortisation expense (2)	(X)	(X)
Impairment of property, plant and equipment (2)	(X)	(X)
Other expenses	(X)	(X)
Finance costs	(X)	(X)

	20.2 R'000	20.1 R'000
Share of profit of associates	X	X
Profit before tax	X	X
Income tax expense	(X)	(X)
Profit for the year from continuing operations	(X)	(X)
Loss for the year from discontinued operations	–	–
Profit for the year	X	X
Other comprehensive income		
Exchange differences on translating foreign operations	X	X
Available-for-sale financial assets	(X)	(X)
Cash flow hedges	X	X
Gains on property revaluation	X	X
Actuarial gains/(losses) on defined benefit pension plans	(X)	(X)
Share of other comprehensive income of associates	X	X
Income tax relating to components of other comprehensive income	(X)	(X)
Other comprehensive income for the year, net of tax	X	X
Total comprehensive income for the year	X	X
Profit attributable to:		
Owners of the parent	X	X
Minority interest	X	X
	X	X
Total comprehensive income attributable to:		
Owners of the parent	X	X
Minority interest	X	X
	X	X
Earnings per share (in currency units):		
Basic and diluted	X	X

(2) In a statement of comprehensive income in which expenses are classified by nature, an impairment of property, plant and equipment is shown as a separate line item. By contrast, if expenses are classified by function, the impairment is included in the function(s) to which it relates, and separately disclosed in the note on profit before tax. The same applies for employee benefit costs, depreciation and amortisation.

The components of other comprehensive income are often influenced by more than one movement during the year. An analysis of the movements on each of the components of other comprehensive income should be provided, either on the face of the statement of comprehensive income or alternatively in the notes.

Note that the movements included in this analysis are those movements that result in an increase or decrease in total equity, as well as reclassification adjustments. These movements do not include normal transfers between reserves – transfers have no effect on the total amount of equity and are disclosed in the statement of changes in equity only. The note, analysing the movements in other components of comprehensive income, will be as follows:

Notes

15. Components of other comprehensive income

Year ended 31 December 20.2

	R'000	20.2 R'000	R'000	20.1 R'000
Other comprehensive income:				
Exchange differences on translating foreign operations		X		X
Available-for-sale financial assets:				
Gains arising during the year	X		X	
Less: Reclassification adjustments for gains included in profit or loss	(X)	(X)	(X)	X
Cash flow hedges:				
Gains/(losses) arising during the year	(X)		(X)	
Less: Reclassification adjustments for gains/(losses) included in profit or loss	X		-	
Less: Adjustments for amounts transferred to initial carrying amount of hedged items	X	(X)	-	(X)
Gains on property revaluation		X		X
Actuarial gains/(losses) on defined benefit pension plans		(X)		X
Share of other comprehensive income of associates		X		(X)
Other comprehensive income		(X)		X
Income tax in respect of components of other comprehensive income		X		(X)
Other comprehensive income for the year		(X)		X

XYZ GROUP
STATEMENT OF CHANGES IN EQUITY FOR THE YEAR ENDED 31 DECEMBER 20.2

	Share capital	Retained earnings	Translation of foreign operations	Available-for-sale financial assets	Cash flow hedges	Revaluation surplus	Total	Minority interest	Total equity
			Attributable to owners of the parent						
Balance at 1 Jan 20.1	X	X	(X)	X	X	–	X	X	X
Changes in accounting policy	–	X	–	–	–	–	X	X	X
Correction of error		X					X	X	X
Restated balance	X	X	(X)	X	X	–	X	X	X
Changes in equity for 20.1									
Dividends	–	(X)	–	–	–	–	(X)	–	(X)
Total comprehensive income for the year	–	X	X	X	(X)	X	X	X	X
Balance at 31 Dec 20.1	X	X	X	X	(X)	X	X	X	X

Changes in equity for 20.2

Issue of share capital	X	–	–	–	–	–	X	–	X
Dividends	–	(X)	–	–	–	–	(X)	–	(X)
Total comprehensive income for the year	–	X	X	(X)	(X)	X	–	–	–
Transfer to retained earnings	–	X	–	–	–	X	–	–	–
Balance at 31 Dec 20.2	X	X	X	X	(X)	X	X	X	X

ANNEXURE – ACCOUNTING POLICIES

IAS 8 (AC 103) defines accounting policies in paragraph .5 as follows: "… are the specific principles, bases, conventions, rules and practices adopted by an enterprise in preparing and presenting financial statements."

The definition contained in IAS 8 (AC 103) .5 includes the following, which requires closer inspection:
- Principles: Accounting principles are the generally accepted rules which have been developed from basic assumptions and are guidelines to be followed in accounting practice to account for transactions and events, for example: the going concern concept, the matching principle, the prudence concept, the accrual basis of accounting, the consistency concept, substance over form and materiality.
- Bases: Accounting bases are methods and procedures used to account for financial transactions, data and information in accordance with accounting principles, which determine how these transactions should be accounted for, in the financial statements, for example: methods of depreciation and inventory cost formulae.
- Conventions: These are generally accepted practical rules whereby information and data are accounted for or treated in the accounting process, for example: the double entry system of accounting for transactions.
- Rules: Accounting rules are the prescribed methods by which transactions and data should be disclosed and accounted for in the financial statements. These methods are generally accepted, for example: disclosure requirements and rules to be observed in the translation of financial statements of foreign operations.
- Practices: These are merely the generally accepted practical application of the above-mentioned accounting bases, conventions and rules in accordance with guidelines encompassed by the accounting principles (which are based on postulates).

From the above it would seem that an entity should indicate that it has complied with the fundamental accounting concepts and the qualitative characteristics contained in the Framework. This is surely not the intention of the preparers of IAS 8 (AC 103) – one can only speculate on what their intention was.

If the requirements of IAS 1, IAS 8 (AC 103), other recently released Statements of Generally Accepted Accounting Practice of the SAICA and the disclosure trends followed by listed companies were to be considered, it would seem that the following disclosure requirements for accounting policies could be applied:
- The fact that fundamental accounting assumptions, principles and postulates have been complied with, need not be disclosed in the financial statements.
- Where fundamental accounting assumptions, principles and postulates are not complied with, the fact and reason therefore must be disclosed; for example, an entity placed under judicial management where the going concern assumption is not applicable.
- All other significant accounting policies must be disclosed, preferably in one location in the financial statements. It would appear that a policy should be disclosed in at least all cases where an accounting standard (100-series) and interpretation (400- and 500-series) is applied by an entity.

The following are examples of areas where an accounting policy would require disclosure:
- revenue recognition;
- consolidation principles, including subsidiaries and associates;
- business combinations;

- joint ventures;
- recognition and depreciation/amortisation of tangible and intangible assets;
- capitalisation of borrowing costs and other expenditure;
- construction contracts;
- investment properties;
- financial instruments and investments;
- leases;
- research and development costs;
- inventories;
- taxes, including deferred taxes;
- provisions;
- employee benefit costs;
- foreign currency translation and hedging;
- definition of business and geographical segments and the basis for allocation of costs between segments;
- definition of cash and cash equivalents;
- inflation accounting; and
- government grants.

Other Statements of Generally Accepted Accounting Practice specifically require disclosure of accounting policies in many of these areas.

SIC 29: DISCLOSURE – SERVICE CONCESSION ARRANGEMENTS

1. Background

An entity (concession operator) may enter into an arrangement with another entity (concession provider) to provide services that give the public access to major economic or social facilities. The concession provider may be a public or private sector entity, including a governmental body.

Examples of service concession arrangements are:
- water treatment and supply facilities;
- motorways, airports;
- car parks, tunnels, bridges; and
- telecommunication networks.

Examples of items that are not service concession arrangements are:
- outsourcing of the employee cafeteria;
- building maintenance; and
- accounting or information technology functions.

A service concession arrangement generally involves the concession provider transferring to the concession operator for the period of the concession:
- the right to provide services that give the public access to major economic and social facilities; and
- in some cases the right to use specified assets.

In exchange for the above, the concession operator:
- commits to provide services according to certain terms and conditions during the concession period; and
- commits to return at the end of the concession period the rights awarded for this period where applicable.

The common characteristic of all such arrangements is that the concession operator receives a right and incurs an obligation to provide public services.

2. Issue

- The issue is what information should be disclosed in the notes to the financial statements of both a concession provider and a concession operator.

- Certain aspects and disclosures on service concession arrangements are addressed by existing Statements of GAAP, such as IAS 16 (AC 123) (Property, plant and equipment), IAS 17 (AC 105) (Leases) and IAS 38 (AC 129) (Intangible assets).
- A service concession arrangement could also involve executory contracts that are not addressed in other Statements of GAAP, unless these contracts are onerous, in which case IAS 37 (AC 130) applies.
- This interpretation addresses additional disclosures of service concession arrangements over and above the matters raised earlier in other statements.

3.   Consensus

All aspects of a service concession arrangement should be considered in determining the appropriate disclosures in the notes to the financial statements. A concession operator and a concession provider should disclose the following in each period:
- a description of the arrangement;
- significant terms of the arrangement that may effect the amount, timing and certainty of future cash flows (e.g., the period of the concession, repricing dates and the basis upon which repricing or renegotiation is determined);
- the nature and extent (e.g., quantity, time period or amount as appropriate) of:
  - rights to use specific assets;
  - obligations to provide or rights to expect provision of services;
  - obligations to acquire or build items of property, plant and equipment;
  - obligations to deliver or rights to receive specified assets at the end of the concession period;
  - renewal and termination options;
  - other rights and obligations (e.g., major overhauls);
  - the classification of the service arrangement; and
  - the amount of revenue and profit or loss recognised on the exchange of construction services for a financial or intangible asset; and
- changes in the arrangement occurring during the period.

The disclosures required in accordance with the first paragraph under the heading Consensus should be provided individually for each service concession arrangement or in aggregate for each class of service concession arrangements.

A class is a grouping of service concession arrangements involving services of a similar nature (e.g., toll collections, telecommunications and water treatment services).

IAS 2 *(AC 108)*

Inventories

❑ **SUMMARY**

Background
Accounting practice
Disclosure

BACKGROUND

Standard IAS 2 gives guidance on the calculation of the cost of inventory to be recognised in the determination of cost of sales and the amount to be recognised as an asset and carried forward until the related revenues are recognised. Furthermore, guidelines are provided on the cost formulas that are used for inventory.

Inventories are assets:
- held for sale in the ordinary course of business; or
- in the process of production for above-mentioned sale; or
- which are either materials or supplies that will be consumed in the production process or used in the rendering of services.

In the case of a service provider, inventories consist of the costs of the service for which the entity has not yet recognised the related revenue, for example, work in progress of professional persons.

The standard applies to all inventory, except the following: work-in-progress under construction contracts, including directly related service contracts, financial instruments and biological assets related to agricultural activity and agricultural produce at point of harvest.

The standard does not apply to the measurement of inventories held by:
- producers of agricultural and forest products, agricultural produce after harvest, minerals and mineral products to the extent that they are normally measured at net realisable value; and
- commodity broker-traders measuring inventories at fair value less costs to sell.

ACCOUNTING PRACTICE

1. Measurement of inventories

Inventories shall be measured at the lower of cost (see paragraph 2 below) and net realisable value (see paragraph 4 below).

2. Cost of inventories

The cost of inventories shall comprise all purchase costs, conversion costs and all other costs incurred in bringing the inventories to their present location and condition.

Goods

Purchase cost
- Purchase price (excluding VAT)
- Import charges/duties
- Other levies/taxes (excluding taxes that can be recovered subsequently)
- Transport and handling charges
- Other direct costs of acquisition

minus
- Trade discounts
- Rebates received
- Other similar items such as settlement discounts.

Costs of conversion
- Direct labour
- Production overheads
  - Variable overheads (vary directly or nearly directly with the volume of production)
  - Fixed overheads (remain fairly constant regardless of production volume) allocated at normal capacity. (Actual level of production may be used if it approximates normal capacity and in periods of abnormally high production.)

Special rules apply to joint products and by-products.

Other costs incurred to bring to present location and condition, such as:
- Design
- Borrowing costs (IAS 23 (AC 114))
- Necessary storage costs prior to a further stage of production (IAS 2.16)

Services

All costs directly engaged in providing the service, for example:
- Consumable goods
- Labour
- Other costs of personnel directly engaged in providing the service
- Attributable overheads

Exclusions

- Abnormal wastage (materials, labour and overheads)
- Storage costs (unless necessary prior to a further stage of production)
- Administrative overheads
- Selling costs
- Interest expense occurring when settlement is deferred.

3.   Cost formulas and techniques for the measurement of cost

Actual cost

- Specific identification
- Weighted average cost (See * below)
- First in, first out (FIFO) (See * below)

*   For inventories with a different nature or use, different cost formulas may be used. For example, raw materials may be valued using FIFO and finished goods using weighted average cost. For example, in one business segment a metal is mixed with other metals to create a new alloy, while another business segment uses the pure metal to manufacture individual items. Under these circumstances the two business segments may value the same metal using weighted average and FIFO (two different cost formulas) respectively.

Standard cost

- Used for convenience if results approximate cost.
- Take into account normal levels of materials, labour, efficiency and capacity.
- Review regularly and revise if necessary.

Retail method

- Used for convenience if results approximate cost.
- Use when it is impractical to use actual costs.
- Reduce sales value by gross margin.
- Average percentage is used for each homogeneous group of items.
- Take into consideration marked down prices.

4.   Net realisable value

Definition

Estimated selling price (ordinary course of business) less costs incurred to make the sale, for example:
- Costs to complete inventory
- Trade discounts
- Advertising costs
- Sales commission

NRV is an entity-specific value, whereas fair value less costs to sell is not.

Write-downs

- Item-by-item basis.
- Similar items may be grouped together, for example, inventory:
  - manufactured in the same production line;
  - with similar purposes or end uses; and
  - produced and marketed in the same geographical area.
- Costs relating to each service provided by a service provider with a specific selling price, is treated as a separate item.

Estimates of net realisable value

- Use most reliable evidence at the time of the estimates.
- Consider fluctuations of price or costs relating to events occurring after balance sheet date in order to complete.
- Take into consideration the purpose for which the inventory is held (e.g. fixed sales contracts).
- Special rules apply for materials and other supplies if the finished products in which they will be incorporated are expected to be sold at or above cost.
- New assessments are made in each subsequent period for items still on hand to determine possible reversals of previous write-downs.

5. Recognition as an expense

The following shall be recognised as expenses, according to the Framework, in the income statement of the related period:
- carrying amount of inventories sold (cost of sales);
- write-downs to net realisable value;
- inventory losses;
- non-allocated production overheads; and
- abnormal amounts of wasted materials, labour and overheads.

Reversals of previous write downs to net realisable value are recognised in the period of reversal and disclosed as a correction of an accounting estimate in accordance with IAS 8 (AC 103).

Inventories allocated to other asset accounts (for example, components of self-constructed property, plant or equipment) are recognised as an expense during the useful life of that asset, as depreciation is written off.

DISCLOSURE

The following are disclosed in the financial statements:
- the accounting policies adopted in measuring inventories (refer to paragraph 3 dealing with actual costs);
- the cost formulas used (refer to paragraph 3 dealing with actual costs);
- the total carrying amount of inventories and the carrying amount in classifications appropriate to the entity;
- the carrying amount of inventories carried at fair value less costs to sell;
- the amount of any reversal of any write-down which is recognised as a reduction of the inventory expense in the period which resulted from an increase in net realisable value;
- the circumstances or events that led to the reversal of a write-down of inventories;
- the carrying amount of inventories pledged as security for liabilities;
- the amount of a write-down to net realisable value;
- costs of inventories recognised as an expense during the period (income statement using functional classification);

or

- the operating costs, applicable to revenues, recognised as an expense during the period, classified by their nature (income statement using classification by nature).

IAS 7 *(AC 118)*

Cash Flow Statements

❑ **SUMMARY**

Background
Presentation and format
Disclosure

BACKGROUND

An entity must prepare a cash flow statement in accordance with the requirements of IAS 7. This cash flow statement will be presented as an integral part of the entity's financial statements for each period for which financial statements are presented.

Users of financial statements specifically need information on cash flow to form an opinion on:
- an entity's ability to generate cash, the timing thereof, and the certainty that it will be generated; and
- the needs of the entity to utilise the cash flows.

The cash flow statement deals with movements in cash and cash equivalents. **Cash** consists of cash on hand and demand (call) deposits. **Cash equivalents** are highly liquid short-term (three months maximum) investments that are normally held for the purpose of meeting short-term cash commitments rather than for the purpose of earning a return such as interest and dividends. Cash equivalents must, therefore, be readily convertible into cash and not be subject to the risks associated with significant changes in value.

PRESENTATION AND FORMAT

The cash flows reported in the cash flow statement should be classified as cash flows from:
- operating activities;
- investing activities; and
- financing activities.

1. Operating activities

Operating activities are the principal revenue-producing activities of the entity that are not investing or financing activities. Cash flows from operating activities generally result from the transactions and other events that enter into the determination of profit or loss.

One of the following methods can be used to report the cash flows from operating activities:
- the direct method (recommended), whereby major classes of gross cash receipts (i.e. cash receipts from customers) and gross cash payments (i.e. cash paid to suppliers and employees) are disclosed; or
- the indirect method, whereby profit or loss is adjusted for the effects of non-cash transactions, any deferrals or accruals of past or future operating cash receipts or payments, and items of income and expense associated with investing or financing cash flows.

Cash flows relating to taxes on income should be disclosed separately. These cash flows should be classified as operating activities. However, if these cash flows relate to a transaction classified as a financing or investing activity (and it is practicable to identify the related tax cash flow) then the tax cash flow should also be classified as an investing or financing activity, as appropriate.

2. Investing activities

- Investing activities represent acquisitions and disposals of long-term assets and other investments not included in cash equivalents.
- Major classes of gross cash receipts and gross cash payments arising from investing activities should be reported separately. Certain exceptions may be reported on a net basis.
- The total cash flow resulting from the purchase or sale of a subsidiary or other business unit, should be presented separately and should be classified as an investing activity.
- Certain transactions, such as the sale of an item of plant, can result in a gain or loss that is included in the determination of profit or loss. The cash flow that results from such transactions is, however, cash flow from investing activities.

3. Financing activities

- Financing activities represent activities that result in changes in the size and composition of the equity capital and borrowings of the entity.
- Major classes of gross cash receipts and gross cash payments arising from financing activities should be reported separately. Certain exceptions may be reported on a net basis.

4. Sundry aspects

- The following cash flows may be reported on a net basis:
    - cash receipts and payments on behalf of customers when these cash flows reflect the activities of the customers rather than those of the entity (for example rents collected on behalf of the owners of properties); and
    - cash receipts and payments for items in which the turnover is quick, the amounts are large, and the maturities are short (for example the acceptance and repayment of demand deposits).
- Cash flows arising from foreign currency transactions must be translated at the exchange rate as at the date of the cash flow.
- The cash flows of a foreign subsidiary must be translated at the exchange rates between the functional currency and the foreign currency at the dates of the cash flows.
- When an investment in another entity has been accounted for according to the cost or equity method, the reporting in the cash flow statement is limited to the cash flow between the entity and the investee (i.e. dividends and advances).
- An entity that accounts for an investment in a jointly controlled entity under the proportionate consolidation method, will account for its proportional share of the jointly controlled entity's cash flow in its consolidated cash flow statement.
- Cash flows from interest and dividends received and paid, must each be disclosed separately. Dividends and interest received may be classified as either operating or investing activities, while dividends and interest paid may be classified as either operating or financing activities. This classification will be consistent from period to period. The writers propose showing these as part of operating activities.

DISCLOSURE

Notes:

- The aggregate of the following in respect of the purchase or sale of a subsidiary or business unit during the period:
    - The total purchase or disposal consideration
    - The portion of the purchase or disposal consideration discharged by means of cash and cash equivalents
    - The amount of cash and cash equivalents in the subsidiary or business unit acquired or disposed of
    - The amount of assets and liabilities, other than cash and cash equivalents in the subsidiary or business unit acquired or disposed of, summarised by each major category
- The components of cash and cash equivalents and a reconciliation of the amounts in the cash flow statement with the equivalent items reported in the balance sheet
- Investing and financing transactions that do not require the use of cash or cash equivalents must be disclosed in the notes in a way that provides all the relevant information about these investing and financing activities
- The amount of significant cash and cash equivalent balances held by the entity that are not available for use by the group, together with commentary by management
- Distinguish in total the cash flows that represent an increase in the operating capacity from those required to maintain the operating capacity
- The amount of undrawn borrowing facilities that may be available for future operating activities and to settle capital commitments, indicating any restrictions on the use of these facilities
- The aggregate amount of cash flows from each of operating, investing and financing activities, related to interests in joint ventures reported using proportionate consolidation
- Segmental cash flows

IAS 8 *(AC 103)*, Circular 7/2005

Accounting Policies, Changes in Accounting Estimates and Errors

❑ SUMMARY

Background
Accounting practice and disclosure

BACKGROUND

The objective of this standard is to prescribe the criteria for selecting and changing accounting policies, together with the accounting treatment and disclosure of changes in accounting policies, changes in accounting estimates and corrections of errors.

The selection and application of accounting policies, and accounting for changes in accounting policies, changes in accounting estimates and corrections of prior period errors must be in accordance with this standard.

ACCOUNTING PRACTICE AND DISCLOSURE

1. Accounting policies

The accounting policy that has to be applied to a transaction is determined by the standard applicable to that transaction, taking into consideration any implementation guidance.

If no standard applies specifically to a transaction, management shall use its judgement in developing and applying an accounting policy to ensure that the information is:
- relevant to the economic decision-making needs of users; and
- reliable, in that the financial statements:
  - represent faithfully the financial position, financial performance and cash flows of the entity;
  - reflect the economic substance of transactions, other events and conditions, and not merely the legal form;
  - are neutral (free from bias);
  - are prudent; and
  - are complete in all material respects.

Management must refer to the following sources when applying their judgement in developing and applying an accounting policy:
- the requirements and guidance in statements and interpretations dealing with similar and related issues; and
- the definitions, recognition criteria and measurement concepts for assets, liabilities, income and expenses in the Framework.

Management may also consider the most recent pronouncements of other standard-setting bodies that use a similar conceptual (accounting) framework to develop accounting standards, other accounting literature and accepted industry practices, to the extent that these do not conflict with the above-mentioned sources.

Accounting policies must be selected and applied consistently for similar transactions, other events and conditions, unless a standard or an interpretation specifically requires or permits categorisation of items for which different accounting policies may be appropriate.

An appropriate accounting policy shall be selected and applied consistently to each category if a standard requires or permits such categorisation.

2. Changes in accounting policy

Changes in accounting policy can be either prospective or retrospective. Retrospective application is applying a new accounting policy to transactions, other events and conditions as if that policy had always been applied. Prospective application of a change in accounting policy and of recognising the effect of a change in an accounting estimate, respectively, are:
- applying the new accounting policy to transactions, other events and conditions occurring after the date as at which the policy is changed; and
- recognising the effect of the change in the accounting estimate in the current and future periods affected by the change.

An accounting policy may only be changed if the change:
- is required by a standard or an interpretation (compulsory); or
- results in reliable and more relevant information about the effects of transactions, other events or conditions on the entity's financial position, financial performance or cash flows (voluntary).

The following are not changes in accounting policies:

- the application of an accounting policy for transactions, other events or conditions that differ in substance from those previously occurring; and
- the application of a new accounting policy for transactions, other events or conditions that did not occur previously or were immaterial.

If the revaluation model is initially applied to assets in accordance with IAS 16 (AC 123) or IAS 38 (AC 129), IAS 8 must not be applied to this change in accounting policy. IAS 16 (AC 123) or IAS 38 (AC 129) must, however, be applied.

Unless it is impracticable to determine the effects of the change in accounting policy:[*]

- an entity shall account for a change in accounting policy resulting from the initial application of a standard or an interpretation in accordance with the specific transitional provisions, if any, in that standard or interpretation; and
- when an entity changes an accounting policy upon initial application of a standard or an interpretation that does not include specific transitional provisions applying to that change, or changes an accounting policy voluntarily, it shall apply the change retrospectively.

Subject to the impracticability to determine the necessary amounts to be disclosed when a change in accounting policy is applied retrospectively in accordance with the previous paragraph marked ([*]), the entity shall:

- adjust the opening balance of each affected component of equity for the earliest prior period presented; and
- the other comparative amounts disclosed for each prior period presented as if the new accounting policy had always been applied.

When it is impracticable to determine the period-specific effects of changing an accounting policy on comparative information for one or more of the prior periods presented:

- The entity shall apply the new accounting policy to the carrying amounts of assets and liabilities as at the beginning of the earliest period for which retrospective application is practicable.
- This earliest period may be the current period, and the entity shall also make a corresponding adjustment to the opening balance of each affected component of equity for that period.

Prospective application of the new accounting policy from the earliest day practicable will only occur if it is impracticable to determine the cumulative effect, at the beginning of the current period, of applying a new accounting policy to all prior periods.

3. Disclosure – changes in accounting policy

When initial application of a standard or an interpretation has an effect on the current period or any prior period, and would have such an effect except that it is impracticable to determine the amount of the adjustment, or might have an effect on future periods, an entity shall disclose:

- the title of the standard or interpretation;
- when applicable, that the change in accounting policy is made in accordance with its transitional provisions;
- the nature of the change in accounting policy;
- when applicable, a description of the transitional provisions;
- when applicable, the transitional provisions that might have an effect on future periods;
- for the current period and each prior period presented, to the extent practicable, the amount of the adjustment:
  - for each financial statement line item affected; and
  - if IAS 33 (AC 104) applies to the entity, for basic and diluted earnings per share;
- the amount of the adjustment relating to periods before those presented, to the extent practicable; and
- if retrospective application as required by the earlier paragraph marked ([*]) is impracticable for a particular prior period, or for periods before those presented, the circumstances that led to the existence of that condition and a description of how and from when the change in accounting policy has been applied.

Financial statements of subsequent periods need not repeat these disclosures.

When a voluntary change in accounting policy has an effect on the current period or any prior period; would have an effect on that period except that it is impracticable to determine the amount of the adjustment; or might have an effect on future periods, an entity shall disclose:

- the nature of the change in accounting policy;
- the reasons why applying the new accounting policy provides reliable and more relevant information;
- for the current period and each prior period presented, to the extent practicable, the amount of the adjustment:
  - for each financial statement line item affected; and
  - if IAS 33 (AC 104) applies to the entity, for basic and diluted earnings per share;
- the amount of the adjustment relating to periods before those presented, to the extent practicable; and
- if retrospective application is impracticable for a particular prior period, or for periods before those presented, the circumstances that led to the existence of that condition and a description of how and from when the change in accounting policy has been applied.

Financial statements of subsequent periods need not repeat these disclosures.

When an entity has not applied a new standard or interpretation that has been issued but is not yet effective, the entity shall disclose:
- this fact;
- known or reasonably estimable information relevant to assessing the possible impact that application of the new standard or interpretation will have on the entity's financial statements in the period of initial application;
- the title of the new standard or interpretation;
- the nature of the impending change or changes in accounting policy;
- the date by which application of the standard or interpretation is required;
- the date at which it plans to apply the standard or interpretation initially; and either
- a discussion of the impact that initial application of the standard or interpretation is expected to have on the entity's financial statements; or
- if that impact is not known or reasonably estimable, a statement to that effect.

4. Changes in accounting estimates

Many items in financial statements cannot be measured accurately but can only be estimated by using judgement, based on the latest available, reliable information. An estimate may change as new information comes to light, circumstances change or more experience is obtained. Examples of estimates used are:
- allowance for credit losses;
- inventory obsolescence;
- the fair value of financial assets or financial liabilities;
- provisions;
- the useful lives, residual values of, or expected pattern of consumption of the future economic benefits embodied in depreciable assets; and
- warranty obligations.

Using reasonable estimates is an essential part of the preparation of financial statements on the accrual basis. Estimates do not make financial statements unreliable.

The effect of a change in an accounting estimate, other than a change to which the paragraph directly below marked with (#) applies, shall be recognised prospectively (from the date of the change in estimate) by including it in profit or loss in:
- the period of the change, if the change affects that period only; or
- the period of the change and future periods, if the change affects both.

\# To the extent that a change in an accounting estimate gives rise to changes in assets and liabilities, or relates to an item of equity, it shall be recognised by adjusting the carrying amount of the related asset, liability or equity item in the period of the change.

5. Disclosure – changes in accounting estimates

An entity shall disclose the nature and amount of a change in an accounting estimate that has an effect in the current period or is expected to have an effect in future periods, except for the disclosure of the effect on future periods when it is impracticable to estimate that effect.

If the amount of the effect in future periods is not disclosed because estimating it is impracticable, an entity shall disclose that fact.

6. Errors

Prior period errors are omissions from, and misstatements in, the entity's financial statements for one or more prior periods arising from a failure to use, or the misuse of, reliable information that:
- was available when financial statements for those periods were authorised for issue; and
- could reasonably be expected to have been obtained and taken into account in the preparation and presentation of those financial statements.

Such errors include mathematical errors, incorrect application of accounting policies, oversights or misinterpretations of facts, and fraud.

Retrospective restatement is correcting the recognition, measurement and disclosure of amounts of elements of financial statements as if a prior period error had never occurred.

Subject to the impracticability to determine either the period-specific effects or the cumulative effect of the error, an entity shall correct material prior period errors retrospectively in the first set of financial statements authorised for issue after their discovery by:
- restating the comparative amounts for the prior period(s) presented in which the error occurred; or
- if the error occurred before the earliest prior period presented, restating the opening balances of assets, liabilities and equity for the earliest prior period presented.

Retrospective restatement shall occur, except to the extent that it is impracticable to determine either the period-specific effects or the cumulative effect of the error.

When it is impracticable to determine the period-specific effects of an error on comparative information for one or more prior periods presented, the entity shall restate the opening balances of assets, liabilities and equity for the earliest period for which retrospective restatement is practicable (which may be the current period).

Prospective corrections of comparative information from the earliest date practicable shall occur if it is impracticable to determine the cumulative effect, at the beginning of the current period, of an error on all prior periods.

7. Disclosure – prior period errors

An entity shall disclose the following when correcting prior period errors retrospectively:
- the nature of the prior period error;
- for each prior period presented, to the extent practicable, the amount of the correction:
  - for each financial statement line item affected; and
  - if IAS 33 (AC 104) applies to the entity, for basic and diluted earnings per share;
- the amount of the correction at the beginning of the earliest prior period presented; and if retrospective restatement is impracticable for a particular prior period:
  - the circumstances that led to the existence of that condition; and
  - a description of how and from when the error has been corrected.

Financial statements of subsequent periods need not repeat these disclosures.

8. Annexure on accounting policy

Refer to the annexure to the chapter on IAS 1 (AC 101); study that now in conjunction with this chapter.

IAS 10 *(AC 107)*

Events After the Reporting Date

❑ **SUMMARY**

Background
Accounting practice
Disclosure

BACKGROUND

IAS 10 deals with events after the reporting date.

1. Objective

The objective of the above-mentioned standard is to prescribe:
* when adjustments to the financial statements shall be made for events after reporting date; and
* disclosure required for the date on which financial statements were authorised for issue as well as events after reporting date.

2. Date of authorisation for issue

In some cases an entity presents its financial statements to shareholders for approval after the financial statements have already been issued. Should this be the case, the date the financial statements are authorised for issue will be the date of original issuance, and not the date of approval by shareholders.

In other cases, management presents its financial statements to a supervisory board (made up solely of non-executives) for approval. Under these circumstances financial statements are authorised for issue when management authorises them for issue to the supervisory board.

ACCOUNTING PRACTICE

1. Events occurring after the reporting date

Events after the reporting date occur between the reporting date (whether favourable or unfavourable) and the date on which the financial statements are authorised for issue (see 2. above). Two types of event can be identified:
* events providing additional evidence of conditions existing at the reporting date, called adjusting events; (the origin of the event is in the current accounting period); and
* events indicative of conditions arising after the reporting date, called non-adjusting events.

Assets and liabilities at reporting date are adjusted if events occurring after the reporting date provide additional information about conditions existing at reporting date, and therefore allow the assets and liabilities to be estimated more accurately.

Assets and liabilities are also adjusted if events after reporting date indicate that part of or all of the business is no longer a going concern.

If events occurring after the reporting date do not relate to conditions which existed at reporting date, assets and liabilities are not adjusted. However, the events must be disclosed if they could influence decisions taken by the users of the financial statements. A list of disclosable non-adjusting events is provided in IAS 10.22.

2. Dividends

When dividends are declared after the reporting date, an entity shall not recognise those dividends as a liability at reporting date.

Therefore, only dividends paid or approved for payment at an annual general meeting during the current year shall be recognised in the financial statements of the current year.

3. Going concern

If management determines after reporting date it intends to liquidate an entity, cease trading or that it has no realistic alternative but to perform either of these actions, they shall not prepare financial statements on a going concern basis.

DISCLOSURE

1. Date of authorisation for issue

- Disclose the date when financial statements were authorised for issue and who gave the authorisation.
- If other parties have the power to amend financial statements after issuance, this fact shall be disclosed.

2. Adjusting events after reporting date – updating

If such an event is adjusted, all disclosures relating to this event shall be updated for the new information.

3. Non-adjusting events after reporting date

Dividends

In terms of IAS 1 (AC 101) .125, dividends declared or proposed before the financial statements were authorised for issue and not recognised as a liability, shall be disclosed in the notes by way of a note dealing with dividends declared or proposed, also disclosing the related dividend per share.

Going concern

IAS 1 (AC 101) .23 requires certain disclosures if:
- the financial statements are not prepared on a going concern basis; or
- management is aware of material uncertainties that may cast significant doubt on an entity's ability to continue to operate as a going concern.

Events occurring after reporting date

In the case of events, which do not result in the adjustment of items of the statement of financial position but nevertheless must be disclosed owing to materiality, the following information shall be provided:
- the nature of the events;
- the estimated financial effect of the event; and
- if the financial effect of the estimation cannot be determined, a statement to that effect.

In addition to this standard, the following Companies Act, 1973, Schedule 4 requirements also apply:

Par 67(2) and 72(b): Directors' report: The fact and circumstances of occurrences between the accounting date and the date of the report shall be noted. In the case of a holding company (parent), these facts must also be disclosed when they relate to the group.

Schematic summary of IAS 10 (AC 107)

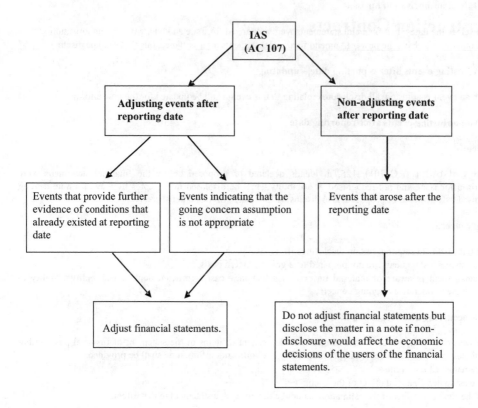

IAS 11 *(AC 109)*

Construction Contracts

❑ **SUMMARY**

Background
Accounting practice
Disclosure

BACKGROUND

A construction contract is a contract specifically negotiated for the construction of an asset or a combination of assets that are closely interrelated or interdependant in terms of:
- design;
- technology and function; or
- the ultimate purpose or use thereof.

Construction contracts include contracts for the:
- rendering of services, for example, architects;
- demolition of assets;
- restoration of assets; and
- the restoration of the environment following the demolition of assets.

Owing to the nature of the activities undertaken in construction contracts, they usually take place over more than one accounting period.

The issues in accounting for construction contracts are primarily:
- proper matching of contract revenue and related costs; and
- the allocation of contract revenue and related costs to the accounting periods in which the construction work was performed.

Two types of contract are distinguished, namely:
- fixed price contracts (usually subject to cost escalation clauses); and
- cost plus contracts (the contract costs plus a profit allowance payable to the contractor).

Some construction contracts may be a combination of both of the above.

The requirements of IAS 11 are usually applied separately to each construction contract. In the following circumstances, however, one may, if certain conditions are met, deviate from this rule:
- The contract covers a number of assets and the construction of each asset is treated as a separate construction contract.
- A group of contracts is treated as a single construction contract.
- The construction of an additional asset is treated as a separate construction contract, when certain conditions apply.

Contract revenue comprises:
- the initial amount of revenue agreed in the contract; and
- variations in contract work, claims and incentive payments to the extent that:
  - it is probable that they will result in revenue; and
  - they are capable of being reliably measured.

The initial amount of revenue agreed upon in the contract can differ from actual revenue, owing to the occurrence of events and uncertainties being resolved, for example:
- cost escalation clauses in a fixed price contract which will result in an increase in revenue; or
- a decrease in revenue as a result of penalties arising from delays.

A **variation** is an instruction by the customer for a change in the scope of the work to be performed under the contract, for example:
- changes in specifications or design of the asset; and
- changes in the duration of the contract.

A **claim** is an amount that the contractor seeks to collect from the customer or another party as reimbursement for costs over and above the contract price. Claims may arise, for example, from:
- customer caused delays;
- errors in specifications or design of an asset; and
- disputed variations in contract work.

Incentive payments are additional amounts paid to the contractor if specified performance standards are met or exceeded, for example, early completion of a contract.

All contract revenue is measured at the fair value of the consideration received or receivable.

Contract costs are costs relating to the contract from the date of securing the contract to the final completion thereof. However, directly related costs and costs incurred in securing the contract are also included as part of the contract costs, if they can be separately identified and measured reliably, and if it is probable that the contract will be obtained. Contract costs comprise the following:

- Directly related costs to the specific contract, including specially manufactured materials delivered on site, even if they have not been installed yet. These costs may be reduced by any incidental income that is not included in contract revenue, for example, income from the sale of surplus materials and the disposal of plant and equipment at the end of the contract. It will therefore also decrease the total estimated costs of a contract.
- Costs that may be attributable to contract activity in general and can be allocated to a specific contract; for example, insurance and overheads. Such costs are allocated according to the normal level of construction activity, by using methods that are systematic and rational, and are consistently applied.
- Costs that are specifically chargeable to the customer under the terms of the contract; for example, administration and development costs.

These types of cost usually do not form part of the contract costs.

ACCOUNTING PRACTICE

When the outcome of a construction contract can be estimated reliably, contract revenue and contract costs associated with the construction contract should be recognised respectively, by reference to the stage of completion (percentage of completion method) of the contract activity at the balance sheet date.

1. Estimated outcome

The outcome of a construction contract can only be estimated reliably when it is probable that the economic benefits associated with the contract will flow to the entity. Furthermore, an entity is generally able to make reliable estimates after it has agreed to a contract that establishes:

- each party's enforceable rights regarding the asset to be constructed;
- the consideration to be exchanged; and
- the manner and terms of settlement.

IAS 11 prescribes specific conditions that are to be met before the outcome of a contract (both a fixed price contract and a cost plus contract) can be estimated reliably. When the outcome of a construction contract cannot be estimated reliably; for example, in the early stages of construction:

- revenue shall be recognised only to the extent that the contract costs incurred are recoverable; and
- contract costs shall be recognised as an expense in the period in which they are incurred.

When the uncertainties that prevented the outcome of the contract being estimated reliably no longer exist, revenue and expenses associated with the construction contract should be recognised as normal.

2. Method of income recognition

The percentage of completion method is applied to ensure that contract revenue is matched with the contract costs incurred in reaching the stage of completion. In terms of this method, both contract revenue and contract costs are recognised in the income statement in the accounting periods in which the work is performed.

The stage of completion of a contract may be determined in a variety of ways. The entity uses the method that measures reliably the work performed. It includes, inter alia, the following:

In proportion to costs incurred

Costs to date/Total estimated costs. Costs to date exclude costs that relate to future activity, such as unused material on site and advance payments to subcontractors. However, it includes materials which have been custom made for the contract and delivered on site, even though it has not been installed yet.

The percentage of work certified (surveys of work performed)

Work certified to date/Contract price.

Physical stage

Number; for example, the number of houses completed in a big housing project.

3. Collectability

When an uncertainty arises about the collectability of an amount already included in contract revenue or already recognised as contract revenue in a previous period, the probable uncollectable amount is recognised as an expense rather than as an adjustment of contract revenue.

4. Contract costs

Even though contract costs are normally recognised as an expense in the accounting period in which the work was performed, any expected excess of total contract costs over total contract revenue is recognised as an expense immediately. Such a construction contract is an onerous contract in terms of IAS 37 (AC 130).

A contractor may have incurred contract costs that relate to future activity on the contract. Such contract costs are recognised as an asset, provided it is probably recoverable. This asset represents an amount due from the customer and is often classified as contract work in progress.

If it is not probable that contract costs will be recovered, then these costs are immediately expensed. Examples of such circumstances include contracts:
- which are not fully enforceable, that is, their validity is seriously in question;
- the completion of which is subject to the outcome of pending litigation or legislation;
- relating to properties that are likely to be condemned or expropriated;
- where the customer is unable to meet its obligations; or
- where the contractor is unable to complete the contract or otherwise meet its obligations under the contract.

5. Expected losses

When it is probable that the total contract costs will exceed total contract revenue, the expected loss shall be recognised as an expense immediately. (See onerous contracts under IAS 37 (AC 130)).

6. Changes in estimates

The effect of a change in the estimate of contract revenue or contract costs, or the effect of a change in the estimate of the outcome of a contract, is accounted for as a change in accounting estimate. (Refer chapter on IAS 8 (AC 103)).

7. Progress payments

In most contracts, the customer is required to make advance and/or progress payments at certain stages of completion, on the basis of progress certificates issued by an architect or engineer. The following types of payment are normally made:

An advance structured as a loan in the contractual agreement

When an amount is received it is immediately recorded as a liability. Depending on the agreement, the contractor may be obliged to pay interest on such an advance. The contract should also indicate whether the loan is to be repaid or offset against a progress certificate as a payment.

This type of advance is normally negotiated by a contractor when the contract is capital intensive and the contractor does not have sufficient funds available to purchase all the machinery and equipment.

- A normal advance: A customer may be requested by the contractor to make an advance before a progress certificate is issued. This will normally happen when the contractor experiences a temporary cash flow problem.
- Progress payments: These are payments made in accordance with issued progress billings.
- Retention monies: Construction contracts normally contain a clause in terms of which a customer has the right to retain certain amounts until specified contractual conditions are satisfied. Retention monies are portions of issued progress billings, which are not paid until the conditions as set out in the contract for payment of such amounts are met, or until defects have been rectified. These amounts should be classified as debtors (receivables) in the financial statements.

These amounts are normally paid as soon as certain conditions in the contract are met.

8. Tax implications

In terms of the South African Income Tax Act, if a receipt precedes an accrual, the receipt must be included in gross income in the year of the receipt and not (if that is later) in the year of accrual.

Accrual takes place when the taxpayer becomes unconditionally entitled to an amount and the inclusion in income will be the face value (and not the net present value). With construction contracts and specifically those that provide for retention monies the accrual will only take place when the suspensive condition is fulfilled. A loan is not a receipt or accrual for purposes of gross income.

If an amount is received in advance in terms of a contract and the expenses related to fulfilling the obligations under the contract will only be incurred in a following year of assessment, the taxpayer can claim an allowance under section 24C. Note, the expenses incurred in the same year as the year of receipt, will be allowed as a deduction for tax purposes in the normal way, if they meet the related requirements.

The section 24C allowance is therefore only for future expenditure. The amount thereof is to be determined by SARS. The request to determine the amount (of the allowance) is made by the taxpayer; the taxpayer should ensure that full consideration is given to this application.

Adjustments to the original contract amount should only influence the section 24C allowance to the extent that it relates to future expenses. Adjustments in respect of expenses actually incurred will not be in connection with future expenditure.

The following aspects are important in respect of the section 24C allowance:
- It may not exceed the amount included in gross income.
- The allowance allowed in the preceding year of assessment is added back in the current year of assessment.
- It is not strictly applied in practice, but the allowance is normally calculated per contract. Losses made on a specific contract may not be brought into account when the future expenses of another contract are determined.

Amounts due under contract of sale, where the ownership or transfer of the 'goods' is only done after receipt of the whole or a portion of the amount payable under the agreement, qualify for the section 24C allowance. This allowance is generally calculated as a percentage of the outstanding amounts at the end of the financial year and normally uses the gross profit as a basis of determination.

DISCLOSURE

Accounting policy

- The methods used to determine the contract revenue recognised
- The methods used to determine the stage of completion of contracts in progress

Income statement

- The amount of contract revenue recognised in the period
- The amount of contract costs recognised for the period

Balance sheet

- The amount of advances received
- The amount of retention monies

Notes

- The aggregate amount of costs incurred and recognised profits (less recognised losses) to date
- The gross amount* due from customers for contract work (to be shown as an asset)
- The gross amount* due to customers for contract work (to be shown as a liability)
- Contingent gains and contingent losses from such items as warranty costs, claims, penalties or possible losses

* This amount can always be calculated as the total of the following:
  - construction work in progress;
  - unbilled contract revenue/contract revenue billed in advance; and
  - provision for losses on construction contracts.

IAS 12 *(AC 102)*, SIC 21 *(AC 421)*, SIC 25 *(AC 425)*, AC 501, AC 502 and Circular 01/06

Income Taxes

❑ **SUMMARY**

Background
Accounting practice
Presentation and disclosure
SIC 21: Income taxes – recovery of revalued non-depreciable assets
SIC 25: Income taxes – changes in the tax status of an entity or its shareholders
AC 501: Accounting for secondary tax on companies
AC 502: Substantively enacted tax rates and tax laws
Circular 01/06: Disclosures in relation to deferred tax

BACKGROUND

1. Introduction

The objective of IAS 12 (AC 102) is to prescribe the accounting treatment for the current and future tax consequences of:
- the future recovery/settlement of the carrying amount of assets/liabilities that are recognised in an entity's balance sheet; and
- transactions and other events of the current period that are recognised in an entity's financial statements.

The standard must be applied in accounting for income taxes, including all domestic and foreign taxes based on taxable profits, which includes withholding taxes. VAT is excluded, as it is not a tax based on taxable profits.

2. Deferred tax

Deferred tax is tax attributable to temporary differences, that is, taxes payable or recoverable in future periods.
- Deferred tax liabilities are the amounts of income taxes payable in future periods in respect of taxable temporary differences.
- Deferred tax assets are the amounts of income taxes recoverable in future periods in respect of:
  - deductible temporary differences;
  - the carryforward of unused tax losses; and
  - the carryforward of unused tax credits.
- Temporary differences are differences between the tax base of an asset or liability and its carrying amount in the balance sheet. They may be either:
  - taxable temporary differences that will result in taxable amounts in future periods; or
  - deductible temporary differences that will result in amounts that are deductible in future periods.

Some temporary differences (related to differences in timing) arise when items of income or expense are included in accounting profit in one period but are included in taxable profit in another period.

Temporary differences also arise when:
- the cost of a business combination (that is an acquisition) is allocated to the assets and liabilities acquired but equivalent adjustments are not made for tax purposes;
- assets are revalued and equivalent adjustments are not made for tax purposes;
- goodwill arises on consolidation;
- on initial recognition of an asset or liability, the tax base differs from the carrying amount, for example when an entity benefits from non-taxable government grants related to assets; and
- the carrying amount of investments in subsidiaries, branches, associates and interests in joint ventures differ from the tax base of such investments or interests.

ACCOUNTING PRACTICE

1. Tax base

The **tax base** of an item is the amount attributed to that item for tax purposes. It is determined as follows:
- Asset: The amount that will be deductible for tax purposes against any taxable economic benefits that will flow to an entity when it recovers the carrying amount of the asset. If the economic benefits will not be taxable, the tax base of the asset is equal to its carrying amount.
- Expense: Some expenses are recognised in full for accounting purposes in the current period, but are allowed as a deduction for tax purposes in current and future periods. The carrying amount of the expense is then nil; the tax base is the amount that will be permitted in future periods.
- Liability: The carrying amount, less any amount that will be deductible for tax purposes in respect of that liability in future periods.
- Revenue received in advance: The carrying amount, less any amount of the revenue that will not be taxable in future periods (or that has already been taxed).

The relationship and effect of the differences between the carrying amount (CA) and tax base (TB) of the above-mentioned elements can be summarised as follows:

Assets and expenses	CA > TB	Taxable temporary difference	DTL
	CA < TB	Deductible temporary difference	DTA
Liabilities and revenue received in advance	CA > TB	Deductible temporary difference	DTA
	CA < TB	Taxable temporary difference	DTL

DTL = Deferred tax liability
DTA = Deferred tax asset

2. Recognition of deferred tax assets and liabilities

2.1 Taxable temporary differences

A deferred tax liability shall be recognised for all taxable temporary differences, except if it arises from:
- the initial recognition of goodwill; or
- the initial recognition of an asset or liability in a transaction that is not a business combination, and at the time of the transaction, affects neither accounting profit nor taxable profit/tax loss.

2.2 Deductible temporary differences

A deferred tax asset shall be recognised for all deductible temporary differences to the extent that it is probable[*] that taxable profit will be available against which the deductible temporary differences can be utilised. A deferred tax asset is, however, not recognised when it arises from:
- the initial recognition of an asset or liability in a transaction which is not a business combination; and
- at the time of the transaction, affects neither accounting profit nor taxable profit/tax loss.

It is probable[*] that taxable profit will be available against which a deductible temporary difference can be utilised when there are sufficient taxable temporary differences relating to the same tax authority and the same taxable entity. If there are insufficient taxable temporary differences, the deferred tax asset is recognised to the extent that it is probable that the entity will have sufficient taxable profit in future periods.

For investments in subsidiaries, branches and associates as well as interests in joint ventures, see 2.5 hereafter.

2.3 Unused tax losses and unused tax credits

If an entity has unused tax losses and unused tax credits, a deferred tax asset should be recognised for the carryforward of these losses and credits to the extent that it is probable that future taxable profit will be available against which the unused tax losses and unused tax credits can be utilised. (Also see AC 501).

2.4 Reassessment of unrecognised deferred tax assets

At each balance sheet date, an entity shall reassess unrecognised deferred tax assets. To the extent that it has become probable that future taxable profit will allow the previously unrecognised deferred tax asset to be recovered, it should be recognised in the current period.

2.5 Investments in subsidiaries, branches, associates and interests in joint ventures

If the carrying amount of investments in subsidiaries, branches, associates and interests in joint ventures becomes different from the tax base thereof (which is often cost), a temporary difference arises. Such differences may result from:
- the existence of undistributed profits;
- changes in exchange rates when the subsidiary is a foreign operation; and
- a reduction in the carrying amount of an investment in an associate owing to an impairment loss.

An entity shall recognise a deferred tax liability for all taxable temporary differences associated with these investments except to the extent that both of the following conditions are satisfied:
- the parent, investor or venturer has the ability to control the timing of the reversal of the temporary differences; and
- it is probable that the temporary differences will not reverse in the foreseeable future.

An entity shall recognise a deferred tax asset for all deductible temporary differences arising from these investments to the extent that it is probable that:
- the temporary differences will reverse in the foreseeable future; and
- taxable profit will be available against which the temporary differences can be utilised.

3. Measurement of current and deferred tax

An entity should measure current tax liabilities/assets at the amount expected to be paid to (recovered from) the tax authorities. This measurement should be based on tax rates (and tax laws) that have been enacted or substantively enacted by the balance sheet date (also see AC 502).

An entity should measure deferred tax assets and liabilities at the tax rates that are expected to apply to the future period when the asset is realised or the liability is settled. This measurement should be based on tax rates (and tax laws) that have been enacted or substantively enacted by the balance sheet date (also see AC 502).

When measuring deferred tax assets and liabilities, the expected manner of recovery of the assets and liabilities should be taken into account. (Refer to SIC 21 at the end of this chapter.)

The carrying amount of a deferred tax asset shall be reviewed at each balance sheet date and shall be reduced to the extent that it is no longer probable that sufficient taxable profit will be available to utilise the asset. If it subsequently becomes probable that sufficient taxable profit will be available, the reduction shall be reversed.

Deferred tax assets and liabilities shall not be discounted.

4. Recognition of current and deferred tax expenses

Current and deferred tax are included in the income statement as income/expense, except to the extent that the tax arises from:
- a transaction or event which is recognised directly in equity; or
- a business combination.

If terms are charged directly to equity, the related current and deferred tax shall also be charged directly to equity. (Also refer to SIC 25 at the end of this chapter.)

When temporary differences arise from a business combination, an entity recognises any resulting deferred tax assets/liabilities as identifiable assets and liabilities at the date of the acquisition. As a result, those deferred tax assets and liabilities affect the amount of goodwill or the amount of any excess at acquisition date and does not effect the income statement.

PRESENTATION AND DISCLOSURE

1. Presentation

Tax assets and tax liabilities shall be presented separately from other assets and liabilities in the balance sheet (from IAS 1 (AC 101)).

Deferred tax assets and liabilities shall be presented separately from current tax assets and liabilities (from IAS 1 (AC 101)).

When an entity makes a distinction between current and non-current assets and liabilities in its financial statements, it shall not classify deferred tax assets/liabilities as being current.

An entity shall offset current tax assets against current tax liabilities only if the entity:
- has a legally enforceable right to set off the recognised amounts; and
- intends either to settle on a net basis, or to realise the asset and settle the liability simultaneously.

An entity shall offset deferred tax assets and deferred tax liabilities only if:
- the entity has a legally enforceable right to set off current tax assets against current tax liabilities; and
- the deferred tax assets and the deferred tax liabilities relate to income taxes levied by the same tax authority on either:

- the same taxable entity; or
- different taxable entities, which intend either to settle current tax liabilities and assets on a net basis, or to realise the assets and settle the liabilities simultaneously in each future period in which significant amounts of deferred tax assets and liabilities are expected to be settled or recovered.

The income tax expense is presented as a separate line item on the face of the income statement.

2. Disclosure

Accounting policy

- State the method used to provide for deferred tax; that is, the balance sheet liability method (from IAS 1 (AC 101) and IAS 8 (AC 103)).

Income statement and notes

The major components of tax expense/income shall be disclosed separately, including the following:
- current tax expense/income;
- any adjustments recognised in the present period for current tax recognised in prior periods;
- the amount of deferred tax expense/income arsing from the origination and reversal of temporary differences;
- the amount of deferred tax expense/income arising from changes in tax rates or the imposition of new taxes;
- the amount of the benefit arising from a previously unrecognised tax loss, tax credit or temporary difference of a prior period that is used to reduce the current tax expense of the current period;
- the amount of the benefit from a previously unrecognised tax loss, tax credit or temporary difference of a prior period that is used to reduce the deferred tax expense of the current period;
- the deferred tax expense/income arising from the write-down, or reversal of a previous write-down, of a deferred tax asset when it is reviewed at each balance sheet date; and
- the amount of tax expense/income relating to changes in accounting policy and errors (see IAS 8 (AC 103)) that are included in the income statement because they cannot be accounted for retrospectively.

The following information shall also be disclosed in addition to the tax expense/income:
- a reconciliation between the tax expense/income and accounting profit/loss in either or both of the following forms:
  - a numerical reconciliation in Rand, disclosing the basis on which the applicable tax rate(s) is (are) computed; or
  - a numerical reconciliation of the average effective tax rate and the applicable tax rate, disclosing the basis on which the applicable tax rate is computed;
- an explanation of changes in the applicable tax rate(s) compared to the previous accounting period;
- in respect of each type of temporary difference, and in respect of each type of unused tax loss and unused tax credit, the amount of the deferred tax income or expense recognised in the income statement, if this is not apparent from the change in the amount recognised in the balance sheet; and
- in respect of discontinued operations, the tax expense/income relating to:
  - the gain or loss on discontinuance; and
  - the profit or loss from the ordinary activities of the discontinued operation for the period, together with the corresponding amounts for each prior period presented.

Balance sheet and notes

The following shall be disclosed:
- the aggregate current and deferred tax relating to items that are charged to equity;
- the amount (and expiry date, if any) of deductible temporary differences, unused tax losses and unused tax credits for which no deferred tax asset is recognised in the balance sheet;
- the aggregate amount of temporary differences associated with investments in subsidiaries, branches and associates and interests in joint ventures, for which deferred tax liabilities have not been recognised;
- in respect of each type of temporary difference, and in respect of each type of unused tax loss and unused tax credit the amount of the deferred tax asset and liability recognised in the balance sheet for each period presented; and

- the amount of a deferred tax asset and the nature of the evidence supporting its recognition, when:
    - the utilisation of the deferred tax asset is dependent on future taxable profits in excess of the profits arising from the reversal of existing taxable temporary differences; and
    - the entity has suffered a loss in either the current or preceding period in the tax jurisdiction to which the deferred tax asset relates.

Other notes

- The amount of income tax consequences of dividends to shareholders of the entity that were proposed or declared before the financial statements were authorised for issue, but that are not recognised as a liability.
- An entity shall disclose the nature of potential income tax consequences that would result from the payment of dividends to its shareholders.
- Also disclose the amounts of potential income tax consequences practically determinable and whether there are any income tax consequences not practically determinable.

SIC 21: INCOME TAXES – RECOVERY OF REVALUED NON-DEPRECIABLE ASSETS

1.   Background

The standard on income taxes requires the measurement of deferred tax liabilities and assets to reflect the tax consequences that would arise from the manner in which the entity, at balance sheet date, expects to recover or settle the carrying amounts of the assets and liabilities that resulted in temporary differences.

When an asset is revalued in South Africa, taxable profit is not affected and the tax base of the asset remains unchanged.

If the future recovery of the revalued carrying amount will be taxable, any difference between this carrying amount and the unadjusted tax base, will be a temporary difference and will thus give rise to a deferred tax asset or liability.

This interpretation is also applicable to investment properties carried at revalued (fair value) amounts that would, in terms of IAS 16 (AC 123), be considered non-depreciable.

2.   Issue

The issue is how to interpret the term 'recovery' in the case of a non-depreciable asset, for example, land, which is revalued under IAS 16 (AC 123) on property, plant and equipment.

3.   Consensus

The deferred tax liability or asset that would arise from the revaluation of a non-depreciable asset such as land, is measured based on the recovery of the carrying amount of that asset through sale, regardless of the basis on which the carrying amount of the non-depreciable asset was determined.

Consequently, if the tax rate applicable to the taxable amount derived from the sale of the asset differs from the tax rate applicable to recovery of the carrying amount of the asset through use, the former tax rate is applied to measure the resulting deferred tax asset or liability. In South Africa, this will be the capital gains tax rate.

SIC 25: INCOME TAXES – CHANGES IN THE TAX STATUS OF AN ENTITY OR ITS SHAREHOLDERS

1.   Background

A change in the tax status of an entity or of a shareholder may have an immediate impact on the current and deferred tax liabilities and assets of an entity. For example, an entity's equity may be restructured, a controlling shareholder may move to a foreign country or an entity may be listed. As a consequence of the above, an entity may gain or lose certain tax incentives or may become subject to a different tax rate.

2. Issue

The issue is how an entity shall account for the tax consequences of such a change in tax status or that of its shareholder.

3. Consensus

- A change in the tax status of an entity or of its shareholders, does not normally have an impact on pre-tax amounts recognised directly in equity.
- Consequently, the current and deferred tax consequences of a change in tax status shall be included in profit or loss for the period, unless those consequences result from transactions or events that gave rise to a direct credit or charge to the recognised amount of equity.
- Tax consequences relating to changes in the recognised amount of equity (in the same or a different period), without going through the income statement, shall be charged or credited directly to equity.

AC 501: ACCOUNTING FOR SECONDARY TAX ON COMPANIES

1. Issues and consensus

Issue 1   How shall STC be presented in the financial statements of an entity?

Consensus 1   STC shall be treated as part of the income tax charge in the income statement for the period.

Issue 2   In terms of IAS 10 (AC 107) .12, dividends declared after the balance sheet date shall not be recognised as a liability at balance sheet date. When shall STC on such declared dividends be raised?

Consensus 2   The income tax consequence of dividends is recognised when a liability to pay the dividend is raised. Consequently, the expense shall be raised in the period when the liability for the dividend is raised.

Issue 3   Certain equity instruments are classified as liabilities under IAS 32 (AC 125) and consequently, dividends paid on such instruments are accrued on a day-to-day basis (similar to interest), even though such dividends may not have been declared. How shall STC on such dividends be treated?

Consensus 3   Where the equity instrument has been classified as a liability and the related dividends are treated the same as interest, the related STC shall be accrued as a liability when the dividend/interest accrues.

Issue 4:   IAS 32 (AC 125) .35 states that the transaction costs of issuing or acquiring own equity shares shall be accounted for as a deduction from equity, net of related taxes. Should the STC on the reacquisition of an entity's own equity instruments be accounted for as a charge to income or as deduction from equity?

Consensus 4   AC 501 requires this STC to be shown as part of the tax charge in the income statement and not as a deduction from equity. This is not in line with IAS 32 (AC 125) .35, which requires STC on reacquisition to be deducted from equity.

Issue 5   In terms of IAS 33 (AC 104) .14(b) earnings for purposes of calculating EPS shall be net of after-tax undeclared cumulative preference dividends. Should the STC on the preference dividend also be deducted when calculating EPS?

Consensus 5   Where the preference dividend has not been declared, both the STC related to the dividend and the preference dividend shall be deducted to calculate EPS. The standard requires an after-tax amount.

Issue 6   Should STC on dividends declared during an interim period be recognised on a discrete basis (in the period in which the dividend is declared) or on an integral basis (forming part of average tax rate)?

Consensus 6   The STC expense shall be recognised in each interim period – based on the dividend accrued during that interim period – as a liability.

Issue 7   Should a deferred tax asset be raised when an entity received a dividend and has not utilised the related STC credits on such dividends received?

Consensus 7   A deferred tax asset shall be raised when an entity received a dividend without utilising the related tax credit in that period and it is probable that such STC credits will be utilised in future.

2.   Disclosure

The following disclosure, which may also be required by IAS 12, shall be made in respect of STC:
- amount provided for STC;
- amount of income tax consequences related to dividends declared or proposed subsequent to balance sheet date, but before the financial statements were authorised for issue;
- the nature of potential income tax consequences that would result from the payment of dividends by an entity (also provide the amounts involved if practicable to determine and state if not practicable to determine);
- an explanation that will assist in understanding the factors affecting the STC charge (this is particularly relevant where STC is a significant component of the tax charge);
- the amount of unutilised STC credits that arise when dividend income exceeds dividends declared, to the extent that a deferred tax asset was not raised; and
- the tax rate reconciliation shall include STC as a reconciling item.

AC 502: SUBSTANTIVELY ENACTED TAX RATES AND TAX LAWS

1.   Background

New tax rates and tax laws may be announced during the annual Budget Statement. IAS 12 (AC 102) requires current and deferred tax assets and liabilities to be measured using tax rates and tax laws enacted or substantively enacted by the balance sheet date.

2.   Issue

If the Minister of Finance announces changes in tax rates and tax laws, the question arises as to when these changes should be regarded as substantively enacted.

3.   Consensus

- Changes in tax rates that are not inextricably linked to other changes in tax laws are regarded as substantively enacted from the time that they are announced.
- Changes in tax rates that are inextricably linked to other changes in tax laws are regarded as substantively enacted when they have been approved by Parliament and signed by the President.
- Other changes in tax laws are regarded as substantively enacted when approved by Parliament and signed by the President.

CIRCULAR 01/06: DISCLOSURES IN RELATION TO DEFERRED TAX

- If the manner of recovery/settlement of an asset/liability would give rise to materially different deferred tax balances, an entity should disclose:
  - the expected manner of recovery;
  - the tax rate used to calculate the deferred tax balance; and
  - possible charges to the above.

IAS 14 *(AC 115)*

Segment Reporting

❏ **SUMMARY**

Background
Accounting practice
Disclosure

IFRS 8 replaced IAS 14 (AC115) during 2006. However, to ensure that the summaries are aligned with the questions in the question book, as well as the fact that IFRS 8 will only become effective for annual periods beginning on or after 1 January 2009, the summary has not been updated.

BACKGROUND

1. Introduction

The standard establishes principles for reporting financial information by segment about:
- the different types of product/service of an entity; and
- the different geographical areas in which it operates.

This information will be useful to:
- better understand the entity's past performance;
- better assess the entity's risk and returns; and
- make more informed judgements about the entity as a whole.

The standard is applicable to entities whose equity or debt are publicly traded on a stock exchange or those entities who are in the process of issuing such publicly traded instruments and that provide complete sets of published financial statements that comply with Statements of GAAP. Should an entity choose to disclose segment information voluntarily, it should comply fully with this standard.

If a parent owns an interest in a subsidiary, associate and/or joint venture, the segment information shall be based on the consolidated data. Otherwise a stand-alone entity whose securities are publicly traded will provide segment information in its own individual financial statements.

2. Types of segment

Segment information should be provided for both of the following:
- Business segment – a distinguishable component of an entity engaged in providing a single product or a group of related products or services and that is subject to risks and returns that are different from those of other business segments. Factors to be considered in determining whether products and services are related, include:
  - nature of the products or services;
  - nature of the production processes;
  - type or class of customer for the products or services;
  - methods used to distribute the products or provide the services; and
  - the nature of the regulatory environment, for example, banking, insurance, or public utilities.
- Geographical segment – a distinguishable component of an entity that is engaged in providing products or services within a particular economic environment and that is subject to risks and returns that are different from those of components operating in other economic environments. Factors to be considered when identifying geographical segments include:
  - similarity of economic and political conditions;
  - relationships between operations in different geographical areas;
  - proximity of operations;
  - special risks associated with operations in a particular area;
  - exchange control regulations; and
  - the underlying currency risks.

A geographical segment may be represented by a single country, a group of two or more countries or even a region within a country. These segments could be based on either the location of an entity's:
- production or service facilities and other assets; or
- its markets and customers.

ACCOUNTING PRACTICE

1. Primary and secondary segments

An entity's internal organisational and management structure and its system of internal financial reporting to the board of directors and the chief executive officer would normally be the basis for identifying the predominant source and nature of risks and differing rates of return facing the entity. Consequently, those should be used to determine which reporting format (business or geographical) is primary and which is secondary.

If the risks and rates of return of an entity are affected predominantly by differences in the products and services it produces, its primary reporting format should be business segments, with secondary information being reported geographically. The following exceptions apply:

- If an entity's risks and rates of return are strongly affected both by differences in the products and services and the geographical areas in which it operates (as evidenced by a matrix approach to managing the company and to reporting internally), it uses business segments as its primary segment reporting format and geographical segments as its secondary reporting format.

- If an entity's internal organisational and management structure and its system of internal financial reporting are based neither on products or services nor on geography, the entity should determine whether its risks and returns are related more to the products and services or more to the geographical areas, in order to identify the primary and secondary segment reporting formats. Management should then look to the next lower level of internal segmentation that reports information along product and service or geographical lines in order to identify the reportable segments.

2. Reportable segments

A segment should be identified as reportable if the majority of its revenue is earned from sales to external customers and:

- its revenue from sales to external customers and from transactions with other segments is ≥ 10% of the total revenue, external and internal, of all segments;
- its segment result (whether profit or loss) is ≥ 10% of the combined result of all segments in profit or in loss, whichever is the greater in absolute amount; or
- its assets are ≥ 10% of the total assets of all segments.

A segment identified as reportable in previous periods shall continue to be a reportable segment for the current period, notwithstanding the fact that its revenue, result (profit) and assets all no longer exceed the 10% thresholds, if management judges it to be of continuing significance.

If an internally reported segment is below all of the thresholds mentioned above, it:

- may be designated as a reportable segment despite its size;
- may be combined into a separately reportable segment with one or more other similar internally reported segment(s) that are also below all of the thresholds of significance; or
- should be included as an unallocated reconciling item if that segment is not separately reported or combined.

If total external revenue for all reportable segments constitutes < 75% of the total reported revenue, additional segments should be identified (even if they do not meet the 10% thresholds) until the 75% level is reached.

If a segment is identified as reportable in the current period because it satisfies the 10% thresholds, comparative segment data should be restated to reflect the newly reportable segment as a separate segment, even if that segment did not satisfy the 10% thresholds in the prior period, unless it is impracticable.

3. Segment result

The segment result is calculated as segment revenue less segment expenses and is determined before deducting the minority interest in group profit.

Segment revenue and **segment expenses** are those items resulting from the operating activities of a segment (external customers or other segments) and that is directly attributable to the segment together with relevant items that can be allocated to the segment on a reasonable basis. It includes proportionately consolidated revenue and expenses from jointly controlled entities and all equity accounted profits/losses. The following items are excluded:

- interest or dividend income, including interest earned on advances or loans to other segments;
- interest paid, including interest incurred on advances or loans from other segments;
- gains and losses on sales of investments or gains and losses on repayments of debt unless the segment's operations are primarily of a financial nature;
- an entity's share of losses of investments accounted for under the equity method;
- income tax expense; and
- general administrative expenses, head office expenses, and other expenses that arise at the entity level and relate to the entity as a whole.

Interest income and interest expense of financial institutions may be reported as a single net amount for segment reporting purposes only if those items are netted in the consolidated or entity financial statements.

4. Segment assets and liabilities

Segment assets and liabilities are those operating assets and liabilities that are employed by or result from a segment's operating activities and that are either directly attributable to the segment or can be allocated to the segment on a reasonable basis.

Symmetry is required for the inclusion of items in segment result and in segment assets or liabilities. If, for example, segment result reflects a depreciation expense, the depreciable asset must be included in segment assets, similarly also goodwill and its impairment expense. To the analogy of the latter example, if segment result includes an interest expense, the interest-bearing liabilities should be included in segment liabilities.

The following rules apply when identifying segment assets and liabilities:
- Income tax assets/liabilities are excluded.
- Assets that are used jointly by two or more segments should be allocated to segments only if their related revenues and expenses are also allocated to those segments.
- Segment assets include investments accounted for under the equity method only if the profit or loss from such investments is included in segment revenue.
- Proportionately consolidated assets and liabilities of jointly controlled entities are included.
- Segment assets are determined after deducting related allowances that are reported as direct offsets in the entity's balance sheet.
- Assets used for general entity or head office purposes are excluded. Similarly, because debt is often issued at the head office level on an entity-wide basis, it is often not possible to directly attribute, or reasonably allocate, the interest-bearing liability to the segment.
- Segment liabilities do not include borrowings, liabilities related to assets that are the subject of finance leases, and other liabilities that are incurred for financing rather than operating purposes.
- Measurements of segment assets and liabilities include adjustments for purposes of a business combination (see IFRS 3 (AC 140)) as well as revaluations allowed by IAS 16 (AC 123) and IAS 38 (AC 129).

Segment revenue, segment expense, segment assets, and segment liabilities are determined before intra-group balances and intra-group transactions are eliminated as part of the consolidation process, except to the extent that such intra-group balances and transactions are between group entities within a single segment.

5. Segment accounting policies

Segment information should be prepared in conformity with the accounting policies adopted for preparing and presenting the consolidated financial statements.

DISCLOSURE

1. Primary segment information

Disclose the following for each reportable segment:
- segment revenue, distinguishing between sales to external customers and revenue from other segments;
- segment result, splitting the result between continuing and discontinued operations;
- the segment results shall be restated for prior periods to effect a split between continuing and discontinued operations in respect of operations classified as discontinued at the latest year end;
- total carrying amount of segment assets;
- segment liabilities;
- cost of property, plant and equipment and intangible assets acquired during the period (that are expected to be used during more than one period);
- depreciation and amortisation expense of segment assets;
- other significant non-cash expenses in terms of IAS 7 (AC 118);
- if segment cash flow disclosures in terms of IAS 7 (AC 118) are disclosed, the depreciation expense and amortisation expense as well as other non-cash expenses need to be disclosed;

- share of profit or loss of an investment accounted for under the equity method, if substantially all of its operations fall within this segment;
- aggregate amount of investments that are equity accounted; and
- a reconciliation between the information of reportable segments and the consolidated financial statements in terms of segment revenue, result, assets and liabilities.

The disclosure (nature and amount) of separately disclosable income/expenses in terms of IAS 1 (AC 101) is encouraged.

2. Secondary segment information

a. If business segments are primary

Disclose the following for each geographical segment whose revenue from sales to external customers is ≥ 10% of total revenue from sales to external customers or whose segment assets are ≥ 10% of total geographical assets:

- segment revenue from external customers;
- total carrying amount of segment assets; and
- total cost of property, plant and equipment and intangible assets acquired that are expected to be used during more than one period.

b. If geographical segments are primary

Disclose the following for each business segment whose revenue from sales to external customers is ≥ 10% of total revenue to external customers or whose segment assets are ≥ 10% of total business assets:

- segment revenue from external customers;
- total carrying amount of segment assets;
- total cost of property, plant and equipment and intangible assets acquired, that are expected to be used during more than one period;
- for primary geographical segments based on location of assets, for which the location of its customers is different from the location of its assets, report revenue from sales to external customers for each customer-based geographical segment whose revenue from sales to external customers is ≥ 10% of total entity revenue from sales to all external customers; and
- for primary geographical segments based on location of customers, for which the entity's assets are located in different geographical areas from its customers, report the following segment information for each asset-based geographical segment whose revenue from sales to external customers or segment assets are ≥ 10% of related consolidated or total entity amounts:
  - total carrying amount of segment assets by geographical location of the assets; and
  - total cost of property, plant and equipment and intangible assets acquired and that are expected to be used during more than one period, by geographical location of assets.

3. Other disclosures required

- If any segment earns a majority of its revenue from sales to other segments and is therefore not a reportable segment, but nonetheless its revenue from sales to external customers is ≥ 10% of total entity revenue from sales to external customers, the following should be disclosed:
  - the fact;
  - revenue from external sales; and
  - revenue from internal sales.
- Basis of pricing intersegment transfers and changes therein.

- Changes in accounting policies adopted for segment reporting:
  - restatement of comparative amounts, unless impracticable to do so;
  - nature of change;
  - reasons for the change;
  - the fact that comparative amounts have been restated or the fact that it is impracticable to do so;
  - financial effect of the change, if reasonably determinable;
  - if an entity changes the identification of its segments and it does not restate prior period segment information on the new basis because it is impracticable to do so, then the entity should report segment data for both the old and the new bases of segmentation in the year of change.
- Types of product and service in each business segment.
- Composition of each geographical segment, both primary and secondary.

An explanation of the reasons why a previously reported segment is no longer reported may also be useful in confirming expectations regarding declining markets and changes in entity strategies.

IAS 16 *(AC 123)* & SIC 21 *(AC 421)*

Property, Plant and Equipment

☐ **SUMMARY**

Background
Accounting practice
Disclosure
SIC 21: Income taxes – recovery of revalued non-depreciable assets

BACKGROUND

This standard prescribes the accounting treatment for property, plant and equipment (PPE) particularly with regard to:
- the timing of recognition of the assets;
- the determination of their carrying amounts; and
- the depreciation charges and impairment losses to be recognised in relation to them.

PPE are distinguished from other assets by applying the following definition. They are tangible assets that
- are held by an entity for use in:
  - production;
  - supply of goods or services;
  - rental to others; or
  - administrative purposes; and
- are expected to be used during more than one period.

Investment properties are generally accounted for under IAS 40 (AC 135), except where IAS 40 (AC 135) refers back to IAS 16.

IAS 16 does not apply to:
- biological assets related to agricultural activity;
- mineral rights and mineral reserves such as oil, natural gas and similar non-regenerative resources; and
- property, plant and equipment classified as held for sale under IFRS 5 (AC 142).

ACCOUNTING PRACTICE

1. Recognition criteria

In accordance with the Framework, an item of PPE is recognised as an asset if the following conditions are met:
- It is probable that the future economic benefits associated with the asset will flow to the entity. Sufficient certainty in this regard is normally obtained from the transfer of rewards and risks of the asset to the entity.
- The cost of the asset shall be measured reliably from the exchange transaction itself (for example, an invoice). In the case of a self-constructed asset, the cost of materials, labour and other inputs of the transaction with external parties are used to measure cost. Investment properties under construction are treated in terms of IAS 16. Once they are completed, they are reclassified to investment property.

The following guidelines are normally applicable to the identification of a separate PPE item:
- Individual insignificant items (for example, moulds and dies) could be aggregated as a single asset item.
- Major spare parts and standby equipment are also PPE if they are expected to be used during more than one period. Other spare parts are inventory.
- Spare parts and servicing equipment, which are related to specific items of PPE, are accounted for as PPE and are depreciated over the useful life of the related asset.
- Component parts of an asset are accounted for as separate items if the related assets have different useful lives or provide economic benefits according to different patterns, for example, an aircraft's frame and its engines.
- Safety and environmental assets[#] do not directly increase the future economic benefits of the entity. Such assets, however, still qualify to be recognised as PPE if such assets enable the entity to increase future economic benefits from related assets in excess of what it could derive if they had not been acquired. Such assets are reviewed for impairment to ensure that the total carrying amount of such an asset and the related assets (see #) does not exceed the total recoverable amount of that asset and its related assets.
- Measurement after recognition shall be effected using either the cost model or revaluation model as accounting policy. The policy shall be applied to an entire class of PPE.

2. Cost model

2.1 Initial cost

A PPE item that qualifies for recognition is measured at its cost. The **initial cost component** of an asset consists of the following:

Includes	**Excludes**

Includes

Purchase price (cash price equivalent) less trade discounts and rebates

Import duties

Non-refundable purchase taxes

Borrowing costs capitalised

Condition necessary to be capable of operating as management intended, for example:

- site preparation;
- initial delivery and handling costs;
- installation and assembly costs;
- employee benefit costs arising from the construction or acquisition of a PPE item;
- professional fees (architect);

- administrative costs, general overhead costs, pre-production costs and start-up costs, only to the extent that it directly relates to the acquisition of the asset;
- the initial estimate of dismantling costs, removal costs and restoring the site on which the asset is located, the obligation which arises at acquisition or through use (if not used to produce inventory) in terms of IAS 37 (AC 130); and
- costs of testing whether the item is functioning properly, after deducting the net proceeds from selling any items produced while bringing the asset to that location and condition

Excludes

Finance costs (unless borrowing costs are capitalised)

Cost to open a new facility

Cost to introduce a new product/service

Cost to conduct business in a new location

Costs of relocating or reorganising part of the business

General overhead costs

Pre-production expenses

Initial operating losses

Internal profits in respect of self-constructed assets

Abnormal amounts of wasted resources in respect of self-constructed assets

Costs and revenue associated with incidental operations

2.2 Deferred settlement terms

The cost of an item of property, plant and equipment is the cash price equivalent at the recognition date.

If payment is deferred beyond normal credit terms, the difference between the cash price equivalent and the total payment is recognised as interest over the period of credit, unless such interest is recognised in the carrying amount of the item in accordance with IAS 23 (AC 114).

2.3 Exchanges of assets.

- One or more items of property, plant and equipment may be acquired in exchange for a non-monetary asset or assets, or a combination of monetary and non-monetary assets.
- The cost of such an item of property, plant and equipment is measured at the fair value, of the asset given up, unless the fair value of the asset acquired is more clearly evident.
- The acquired item is measured in this way even if an entity cannot immediately derecognise the asset given up.
- An item may not be measured at fair value if:
  - the exchange transaction lacks commercial substance; or
  - the fair value of neither the asset received nor the asset given up is reliably measurable.
- If the acquired item is not measured at fair value, the cost of the asset acquired is measured at the carrying amount of the asset given up.
- An entity determines whether an exchange transaction has commercial substance by considering the extent to which its future cash flows are expected to change as a result of the transaction.
- An exchange transaction has commercial substance if:
  - the configuration (risk, timing and amount) of the cash flows of the asset received differs from the configuration of the cash flows of the asset transferred*; or

- the entity-specific value of the portion of the entity's operations affected by the transaction changes as a result of the exchange[#]; and
- the difference in (*) or (#) is significant, relative to the fair value of the assets exchanged.

2.4 Subsequent costs

- An entity shall only recognise subsequent costs incurred in respect of a PPE item as an asset if it meets the normal recognition criteria for an asset used to determine initial recognition of an item of PPE.
- An entity does not recognise in the carrying amount of an item of property, plant and equipment the costs of the day-to-day servicing of the item, but these costs are recognised in profit or loss as incurred and are called repairs and maintenance.
- Certain parts of some items of property, plant and equipment may require replacement at regular intervals. For example, a furnace may require relining after a specified number of hours of use, or aircraft interiors such as seats and galleys may require replacement several times during the useful life of the airframe:
  - An entity recognises in the carrying amount of an item of property, plant and equipment the cost of replacing part of such an item when that cost is incurred if the recognition criteria are met.
  - The carrying amount of those parts that are replaced is derecognised in accordance with the derecognition provisions of this statement.
  - This occurs regardless of whether the replaced part had been depreciated seperately.
  - If necessary the estimated cost of the replacement component may be used as an indication of what the cost of the replaced part was at the time it was acquired or constructed initially.
- A condition of continuing to operate an item of property, plant and equipment (for example, an aircraft) may be performing regular major inspections for faults regardless of whether parts of the item are replaced or not.
  - When each major inspection is performed, its cost is recognised in the carrying amount of the item of property, plant and equipment as a replacement provided the recognition criteria are satisfied.
  - Any remaining carrying amount of the cost of the previous inspection (as distinct from physical parts) is derecognised.
  - This occurs regardless of whether the cost of the previous inspection was identified in the transaction in which the item was acquired or constructed.
  - If necessary, the estimated cost of a future similar inspection may be used as an indication of what the cost of the existing inspection component was when the item was acquired or constructed.

3. Revaluation model

3.1 General

An entity may choose to carry a PPE item at a revalued amount (fair value less subsequent accumulated depreciation) after initial recognition at cost. A revaluation can only be done if the item's fair value can be measured reliably. The negative impact of price changes on financial statements is partly solved with the revaluation of PPE items.

The revaluation of PPE items has, in broad terms, the following impact on financial statements:
- Income statement – improves matching of current cost and revenue.
- Balance sheet – disclosure of property, plant and equipment (PPE) at more realistic values.

The following principles are applicable when property, plant and equipment are revalued:
- The items in the entire class of PPE are revalued simultaneously on a continual basis, provided the revaluations are completed within short periods of time. A class would be, for example, land, buildings, motor vehicles and furniture.
- The valuation value of property, plant and equipment replaces the historical cost price for purposes of calculating:
  - depreciation for the period;
  - the carrying amount of PPE; and
  - the gain/loss on disposal of PPE.
- The valuation must be carried out by a competent person.
- The fair value is usually the market value for existing use. Items of a specialised nature are valued at net replacement value.

- Frequency of revaluations depends upon the volatility of the fair values of PPE. Usually three to five years will be sufficient, except in those circumstances where the fair value and carrying amount differ materially.

3.2 Recording a revaluation

Surpluses on revaluation are transferred directly to a revaluation surplus. IAS 16 does not indicate if these are distributable. In practice, however, it will most probably be regarded as non-distributable.

Deficits on revaluation are accounted for in profit or loss (the income statement) to the extent that it cannot be charged against an earlier surplus in respect of that asset. Deficits on one asset cannot be set off against surpluses of another.

Surpluses reversing previous deficits written off (in income statement), are first credited to profit or loss (the income statement). Any remaining surplus is transferred to a revaluation surplus.

The revaluation surplus that realises with the derecognition of assets or by using assets is transferred directly to retained earnings (not via the income statement).

Depending on the policy being used by the entity, the entity can choose not to make these transfers while the asset is used but only when the asset is sold (IAS 16.41).

If a transfer to retained earnings while the asset is being used is the policy of the entity, an amount equal to the difference between depreciation based on revalued amount and depreciation based on historical cost is transferred to retained earnings annually. When the asset is sold, the remaining balance on the surplus account is transferred to retained earnings. Alternatively, the whole surplus can be transferred when the asset is sold, without any transfer while the asset is used.

The transfer is an after tax amount if deferred tax had been provided on the revaluation. (See SIC 21 in Chapter IAS 12 (AC 102) for deferred tax on non-depreciable assets.)

The carrying amount always represents the most recent net valuation less depreciation since date of such valuation. Furthermore, a change in the revision of the useful life of a revalued asset shall not affect the depreciation already recognised.

Decreases to recoverable amounts are accounted for in profit or loss (the income statement) except in those circumstances where revaluation surpluses are available in the revaluation surplus.

There is a deferred tax implication with the revaluation of PPE. The difference between the new carrying amount of a revalued asset and its tax base is a temporary difference and gives rise to a deferred tax liability or asset.

At depreciable assets where the carrying amount will be recovered through use only, a tax rate of 29% will be used, and at non-depreciable assets 14,5%.

Once the asset meets the criteria to be classified as held for sale in terms of IFRS 5 (AC 142), the deferred tax on the revaluation shall be adjusted to reflect the expected tax effect of the disposal. If classified as held for sale, depreciation will cease.

4. Depreciation

Depreciation is a measure that reflects the consumption of economic benefits embodied in an asset. Depreciation is therefore recognised even when the fair value of the asset exceeds its carrying amount. Depreciation is a method of cost allocation and not a method of valuation or capital maintenance. The following principles apply:

- Each part of an item of PPE with a cost that is significant in relation to the total cost of the PPE item shall be depreciated separately.
- The depreciable amount shall be allocated on a systematic basis over its useful life. Various factors such as physical wear and tear, technical obsolescence, legal limits, etcetera are taken into account when determining its useful life.
- The depreciation method used shall reflect the pattern of expected consumption of economic benefits. The following methods are generally used:

- straight-line method;
- diminishing balance method;
- sum of the digits method; or
- method based on production.
- Depreciation commences when an asset is available for use.
- Depreciation ceases at the earlier of the date the asset is classified as held for sale in terms of IFRS 5 (AC142) and the date the asset is derecognised.
- The depreciation charge is recognised in profit or loss (the income statement) as an expense, unless it is included in the carrying amount of a manufactured asset.
- If an item of PPE is impaired in the current year, depreciation from the next year shall be based on the new carrying amount.
- Land and buildings are separable assets. Buildings are depreciable assets, but land is non-depreciable.
- The depreciable amount of an asset is determined after deducting its residual value. The residual value is reviewed annually at year-end and if expectations differ from previous estimates, the depreciation charge for the current and future periods shall be adjusted in terms of the rules for changes in accounting estimates as contained in IAS 8 (AC 103).
- The useful life of PPE items shall be reviewed annually at year-end and, if expectations are significantly different from previous estimates, the depreciation charge for the current and future periods shall be adjusted in terms of the rules for changes in accounting estimates as contained in IAS 8 (AC 103).
- The depreciation method applied shall be reviewed annually at year end and, if there has been a significant change in the expected pattern of economic benefits from those assets, the method shall be changed. It shall be accounted for as a change in accounting estimate, and the depreciation charge for the current and future periods shall be adjusted in terms of IAS 8 (AC 103).

5. Recoverable amount (Also refer to IAS 36 (AC 128) – Impairment of assets)

- The carrying amount of an item of PPE shall be compared (usually at the balance sheet date) with its recoverable amount if there are indications of impairment. If the recoverable amount is lower, the difference shall immediately be recognised as an expense, unless it reverses a corresponding amount in the revaluation surplus.
- IAS 36 (AC 128) explains the detail on impairment, testing for impairment and reversals of earlier impairment losses.

6. Compensation for impairment

- Compensation from third parties for items of property, plant and equipment that were impaired, lost or given up, shall be included in profit or loss when the compensation becomes receivable.
- The losses or impairments of assets, the compensation received from third parties to compensate for these losses and the acquisition of replacement assets are all separately accounted for, as they are separate economic events.

7. Derecognition

- The carrying amount for an item of PPE shall be derecognised:
  - on disposal; or
  - when no further future economic benefits are expected from use or sale of the asset.
- The gain or loss arising from the derecognition is recognised in profit or loss when the item is derecognised. Gains do not represent revenue.
- The gain or loss is the difference between the net disposal proceeds and the carrying amount of the disposed asset.

DISCLOSURE

The following disclosure requirements are prescribed by IAS 16 and Schedule 4 of the Companies Act, 1973 (as amended).

Accounting policies

- Measurement bases used for determining the gross carrying amount for each class of asset
- Depreciation methods for each class of asset
- Useful lives or depreciation rates for each class of asset
- Methods and significant assumptions applied in estimating fair values of revalued items

Income statement and notes thereto

- Depreciation charged in arriving at profit or loss for the period
- The effect of material changes in estimates of:
  - residual values;
  - demolishing, removal or restoration costs (estimates);
  - useful lives; and
  - depreciation methods
- Gains/losses on disposal of PPE items (Schedule 4, par 42 (n))
- Monetary and non-monetary compensation recognised due to the impairment or loss of an item of PPE

Balance sheet and notes thereto

- Gross carrying amount and accumulated depreciation (including accumulated impairment losses) for each class of asset at the beginning and the end of the period
- Detailed reconciliation of movements in the carrying amount during the period – see IAS 16.73(e)
- Amount expended on PPE in the course of construction on which depreciation has not yet been provided
- Disclose with respect to PPE pledged as security for either their own or a third parties' liabilities and restrictions on title (also refer schedule 4, par 36):
  - details; and
  - amounts secured
- Amounts for contractual for commitments (in respect of the acquisition of PPE) (also refer schedule 4, par 36):
  - authorised and contracted for;
  - authorised and not contracted for; and
  - source of funding
- Gross carrying amount of fully depreciated PPE items still in use
- Carrying amounts of the following PPE items:
  - temporary idle; and
  - not in use and held for disposal, but not classified as held for sale in terms of IFRS 5 (AC 142)
- Fair value of each class of PPE which materially differs from that of the carrying amount, provided the cost model used
- The following additional disclosure requirements regarding land and buildings must also be shown (Schedule 4, par 22 (3)):
  - description;
  - location;
  - date of acquisition;
  - purchase price; and
  - costs of additions/improvements.
- When PPE is shown at revaluation; the following additional disclosure requirements are applicable:
  - the methods and significant assumptions applied on estimating the fair value of revalued items;
  - effective date of the revaluation;
  - if an independent valuer was involved;
  - the extent to which the item's fair value was determined directly by reference to observable prices in an active market or recent arm's length transactions or where estimated using other valuation techniques such as indices; and
  - carrying amount of each class of PPE which would have been included in the financial statements if the assets were carried at cost less accumulated depreciation.
- Futhermore, Schedule 4, par 22(4) requires the following additional information when land and buildings have been revalued:
  - the most recent year in which asset was revalued (if valued in the current year);

- name and qualifications of valuer; and
- policy regarding the frequency of valuations.
- The date of acquisition and purchase price do not have to be provided.

Other notes

- Revaluation surplus, with details of:
  - movements for the period; and
  - any limitations on the distribution of the balance to shareholders

SIC 21: INCOME TAXES – RECOVERY OF REVALUED NON-DEPRECIABLE ASSETS

Refer to the chapter on IAS 12 (AC 102) for a summary of this interpretation.

IAS 17 *(AC 105)*, Circular 12/2006, SIC 15 *(AC 415)*, SIC 27 *(AC 427)* and IFRIC 4 *(AC 437)*

Leases

❑ **SUMMARY**

Background
Accounting practice: lessees
Disclosure: lessees
Accounting practice: lessors
Disclosure: lessors
Tax
SIC 15: Operating leases – incentives
SIC 27: Evaluating the substance of transactions involving the legal form of a lease
IFRIC 4: Determining whether an arrangement contains a lease
Circular 12/2006: Operating leases

BACKGROUND

This standard deals with the methods of accounting for leases in the financial statements of lessees and lessors. The accounting treatment applicable to finance leases also applies to other instalment credit agreements. The standard does not apply to the following leases:

- lease agreements for the exploration or use of minerals, oil, natural gas and similar non-regenerative resources; and
- licensing agreements for items such as video recordings, plays and manuscripts.

The statement does not apply as basis of the measurement by:

- lessees of investment property under finance leases (see IAS 40 (AC135));
- investment property provided by lessors under operating leases (see IAS 40(AC 135));
- lessees of biological assets held under finance leases; and
- lessors of biological assets under operating leases.

The accounting treatment of leases shall show the financial substance of the transaction, irrespective of whether it corresponds with the legal form of the agreement (substance over form).

Classification of leases

Two types of lease are defined, namely finance leases and operating leases. In the case of a **finance lease**, the risks and rewards incidental to ownership of the leased asset are substantially transferred between the two parties involved. In the case of an **operating lease**, these risks and rewards are not transferred substantially between the two parties. Risks include:

- losses from idle capacity;
- losses from technological obsolescence; and
- variations of return owing to changing economic conditions.

Rewards include:

- profitable operation over the asset's economic life;
- gain from appreciation in value; and
- realisation of a residual value.

As a lease agreement is signed by both the lessor and the lessee, both parties to the lease would normally classify the lease in the same way. However, differing circumstances may sometimes lead to different classifications.

The following situations could, individually or in combination, lead to a lease being classified as a finance lease:

- Any losses of the lessor associated with cancelling the lease contract are borne by the lessee.
- Gains or losses arising from changes in the fair value of any residual value of the lease asset, accrues to the lessee.
- Lessee can rent the asset at a bargain rental during a renewal period.

Note that a lease is classified at the inception of the lease, and reclassification at a later stage will be deemed a new agreement.

Leases of land and buildings are classified as either operating or finance leases in the same way as leases of other assets. The land and building elements of a lease are considered separately for classification purposes and the land element is normally classified as an operating lease, unless ownership will pass to the lessee at the end of the lease, in which case it is a finance lease. The buildings element of the lease is classified as either a finance or operating lease, applying the normal principles for classification of leases.

The conditions indicating whether a lease is an operating or finance lease are summarised in the following diagram:

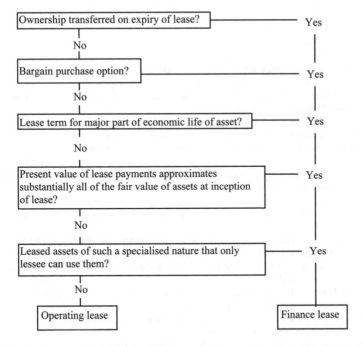

Note: Any one of the conditions indicates that the lease is classified as a finance lease. Also note the difference in substance between a finance lease and an operating lease. With finance leases the intention is to purchase the asset, but the transaction is concluded technically as a lease. The conditions in IAS 17.10 are only guidelines to interpret substance. Therefore, if ownership is passed on to the lessee, or if the asset is used up over the lease period, then it is a finance lease.

Leases will be classified as non-cancellable if they are only cancellable:
- upon the occurrence of some remote contingency;
- with the permission of the lessor;
- if the lessee enters into a new lease for the same or an equivalent asset with the same lessor; or
- upon payment by the lessee of an additional amount so that, at inception, continuation of the lease is reasonably certain.

Listed below are a number of practical examples of the types of lease agreement:
- operating leases:
  - office rental;
  - rent of a vehicle for business purposes; and
  - video rentals.
- finance lease:
  - vehicles;
  - equipment;
  - office equipment; and
  - full maintenance lease – the lessor usually carries the risks of:
    - maintenance costs;
    - residual value; and
    - breakdown.
- hire purchase:
  - as with finance leases.

Maintenance leases are generally classified as finance leases, but may sometimes be classified as operating leases. The normal conditions for classification must be applied, with specific attention being paid to risks associated with finance leases.

ACCOUNTING PRACTICE: LESSEES

1. Finance lease

Assets held under finance leases are capitalised in the financial statements of lessees at the commencement of the lease term. This is in accordance with the principle of substance over form as there is no significant practical difference between an asset acquired by means of an outright purchase or by means of a finance lease. The accounting treatment of finance leases is as follows:

- The fair value of the leased asset at the inception of the lease is the amount capitalised. Fair value means the cost of the asset (cash selling price of lessor) in accordance with the lease agreement plus value-added tax, if the value-added tax cannot be claimed back from the South African Revenue Service.
- If the present value of minimum lease payments is lower than fair value, that lower amount shall be used to capitalise the asset. The discount rate used to determine the present value is either the rate implicit in the agreement or the lessee's incremental borrowing rate.
- A corresponding lease liability is raised.
- Initial direct costs associated with negotiating and securing the leasing arrangement are added to the capitalised cost of the leased asset.
- Depreciation is written off on the capitalised value of the leased depreciable asset over the useful life of the asset in terms of IAS 16 (AC 123) and IAS 38 (AC 129), unless there is no reasonable certainty that the lessee will obtain ownership by the end of the lease term, in which case the asset is fully depreciated over the shorter of the lease term or its useful life.
- Lease payments are split between the capital portion (set off against the lease liability) and the finance portion (recognised as finance cost in profit or loss (the income statement). Finance charges are calculated at the rate stipulated in the lease contract. The total finance charge is equal to the difference between the total minimum finance lease payments and the capitalised value.
- If a leased asset has become impaired, the normal principles associated with impairment as contained in IAS 36 (AC 128) shall be applied.

2. Operating leases

Operating leases are not capitalised.

Operating lease payments are charged as an expense against income on a straight-line basis, unless another systematic basis gives a better match of the lease payments with the benefits derived from the leased asset. (Also refer circular 12/2006 at the back of this summary.) Sometimes lease payments are calculated on factors not directly related to the period of the lease benefit, for example, where the lessee must make payments before the leased asset is put to use. (See SIC 15 at the back of this summary.) To ensure the matching of lease payments with income, it may sometimes be necessary to defer, or provide for lease charges.

3. Sale and leaseback

A sale and leaseback transaction comprises the sale of an asset and the leasing of that asset back from its new owner. The lease can be a finance lease or an operating lease.

3.1 Sale and leaseback – finance leases

The substance of this type of transaction is that finance is obtained with an asset provided as security. There is therefore in substance no sale or lease transaction, only a financing transaction.

The asset is therefore not derecognised but accounted for as a leased asset under a finance lease in the same way as any other finance lease, using the new selling price as the cost of the leased asset and raising a corresponding liability. The asset must also be reclassified as a leased asset in the property, plant and equipment note.

If the sales proceeds exceed the original carrying amount of the asset, the excess so recognised shall be deferred in the financial statements of the seller (lessee) and amortised over the lease term. This deferred excess not yet amortised shall either be treated as a deduction from the asset or an equity item in the statement of changes in equity.

3.2 Sale and leaseback – operating leases

The substance of a sale and leaseback operating lease is that ownership is transferred from the seller to the buyer. There are therefore two transactions: a sales transaction and a lease transaction (an operating lease).

The lease payments and the selling price are usually interdependent, as they are negotiated as a package. The selling price therefore does not always present fair value.

If the selling price is equal to the fair value, the profit or loss on the sale transaction will be recognised immediately in profit or loss (the income statement). The lease transaction will be accounted for as for a normal operating lease.

If the selling price is below the fair value, the difference between the carrying amount and the fair value (a profit or loss) will be recognised immediately in profit or loss (the income statement). If the difference between the selling price and fair value (a loss) is compensated by future lease payments being at below market rates, this loss shall be deferred and amortised in proportion to the lease payments over the period for which the asset will be used (lease term), otherwise this loss shall be recognised immediately.

If the selling price is above the fair value the difference between the carrying amount and the fair value (a profit or loss) will be recognised immediately in profit or loss (the income statement). The excess of the selling price over the fair value (a profit) shall be deferred and amortised over the period for which the asset will be used (the lease term).

If the fair value at the time of a sale and leaseback transaction (operating lease) is below the original carrying amount of the asset, the difference between the original carrying amount of the asset and the fair value shall be recognised immediately as a loss. This means that the carrying amount shall be written down to fair value and the resulting loss will be recognised immediately.

4. Summary

The classification of lease agreements and their accounting can be set out as follows:

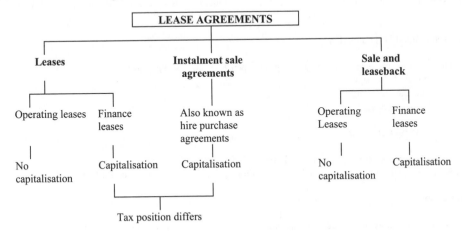

DISCLOSURE – LESSEES

1. Finance lease

The lessee shall, in addition to meeting the disclosure requirements of IAS 16 (AC 123), IAS 36 (AC 128), IAS 38 (AC 129), IAS 40 (AC 135) and IFRS 7 (AC 144), also disclose the following:

Income statement and notes

- Contingent rents recognised as an expense in the period.

Balance sheet and notes thereto

- Assets – described as 'finance leased assets', show cost and accumulated depreciation and accumulated impairment losses for main categories of leased assets.
- Finance lease liability – give details as for any other long-term loan.
- A reconciliation between the total of future minimum lease payments at the balance sheet date and their present value. Also disclose the total of minimum lease payments at the balance sheet date, and their present value for each of the following periods:
  - not later than one year;
  - later than one year and not later than five years; and
  - later than five years.
- The total of future minimum sublease payments expected to be received under non-cancellable subleases at the balance sheet date.
- A general description of the lessee's material leasing arrangements including, but not limited to, the following:
  - the basis on which contingent rent payments are determined;
  - the existence and terms of renewal or purchase options and escalation clauses; and
  - restrictions imposed by lease arrangements, such as those concerning dividends, additional debt, and further leasing.

2. Operating leases

The lessee shall, in addition to meeting the disclosure requirements of IFRS 7 (AC 144), also disclose the following:

Income statement and notes thereto

- Lease and sublease payments recognised as an expense, distinguishing between:
  - minimum lease payments;
  - contingent rents; and
  - sublease payments.

Balance sheet and notes thereto

- Assets – deferred operating lease expenditure (included under other current assets).
- Liabilities – provision for operating lease expenditure (included under other current liabilities).

Other notes

- The total of future minimum lease payments under non-cancellable operating leases for each of the following periods:
  - not later than one year;
  - later than one year and not later than five years; and
  - later than five years.
- The total of future minimum sublease payments expected to be received under non-cancellable subleases at the balance sheet date.
- A general description of the lessee's significant leasing arrangements including, but not limited to, the following:

- the basis on which contingent rent payments are determined;
- the existence and terms of renewal or purchase options and escalation clauses; and
- restrictions imposed by leasing arrangements, such as those concerning dividends, additional debt, and further leasing.

3. Sale and leaseback – finance leases

As for normal finance leases, but note the treatment of the deferred profit arising from such transactions:
- show as deferred profit in statement of changes in equity; or
- show as a deduction from the capitalised leased asset in the property, plant and equipment reconciliation.
- Sale and leaseback transactions may lead to separately disclosable items in terms of IAS 1 (AC 101).

4. Sale and leaseback – operating leases

- Profit or loss on sale of asset (after adjustment for difference between the selling price and open market value).
- The portion of the adjustment (profit or loss) written off for the current period.
- Sale and leaseback transactions may lead to separately disclosable items in terms of IAS 1 (AC 101).
- The description of significant leasing arrangements shall disclose any unique and unusual arrangements related to sale and leaseback transactions.

ACCOUNTING PRACTICE – LESSORS

1. Finance leases

Should a lease be classified as a finance lease, the leased asset will no longer be shown in the books of the lessor as property, plant and equipment, but as a receivable item, as follows:
- Gross investments - unearned finance income = net investment.
- Gross investment equals the total minimum future lease payments from the viewpoint of the lessor plus any unguaranteed residual value.
- Minimum lease payments equals the total of lease payments by lessee over the lease term, guaranteed residual value and bargain purchase options.

The leased asset is presented in the balance sheet as a receivable amount at the **net investment** (gross investment less unearned finance income) thereof. Every year, the unearned finance income recognised in profit or loss (the income statement) shall be based on a pattern to reflect a constant periodic rate of return on the net investment outstanding.

Lease payments received by the lessor (excluding costs for service) are set off against the gross investment.

The estimated unguaranteed residual values used in determining the gross investment in a lease shall be reviewed regularly. If a reduction in the estimated unguaranteed residual value takes place, the allocation of income over the lease term is revised as if the lower unguaranteed residual value was the residual value from day one of the lease. The cumulative adjustment is however accounted for in the current period and not retrospectively.

If an asset under a finance lease is classified as held for sale in terms of IFRS 5 (AC 142), this asset should be accounted for in terms of IFRS 5 (AC 142).

Initial direct costs associated with securing a finance lease are included in the initial measurement of the finance lease receivable and reduce the amount of income recognised over the term of the lease. This is effected by calculating an interest rate implicit in the lease that discounts the minimum lease payments and unguaranteed residual value to an amount equal to the fair value of the leased asset plus any initial direct costs to the lessor.

Manufacturers or dealers often give customers the option to either buy or lease an asset. If the customer chooses to lease an asset under a finance lease, the manufacturer or dealer lessor realises two types of income:
- the profit or loss on the 'sale' of the asset and
- finance income over the lease term.

The profit or loss from the above transaction is accounted for on the normal basis used by the entity. If the interest rate on such a sale is not market related (artificially low) as a result of marketing strategy, the profit or loss is restricted to that which would apply if market rate of interest were charged. Finance income earned will be calculated on the basis of normal trading interest rates.

Initial direct costs associated with a transaction with a manufacturer or dealer shall be recognised as an expense in profit or loss (the income statement) at the commencement of the lease term, as they are related mainly to earning selling profit.

2. Operating leases

Operating leased assets are treated as property, plant and equipment or another appropriate type of asset and, if depreciable, they shall be depreciated or amortised on the same basis as other assets of a similar nature.

To determine whether a leased asset has become impaired and how such impairment or reversal thereof shall be treated, IAS 36 (AC 128) shall be applied.

Lease income is recognised on the straight-line basis over the lease term, even though receipts may not be on such a basis, unless another systematic basis is more representative of the time pattern of the earnings process from the operating lease (also refer to circular 12/2006 at the back of this summary).

Costs incurred to earn lease income shall be recognised immediately as an expense in the income statement.

The depreciation policy on depreciable leased assets shall be consistent with the lessor's normal depreciation policy for similar assets.

Initial direct costs are added to the carrying amount of the leased asset and is recognised as an expense over the lease term on the same basis as the lease income (normally straight-line).

DISCLOSURE – LESSORS

1. Finance leases

Lessors shall, in addition to the disclosure requirements in IFRS 7 (AC 144), also disclose the following:

Accounting policy note

- State the basis of allocation of finance income.

Income statement and notes thereto

- Contingent rents recognised in income for the period.

Balance sheet and notes thereto

- A reconciliation between the total gross investment in the lease at the balance sheet date, and the present value of minimum lease payments receivable at the balance sheet date (providing the split required below).
- Disclose the total gross investment in the lease and the present value of minimum lease payments receivable at the balance sheet date, for each of the following periods:
  - not later than one year;
  - later than one year and not later than five years; and
  - later than five years.
- Unearned finance income (shown as part of above reconciliation).
- The unguaranteed residual values accruing to the benefit of the lessor.
- The accumulated allowance for uncollectable minimum lease payments receivable.
- A general description of the lessor's material leasing arrangements.

2. Operating leases

Income statements and notes thereto

- Total contingent rents recognised in income during the period.

Other notes

- The future minimum leases payments under non-cancellable operating leases in the aggregate and for each of the following periods:
  - not later than one year;
  - later than one year and not later than five years; and
  - later than five years.
- A general description of the lessor's leasing arrangements.

In addition to the above, the disclosure requirements contained in IAS 16 (AC 123), IAS 36 (AC 128), IAS 38 (AC 129), IAS 40 (AC 135) (depending on the type of asset) and IFRS 7 (AC 144) shall be adhered to.

SIC 15: OPERATING LEASES – INCENTIVES

1. Background

A lessor may sometimes provide incentives to a lessee to entice the latter to enter into a new operating lease agreement or to renew an existing one. Examples of such incentives are:
- up-front cash payments to the lessee;
- reimbursement or assumption of certain costs of the lessee (such as relocation costs) by the lessor;
- leasehold improvements by the lessor; and
- initial rent-free periods or periods of reduced rent.

2. Issue

The issue is how these incentives relating to operating leases shall be accounted for in the financial statements of the lessee and lessor.

3. Consensus

- All such incentives shall be recognised as an intergral part of the net consideration agreed for the use of the leased asset.
- The lessor shall use the aggregate cost of the incentive to reduce rental income over the lease term. Use a straight-line basis unless another systematic basis is more appropriate.
- The lessee shall use the aggregate benefit of incentives to reduce the rental expense over the lease term. Use a straight-line basis unless another systematic basis is more appropriate.

SIC 27: EVALUATING THE SUBSTANCE OF TRANSACTIONS INVOLVING THE LEGAL FORM OF A LEASE

1. Background

- In terms of IAS 17 (AC 105), an arrangement can only be accounted for as a lease if the arrangement in substance conveys the right to use the asset.
- An entity may enter into a transaction or a series of structured transactions (an arrangement) with an unrelated party or parties (an investor) that involves the legal form of a lease. For example, an entity may lease assets to an investor and lease the same assets back, or alternatively, legally sell assets and lease the same assets back.
- It should therefore be considered whether such a transaction is in substance a lease.
- The form of each arrangement and its terms and conditions can vary significantly. It may be that the arrangement is designed to achieve a tax advantage for the investor that is shared with the entity in the form of a fee, and not to convey the right to use an asset.

2. Issue

When an arrangement with an investor involves the legal form of a lease, the following are issues to consider:
- How does one determine whether a series of transactions is linked and should be accounted for as one transaction?
- Does the arrangement meet the definition of a lease under IAS 17 (AC 105) and, if not:
  - Whether a separate investment account (asset) and lease payment obligations (liability) exist?
  - How should the entity account for other obligations resulting from the arrangement?
  - How should the entity account for a fee it might receive from an investor?

3. Consensus

- A series of transactions that involve the legal form of a lease is linked and shall be accounted for as one transaction if the overall economic effect cannot be understood without reference to the series of transactions as a whole.
- This will typically arise when the transactions are closely interrelated, negotiated as a single transaction, and take place at the same time or as a continuous sequence.
- The accounting must however reflect the substance of the arrangement and not its legal form. All aspects and implications of an arrangement must therefore be evaluated to determine its substance, with weight given to those aspects and implications that have an economic effect.
- IAS 17 applies when the substance of an arrangement includes the transfer of the right to use an asset for an agreed period of time. The following will individually serve as indicators that an arrangement may not, in substance, involve a lease under IAS 17:
  - An entity retains all the risks and rewards incident to ownership of an underlying asset and enjoys substantially the same rights of use in respect of the asset before and after the arrangement.
  - The primary reason for the arrangement is to achieve a particular tax result, and not to transfer the right to use an asset.
  - The arrangement includes an option on terms that will make sure that the option is exercised.
- Indicators that collectively demonstrate that, in substance, a separate investment account and lease payment obligations do not meet the definitions of an asset and a liability in the framework are the following:
  - The entity is not able to control the investment account for its own benefit and does not have an obligation to pay the lease payments.
  - The entity has only a limited risk of reimbursing the entire amount of the fee paid to it or possibly paying some additional amount under other obligations (e.g., guarantee).
  - Except for the initial cash flows at inception of the arrangement, the only other cash flows expected under the arrangement are the cash flows from the investment account to satisfy the lease payment obligations.
- The fee paid by the investor shall be evaluated in terms of the criteria in IAS 18 (AC 111) .20 to determine when the entity can recognise the fee as income.
- The factors contained in SIC 27 (AC 427) .08 will individually demonstrate that recognition of the entire fee as income, if received at the beginning of the arrangement, is inappropriate.
- The fee shall be presented in the income statement based on its economic substance and nature.

4. Disclosure

- In the case where an arrangement does not, in substance, involve a lease under IAS 17 all related aspects shall be considered in determining the appropriate disclosures that would lead to understanding of the arrangement and the accounting treatment adopted.
- An entity shall disclose the following in each period during which an arrangement is in existence:
  - a description of the arrangement including:
    - the underlying asset and any restrictions on its use;
    - the life and other significant terms of the arrangement;
    - the transactions that are linked together, including any options; and
  - the accounting treatment applied to any fee received, the amount recognised as income in the period, and the line item of the income statement in which it is included.
- The above disclosures shall be provided individually for each arrangement or in aggregate for each class of arrangement. A class is a grouping of arrangements with underlying assets of a similar nature (e.g. power plants).

IFRIC 4: DETERMINING WHETHER AN ARRANGEMENT CONTAINS A LEASE

1. Background and issues

- A lease is defined in IAS 17 as an agreement whereby the lesser transfers to the lessee the right to use an asset for an agreed period of time in return for a payment or series of payments.
- All arrangements meeting the definition of a lease should be accounted for in accordance with IAS 17 regardless of whether they take the legal form of a lease.
- Arrangements have developed in recent years that do not take the legal form of a lease, but transfer the right to use an asset in return for a payment or series of payments.
- IFRIC 4 was issued to assist in determining whether those arrangements are, or contains a lease that should be accounted for in accordance with IAS 17.
- The issues discussed by IFRIC 4 are the following:
  - How does one determine whether an arrangement is a lease, or contains a lease as defined in IAS 17 (refer 2)?
  - When should the assessment or a reassessment of whether an arrangement is a lease or contains a lease, be made (refer3)?
  - If an arrangement is a lease, or contains a lease, how should the payments for this lease be separated from payments for any other elements in the arrangement (refer 4)?

2. Determining whether an arrangement is, or contains, a lease as defined in IAS 17

- It should be based on the substance of the arrangement.
- The following two criteria must be met:
  - Fulfilment of arrangement is dependent on the use of a specific asset.
    - The asset can explicitly or implicitly be identified.
    - Even if an asset is explicitly identified in the arrangement, it can only be the subject of the lease if the supplier does not have the right and ability to use other assets not specified in the arrangement to deliver the goods or services specified in the arrangement.
    - An asset can be identified by implication if it is not economically feasible or practicable for the supplier to perform the obligation through the use of other assets or the supplier owns only one suitable asset to perform its obligation in terms of the arrangement.
  - The arrangement conveys a right to use an asset. (You must be able to control the use of the underlying asset). Control is present if any of the following conditions are met:
    - The purchaser (lessee) has the ability or right to operate the asset in a manner it determines while obtaining or controlling more than an insignificant amount of the output or other utility of the asset. May be evident by the purchaser's ability to hire, fire or replace the operator of the asset; or the purchaser's ability to specify significant operating policies and procedures in arrangement with supplier (as opposed to the right to monitor the suppliers activities).
    - The purchaser (lessee) has the ability or right to control physical access to the underlying asset while obtaining or controlling more than an insignificant amount of the output or other utility of the asset. The purchaser controls the use of the underlying asset through access and therefore has the ability to restrict the access of others to the economic benefits of the underlying asset.
    - Fact and circumstances indicate that chances are remote that one or more parties other than the purchaser will take more than an insignificant amount of the output or other utility that will be produced or generated by the asset during the term of the arrangement. Furthermore the price that the purchaser will pay for the output is neither contractually fixed per unit of output nor equal to the current market price per unit of output as of the time of delivery of the output. (Note that if the price that the purchaser pays for the output is determined on a per unit bases, this indicates that the purchaser is paying for the product rather than for the right to use the underlying asset that produces the product).

3. Assessing or reassessing whether an arrangement is, or contains a lease

- The assessment of whether an arrangement contains a lease should be made at the inception of the arrangement on the basis of all the facts and circumstances.
- A reassessment of whether the arrangement contains a lease after the inception of the arrangement will only be made if any of the conditions listed in IFRIC 4.10 are present.

4. Separating payments for the lease from other payments

- If an arrangement is determined to contain a lease the requirements of IAS 17 must be applied to the lease element of the arrangement, unless exempted in terms of IAS 17.02.
- Many of the arrangements that fall within the scope of IFRIC 4 are likely to involve services, as well as the right to use an asset (multiple element arrangement).
- In terms of IAS 17.04 minimum lease payments includes only payments for the lease (right to use asset) and excludes payments for other elements in the arrangement.
- At inception of the arrangement the payment required under the arrangement must therefore be separated into those for the lease element and those for other elements of the arrangement based on their relative fair values.
- If a purchaser concludes that it is impracticable to separate the payments reliably, it should act as follows:
  - In the case of a finance lease, recognise an asset and a liability at the amount equal to the fair value of the underlying asset that was identified as the subject of the lease. Subsequently the liability should be reduced as payments are made and an imputed finance charge on the liability should be recognised using the purchaser's incremental borrowing rate of interest.
  - In the case of an operating lease, treat all payments under the arrangement as lease payments for the purpose of complying with the disclosure requirements of IAS 17 (AC 105), but:
    - disclose those payments separately from minimum lease payments of other arrangements that do not include payments for non- lease elements; and
    - state that the disclosed payments also include payments for non-lease elements in the arrangement.

CIRCULAR 12/2006: OPERATING LEASES

1. Background

- Circular 12/2006 was issued to explain the requirements of IAS 17 in respect of operating leases, which include fixed rental increases.
- It appeared that certain entities in South Africa recognised lease expenditure and lease income on a basis that was inconsistent with international practice.

2. Issues

- In terms of IAS 17.33 and .50, lease income and lease expenditure should be recognised on a straight-line basis over the lease term, unless a systematic basis is more representative of the time pattern of the user's benefit.
- The issue is if cash flow can be seen as 'another systematic basis' that is 'more representative of the time pattern of the user's benefit'?

3. Conclusion

- The time pattern of user's benefit is only affected by factors which impact physical usage.
- Therefore, if physical usage in each period of the lease is the same, equal lease expense/income must be recognised for each lease period (straight-line basis), irrespective that cash flows differ.
- The conclusions reached in this circular is effective immediately and entities that have not been straight lining lease expense/income must adjust financial statements by accounting for and disclosing the adjustment as an error in accordance with IAS 8 (AC 103).
- Contingent rental is not included in the lease payments to be recognised on a straight-line basis over the lease term, but is recognised as an income/expense in the income statement in the period that it arises.

IAS 18 *(AC 111)* and SIC 31 *(AC 431)*, Circular 9/06

Revenue

❑ **SUMMARY**

BACKGROUND

This standard deals with the bases for recognising revenue in the income statements of entities and specifically when revenue should be recognised. This statement only prescribes the treatment of revenue from normal activities (ordinary transactions and events). Guidelines are given for:
- the timing of recognition;
- the amount to be recognised (measurement); and
- disclosure requirements (reporting).

ACCOUNTING PRACTICE

1. Definition of revenue

This statement deals with the recognition of revenue resulting from the following transactions and events:
- sale of goods;
- rendering of services; and
- interest, royalties and dividends received by others for the use of the entity's assets.

Revenue is defined as the:
- gross inflow of economic benefits;
- during the period;
- arising in the course of ordinary activities;
- which result in increases in equity;
- other than increases relating to contributions from equity participants.

Revenue excludes amounts collected on behalf of third parties such as value-added tax. Similarly, in an agency relationship, the commission received by an agent represents the revenue earned by the agent and revenue does not include the selling price of the product sold on behalf of the principal.

2. Measurement of revenue

Revenue shall be measured at the fair value of the consideration received or receivable. **Fair value** is defined as the amount for which an asset could be exchanged, or a liability settled, between knowledgeable, willing parties in an arm's length transaction.

The following are taken into account in the determination of fair value of the amount received or receivable:
- Trade discounts and volume rebates are deducted in determining the fair value. Settlement discounts granted to debtors are also deductible (refer to Circular 09/06).
- When the inflow of cash is deferred; for example, the provision of interest-free credit, it effectively constitutes a financing transaction. The imputed rate of interest is calculated at the prevailing rate for a similar instrument of an issuer with a similar credit rating or a rate that discounts the nominal amount of the instrument to the current cash sales price. This interest will then be separately recognised and disclosed on a time proportion basis and in terms of IAS 39 (AC 133).
- When goods or services are exchanged for that of a similar nature and value, no revenue recognition takes place.
- When goods or services are rendered in exchange for dissimilar goods or services, revenue is measured at the fair value of the goods or services received. If it cannot be measured reliably, the fair value of the goods or services given up is used.
- When the selling price of a product includes an identifiable amount for subsequent servicing, that amount is deferred and recognised over the period during which the service is performed.
- If an entity concludes an agreement on the selling date to repurchase the goods at a later date, the sale is not accounted for as revenue; for example, repurchase agreements (the sale of prime gilts with an agreement to repurchase it at the selling price plus interest for the period for which it was held).

3. Recognition of revenue from sale of goods

When all the following conditions have been satisfied, the revenue from the sale of goods shall be recognised:
- The significant risks and rewards of ownership of the goods has been transferred to the buyer.

- The entity retains neither continuing managerial involvement to the degree usually associated with ownership nor effective control over the goods sold.
- The amount of revenue can be measured reliably.
- It is probable that the economic benefits associated with the transaction will flow to the entity.
- The costs incurred or to be incurred in respect of the transaction can be measured reliably.

Revenue and expenses that relate to the same transaction or event are generally recognised simultaneously.

When uncertainty arises about the collectability of an amount already included in revenue, such amounts are treated as expenses rather than as an adjustment to revenue recognised.

If legal title is retained solely to protect the collectibility of the amount due, revenue should be recognised (substance over form).

Revenue cannot be recognised when the related expenses cannot be measured reliably. Consideration already received for the sale transaction is recognised as a liability until revenue recognition can take place.

4. Recognition of revenue from rendering of services

When reliable estimation of the outcome of a transaction involving the rendering of services is possible, revenue associated with the transaction should be recognised by reference to the stage of completion of the transaction at the reporting date. Estimation of the outcome of a transaction is possible when all the following conditions are satisfied:
- The amount of revenue can be measured reliably.
- It is probable that the economic benefits associated with the transaction will flow to the entity.
- The stage of completion at reporting date can be measured reliably.
- The costs incurred for the transaction and the costs to complete the transaction can be measured reliably. (Refer to SIC 27 in the chapter on IAS 17 (AC105) and SIC 31 at the back of this summary.)

When, for some reason or other, the outcome of a transaction involving the rendering of services cannot be estimated reliably, revenue should be recognised only to the extent of the expenses recognised that are recoverable.

The stage of completion of a transaction may be determined by a variety of methods. An entity should use the method that measures reliably the services performed, for example, surveys of work performed, services performed to date as a percentage of total services to be performed or the proportion that costs incurred to date bear to the estimated total costs of the transaction.

Note that progress payments and advances received from customers often do not reflect the stage of completion of the services performed.

5. Recognition of revenue from the use of an entity's assets

Interest, royalties and dividends received by others from the use of the entity's assets shall be recognised when:
- it is probable that the economic benefits associated with the transaction will flow to the entity; and
- the amount of the revenue can be measured reliably.

Revenue is recognised as follows:
- Interest – Using the effective interest method in IAS 39 (AC 133) (i.e. on a time proportion basis).
- Royalties – Accrual basis (according to the substance of the relevant agreements).
- Dividends – When the shareholder's right to receive payment is established.

DISCLOSURE

An entity shall disclose the the accounting policies adopted for:
- the recognition of revenue; and
- the determination of the stage of completion in the case of the rendering of services.

NOTES TO THE STATEMENT OF COMPREHENSIVE INCOME (INCOME STATEMENT)

- The amount of each significant category of revenue, for example:
  - the sale of goods;
  - the rendering of services;
  - interest;
  - royalties; and
  - dividends.
- The amount of revenue arising from the exchange of goods or services included in each significant category of revenue.

SIC 31: REVENUE – BARTER TRANSACTIONS INVOLVING ADVERTISING SERVICES

1. Background

- An entity (seller) may enter into a barter transaction agreeing to provide advertising services to the customer in exchange for receiving advertising services. Advertisements may appear on the Internet, poster sites, television, radio, in magazines or journals, or in another medium.
- Equal or approximately equal amounts of cash or other consideration may or may not be exchanged between the entities.
- A seller that provides advertising services in the course of its ordinary activities recognises revenue under IAS 18 from a barter transaction involving advertising when:
  - the services exchanged are dissimilar (IAS 18.12); and
  - the amount of revenue can be measured reliably (IAS 18.20(a)).
- An exchange of similar advertising services is not a transaction that generates revenue under IAS 18 and therefore, this interpretation is only applicable to an exchange of dissimilar advertising services.

2. Issue

Under what circumstances can a seller reliably measure revenue at the fair value of advertising services received or provided in a barter transaction?

3. Consensus

- Revenue from a barter transaction involving advertising cannot be measured reliably at the fair value of advertising services received.
- However, a seller can reliably measure revenue at the fair value of the advertising services it provides in a barter transaction, by reference only to non-barter transactions that:
  - involve advertising similar to the advertising in the barter transaction;
  - occur frequently;
  - represent a predominant number of transactions and amount when compared to all transactions to provide advertising that is similar to the advertising in the barter transaction;
  - involve cash and/or another form of consideration (e.g. marketable securities, non-monetary assets and other services) that has a reliably measurable fair value; and
  - do not involve the same counterparty as in the barter transaction.

IAS 19 *(AC 116)*

Employee Benefits

❑ **SUMMARY**

Background
Accounting practice and disclosure of the different categories of employee benefits

Please note the following when using this summary and chapter on IAS 19:
- IAS 19 must be used in conjunction with this summary.
- Appendix A to IAS 19 must be used when working through the six steps associated with defined benefit plans under 2.2.
- A detailed discussion of the determination of the defined benefit obligation is not conducted, as it is too specialised for this work. Learners must, however, be able to use the defined benefit obligation/asset figure in calculations and disclosure, if it is provided.

BACKGROUND

1. Introduction

The objective of this standard is to prescribe the accounting treatment and disclosure of employee benefits by an employer except those benefits to which IFRS 2 (AC 139) (Share-based payments) applies. The statement requires an employer to recognise the following:

- a liability for future benefits to be paid to an employee who provided a service in exchange for such future employee benefits; and
- an expense when an employee renders a service in exchange for employee benefits.

Employee benefits are all forms of consideration given by an entity in exchange for services rendered by employees. Employee benefits include not only benefits provided to employees, but also benefits provided to their dependants (spouses, children etc.).

This standard covers several different categories of employee benefits and, since each identified category has different characteristics, different requirements are established for each category.

ACCOUNTING PRACTICE

1. Short-term employee benefits

Short-term employee benefits are defined as employee benefits (other than termination benefits) which fall due within 12 months after the end of the period in which the employees render the related service. Short-term employee benefits include the following:

- wages, salaries and social security contributions;
- short-term compensated absences (such as paid annual leave and paid sick leave);
- profit sharing and bonuses payable within twelve months after the period in which the employees rendered the related services; and
- non-monetary benefits (medical care, housing, cars or subsidised goods or services).

1.1 Recognition and measurement related to all short-term employee benefits

When an employee renders services to an entity during an accounting period, the undiscounted amount of short-term employee benefits expected to be paid in exchange for that service shall be recognised:

- as a liability (accrued expense), after deducting any amount already paid (should the amount already paid exceed the undiscounted amount of the benefits, the excess is recognised as an asset (prepaid expense) to the extent that the prepayment will lead to, for example, a reduction in future payments or a cash refund); and
- as an expense, unless another Statement of GAAP requires or permits the inclusion of the benefits in the cost of an asset, for example where wages form part of the cost of inventories.

1.2 Short-term compensated absences

The expected cost of short-term compensated absences shall be recognised as follows:

- In the case of accumulating compensated absences (carry forward to next period if not used), recognise when the employees render service that increases their entitlement to future compensated absences (for example, paid annual leave).
- In the case of non-accumulating compensated absences (lost if not used – do not carry forward to next period), recognise when the absences occur (for example, sick, maternity and paternity leave).

Accumulating compensated benefits may either be vesting or non-vesting. Vesting benefits result in an entitlement to a cash payment in respect of unused benefits when an employee leaves an entity. Non-vesting benefits will not entitle employees to a cash payment in respect of unused benefits upon leaving an entity.

The expected cost of accumulating compensated absences shall be measured as the additional amount that the entity expects to pay as result of the unused entitlement that has accumulated at the balance sheet date.

1.3 Profit sharing and bonus plans

The expected cost of profit sharing and bonus payments shall be recognised when, and only when:
- the entity has a present legal or constructive obligation to make such payments as a result of past events; and
- the entity can make a reliable estimate of the amount of the obligation.

A present obligation will exist only if the entity has no realistic alternative but to make the payments.

As the obligation under profit sharing and bonus plans arises from employee service and not from a transaction with the owners of the business, it is accounted for as an expense and not as a distribution of profits.

If the profit sharing and bonus payments are not due wholly within 12 months after the end of the period in which the services were rendered, they are classified as other long-term employee benefits.

1.4 Disclosure

This statement does not require specific disclosures regarding short-term benefits, but other Statements of Generally Accepted Accounting Practice may require disclosure, for example:
- IAS 1 (AC 101) (Presentation of financial statements) requires that an entity shall disclose employee benefit expense.
- IAS 24 (AC 126) (Related party disclosures) requires disclosures about employee benefits for key management personnel.

2. Post-employment benefits – the distinction between defined benefit and defined contribution plans

Post-employment benefits include, for example, the following:
- retirement benefits such as pensions; and
- other benefits after retirement, such as post-employment medical aid contributions.

Arrangements whereby an entity provides post-employment benefits are referred to as post-employment benefit plans, which can be divided into two classes (depending on the plan's economic substance):
- defined contribution plans (example: provident fund); and
- defined benefit plans (example: pension fund).

Under defined contribution plans, the following applies:
- The entity's legal or constructive obligation is limited to the amount it agrees to contribute to the fund. As a result, the amount of the benefits received by the employee is determined by the amount of contributions paid into the fund by the entity (and perhaps also by the employee) together with investment returns on these contributions.
- Actuarial risk (that benefits will be less than expected) and investment risk (that assets will be insufficient to meet expected benefits) fall on the employee.

Under defined benefit plans, the following applies:
- The entity has an obligation to provide the agreed benefits to current and former employees.
- The actuarial risk (that benefits will cost more than expected) and investment risk (that assets will be insufficient to meet expected benefits) fall on the employer.

IAS 19.29 to .42 explains the distinction between defined benefit and defined contribution plans in the context of multi-employer plans, state plans and insured benefits.

2.1 Recognition and measurement – defined contribution plans

When an employee has rendered service to an entity during a period, the contribution payable to a defined contribution plan in exchange for that service should be recognised as a liability and as an expense. Any amount already paid should be deducted from the liability. If the amount paid exceeds the contribution due, the excess is recognised as an asset to the extent that it will lead to a reduction in future payments or to a cash refund.

Where contributions to a defined contribution plan fall due more than twelve months after the end of the period in which the related service is rendered, such contributions should be discounted.

2.1.1 Disclosure – defined contribution plans

Income statement and notes

Disclose the amount recognised as an expense for defined contribution plans in an appropriate note to the income statement.

Attention shall also be paid to the disclosure requirements of IAS 24 (AC 126), as it relates to contributions made for key management personnel.

2.2 Recognition and measurement – defined benefit plans

Accounting for this type of plan is complex because:
- actuarial assumptions are required to measure the obligation and the related expense;
- there is a possibility of actuarial gains and losses; and
- obligations under these plans are measured on a discounted basis (similar to provisions), as they will be settled many years after an employee rendered the related services.

Defined benefit plans can be funded (contributions of employer and employee transferred into a separate fund or entity), partly funded or unfunded.

In the case of funded plans, the post-employment benefits are paid by the fund, but the employer underwrites the actuarial and investment risks associated with the plan. As a consequence, the expense recognised for a period is not necessarily equal to the contribution due for the period.

An entity shall account not only for its legal obligation under the formal terms of a defined benefit plan, but also for any constructive obligation that arises from the entity's informal practices.

The following steps shall be followed when accounting for a defined benefit plan:
1. Use actuarial techniques to make a reliable estimate of the amount of benefit employees have earned in return for service rendered in current and past periods (IAS 19.67 – 91).
2. Discount that amount of benefits using the Projected Unit Credit Method to determine the present value of the defined benefit obligation and the current service cost for the period (IAS 19.64 – .66).
3. Determine the fair value of plan assets and reimbursement rights (IAS 19.102 – .104).
4. Determine the total amount of actuarial gains or losses and calculate the portion of of those gains or losses that shall be recognised (IAS 19.92 – .95).
5. If a plan has been introduced or changed in the current period, determine the resulting past service cost (IAS 19.96 – .101).
6. If a plan has been curtailed or settled in the current period, determine the resulting gain or loss (IAS 19.109 – .115).

If an entity has more than one defined benefit plan, the above procedures shall be applied separately for each material plan.

In order to perform steps 1 and 2 discussed above, the following need to be considered (IAS 19.64 - .91):
- The Projected Unit Credit Method shall be used to determine the present value of the defined benefit obligation (see IAS 19.64).
- Certain unbiased and mutually compatible actuarial assumptions will have to be considered. These actuarial assumptions will be an entity's best estimates on a number of variables that could have an impact on the ultimate cost of providing post-employment benefit costs. Two types of actuarial assumption are applicable:
  - Demographic assumptions about future characteristics of current and former employees (and their dependants) who are eligible for benefits. The following matters will be dealt with:
    - mortality;
    - rates of employee turnover;
    - claim rates under medical plans; and
    - the proportion of plan members with dependants who will be eligible for post-employment benefits.
  - Financial assumptions such as:
    - the discount rate to determine the present value of related liabilities;
    - future salary and benefit levels;

- expected rate of return on plan assets and any reimbursement right of the defined benefit plan; and
- in the case of medical benefits, future medical costs and the cost of administering claims and benefit payments.

Actuarial gains or losses may arise from the defined benefit obligation as actuarial assumptions may not be precisely in line with reality.

In order to perform step 3 as discussed above, the following need to be considered (IAS 19.102 – .104):
- Plan assets comprise:
  - assets held by a long-term employee benefit fund; and
  - qualifying insurance policies.
- Assets held by a long-term employee benefit fund are assets (other than non-transferable financial instruments issued by the reporting entity) that:
  - are held by an entity (a fund) that is legally separate from the reporting entity and exists solely to pay or fund employee benefits; and
  - are available to be used only to pay or fund employee benefits, are not available to the reporting entity's own creditors (even in bankruptcy), and cannot be returned to the reporting entity, unless either:
    - the remaining assets of the fund are sufficient to meet all the related employee benefit obligations of the plan or the reporting entity; or
    - the assets are returned to the reporting entity to reimburse it for employee benefits already paid.
- A qualifying insurance policy is an insurance policy issued by an insurer that is not a related party (as defined in IAS 24 (AC 126), the statement on related party disclosures) of the reporting entity, if the proceeds of the policy:
  - can be used only to pay or fund employee benefits under a defined benefit plan;
  - are not available to the reporting entity's own creditors (even in bankruptcy), and cannot be paid to the reporting entity, unless either:
    - the proceeds represent surplus assets that are not needed for the policy to meet all the related employee benefit obligations; or
    - the proceeds are returned to the reporting entity to reimburse it for employee benefits already paid.
- Plan assets are valued at fair value, which would generally be the market value of the assets in the plan.
- Reimbursement rights arise when it is virtually certain that another party will reimburse some or all of the expenditure required to settle a defined benefit obligation. In such a case the entity shall recognise its right to reimbursement as a separate asset (distinct from other plan assets) and shall measure the asset at fair value. In all other respects, that asset shall be treated in the same way as other plan assets.

Actuarial gains or losses may result from plan assets and reimbursement rights owing to certain actuarial assumptions not being precisely in line with reality.

In order to perform step 4 as discussed above, the following shall be considered (IAS 19.92 – .95):
- Firstly refer to Appendix A of IAS 19 for a detailed explanation of how to determine the actuarial gains and losses on a defined benefit obligation and plan assets for any specific period.
- Secondly, when measuring a defined benefit liability (i.e. defined benefit obligation less plan assets) an entity must recognise a portion[*] of its actuarial gains and losses as income or expense if the net cumulative unrecognised actuarial gains and losses at the end of the previous reporting period exceeded the greater of:
  - 10% of the present value of the defined benefit obligation at that date; and
  - 10% of the fair value of any plan assets at that date.

These limits shall be calculated as absolute amounts and applied separately for each defined benefit plan.

* The portion to be recognised:
  - For each defined benefit plan, it is the excess determined under the previous paragraphs divided by the expected average remaining working lives of those employees who participate in that plan. The portion to be recognised shall be recalculated every year.
  - An entity may, however, adopt any systematic method that results in faster recognition of actuarial gains and losses. The same basis should be applied to both gains and losses and the basis should be applied consistently from period to period.
  - An entity may adopt a policy of recognising all actuarial gains and losses in the period in which they arise. If an entity adopts this policy, the gains and losses may be recognised outside profit or loss.

- Now refer to Appendix A of IAS 19 for an illustration on how to calculate the portion of the cumulative actuarial gains that will be recognised in the income statement.

In order to perform step 5 as discussed above, consider the following (IAS 19.96 – .101):
- Past service cost is defined as the increase in the present value of the defined benefit obligation for employee service in prior periods, resulting in the current period from the introduction of, or changes to, post-employment benefits or other long-term employee benefits. Past service cost may be either positive (where benefits are introduced or improved) or negative (where existing benefits are reduced).
- When past service cost arises, it will decrease or increase the defined benefit obligation of the plan.

An entity shall recognise past service cost as an expense on a straight-line basis over the average period until the benefits vest. To the extent that the benefits are already vested when the plan is introduced/changed, the past service cost shall be recognised immediately.

In order to perform step 6, the following shall be considered (IAS 19.109 – .115).

A **curtailment** occurs when an entity either:
- has a present obligation (legal or constructive) to make a material reduction in the number of employees covered by a plan; or
- amends the terms of a defined benefit plan with the result that a material element of future service by current employees will no longer qualify for benefits, or will qualify only for reduced benefits.

A **settlement** occurs when an entity enters into a transaction with its employees in terms of which the legal or constructive obligation for part or all of the benefits provided under a defined benefit plan is eliminated, for example, when a lump-sum cash payment is made to employees in exchange for their rights to receive specified post-employment benefits.

Gains or losses on the curtailment or settlement of a defined benefit plan should be recognised when the curtailment or settlement occurs. The gain or loss on a curtailment or settlement comprises the following:
- any resulting change in the present value of the defined benefit obligation;
- any resulting change in the fair value of the plan assets; and
- any related actuarial gains and losses and past service cost that had not previously been recognised.

2.2.1 Balance sheet recognition – defined benefit plans

The defined benefit liability on the balance sheet is the net total of the following amounts (IAS 19.54):
- the present value of the defined benefit obligation at the balance sheet date as calculated in terms of IAS 19.64 (refer to steps 1 and 2 under 2.2);
- plus any actuarial gains (less any actuarial losses) not recognised because of the treatment set out in IAS 19.92 – .93 (step 4 under 2.2);
- minus any past service cost not yet recognised (see IAS 19.96) (step 5 under 2.2);
- minus the fair value, at the balance sheet date, of plan assets (if any) out of which the obligations are to be settled directly (see IAS 19.102 – .104) (step 3 under 2.2).

The present value of defined benefit obligations and the fair value of any plan assets and reimbursement rights shall be determined with sufficient regularity to ensure that the amounts recognised in the financial statements do not differ materially from the amounts that would be determined at the balance sheet date.

Sometimes the amount determined from the four components in the previous paragraph may be negative (an asset). The resulting asset shall be measured at the lower of:
- the amount determined under IAS 19.54; and
- the net total of[#]:
  - any cumulative unrecognised actuarial losses and past service cost (see IAS 19.92, .93 and .96); and
  - the present value of any economic benefits available in the form of refunds from the plan or reductions in future contributions to the plan[@].

The application of the previous paragraph may not result in a gain being recognised by the entity solely as a result of the fund's actuarial loss or past service cost in the current period. Similarly, the entity may not recognise a loss solely as a result of the fund's actuarial gain in the current period.

If the above situation arises, the entity shall recognise immediately under IAS 19.54, to the extent that it arises while the defined benefit asset is determined in terms of paragraph (#) under 2.2.1:

- Net actuarial losses or past service cost of the current period to the extent that they exceed any reduction in the present value of economic benefits specified in paragraph (@).
- If there is no change or increase in the present value of the economic benefits mentioned in paragraph (@), the entire net actuarial losses and past service cost of the current period shall be recognised immediately.
- Net actuarial gains of the current period after deducting past service cost of the current period to the extent that they exceed any increase in the value of the economic benefits mentioned in paragraph (@).
- If there is no change or decrease in the present value of economic benefits, the entire net actuarial gains of the current period after deduction of past service cost of the current period shall be recognised immediately.

2.2.2 Income statement recognition – defined benefit plans

An entity shall recognise the net total of the following amounts as an expense or income, except to the extent that another Statement of Generally Accepted Accounting Practice requires or permits their inclusion in the cost of an asset, for example when these costs are capitalised to inventories or PPE:

- Current service cost (see IAS 19.63 – .91). Current service cost is the increase in the present value of the defined benefit obligation resulting from employee service in the current period.
- Interest cost (see IAS 19.82). Interest cost is the increase during a period in the present value of a defined benefit obligation which arises because the benefits are one period closer to settlement.
- The expected return on any plan assets and any reimbursement right (see IAS 19.105 – .107). This is the actuarial estimate in respect of the return that is expected on plan assets and on reimbursement rights and is not necessarily the actual return that realises on plan assets and reimbursement rights.
- Actuarial gains and losses, to the extent that they are recognised under IAS 19.92 and .93. This is the amount to be calculated and recognised in terms of Step 4 under 2.2.
- Past service cost, to the extent that IAS 19.96 requires an entity to recognise it. This is the amount determined and recognised in terms of Step 5 under 2.2.
- The effect of any curtailments or settlements (see IAS 19.109 and .110). This is the amount determined and recognised in terms of Step 6.
- The effect of the limit in IAS 19.58(b), unless it is recognised outside profit or loss. If actuarial gains and losses are recognised outside profit or loss, the effect of the limit in IAS 19.58(b) is also recognised outside profit or loss.

2.2.3 Presentation of defined benefit plans

An entity shall offset an asset (when plan assets exceed the plan obligation) relating to one plan against a liability (when plan obligation exceeds plan assets) relating to another plan when, and only when, the entity:

- has a legally enforceable right to use a surplus in one plan to settle obligations under the other plan; and
- intends either to settle the obligations on a net basis, or to realise the surplus in one plan and settle its obligation under the other plan simultaneously.

This standard does not specify whether an entity shall distinguish between current and non-current portions of the assets and liabilities relating to post-employment benefits, but it would seem appropriate to disclose such assets and liabilities as non-current items in the balance sheet.

2.2.4 Disclosure of defined benefit plans

Accounting policy
- The entity's accounting policy for recognising actuarial gains and losses.
- A general description of the type of plan, indicating whether it is a flat salary or final salary pension plan.

Balance sheet and notes
- A reconciliation of the opening and closing balances of the present value of the defined benefit obligation, showing separately:
  - current service cost;
  - interest cost;
  - contributions;
  - actuarial gains and losses;
  - foreign currency movements;

- benefits paid;
- post service cost;
- business combinations;
- curtailments; and
- settlements.
- The defined benefit obligation should be analysed into amounts arising from unfunded, partly funded and wholly funded plans.
- A reconciliation of the opening and closing balances of the fair value of plan assets/reimbursement rights, showing separately:
  - expected return on plan assets;
  - actuarial gains and losses;
  - foreign currency movements;
  - contributions;
  - benefits paid;
  - business combinations; and
  - settlements.
- A reconciliation of the assets and liabilities recognised in the balance sheet, showing at least:
  - the present value at the balance sheet date of the defined benefit obligation;
  - the fair value of any plan assets at the balance sheet date;
  - the fair value at the balance sheet date of any reimbursement rights recognised as an asset under IAS 19.104(a) with a brief description of the link between the reimbursement rights and the related obligation;
  - the net actuarial gains or losses not recognised in the balance sheet;
  - the past service cost not yet recognised in the balance sheet;
  - any amount not recognised as an asset, because of the limit in IAS 19.58(b); and
  - other amounts recognised in the balance sheet.
- The amounts included in the fair value of plan assets for:
  - each category of the reporting entity's own financial instruments; and
  - any property occupied by, or other assets used by, the reporting entity.
- The percentage or amount that each major category of plan assets constitutes of the fair value of the total plan assets.
- The basis used to determine the overall expected rate of return on assets, including the effect of the major categories of plan assets.
- The effect of an increase of one percentage point and the effect of a decrease of one percentage point in the assumed medical cost trend rates on:
  - current service cost and interest cost; and
  - the accumulated post-employment benefit obligation.
- The amounts for the current annual period and previous four annual periods of:
  - the present value of the defined benefit obligation, the fair value of the plan assets and the surplus of deficit in the plan; and
  - the experience adjustments arising on the plan liabilities and the plan assets.
- The employer's best estimate of contributions expected to be paid to the plan during the next financial year.
- The principal actuarial assumptions used as at the balance sheet date, including, where applicable:
  - the discount rates;
  - the expected rates of return on any plan assets for the period presented in the financial statements;
  - the expected rates of return for the periods presented in the financial statements on any reimbursement rights recognised as an asset;
  - the expected rates of salary increases (and of changes in an index or other variable specified in the formal and constructive terms of a plan as the basis for future benefit increases);
  - medical cost trend rates; and
  - any other material actuarial assumptions used.

An entity shall disclose each actuarial assumption in absolute terms (for example, as an absolute percentage) and not just as a margin between different percentages or other variables.

The most important distinction between a qualifying insurance policy and reimbursement right (which could also result from an insurance policy), from the perspective of disclosure, lies in the fact that a qualifying insurance policy is dealt with and presented as part of plan assets, whilst reimbursement rights are shown as a separate asset.

Income statement and notes
- The total expense recognised in the income statement for each of the following:
  - current service cost;
  - interest cost;
  - expected return on plan assets;
  - expected return on any reimbursement right recognised as a asset;
  - actuarial gains and losses recognised;
  - past service cost recognised;
  - the effect of any curtailment or settlement; and
  - the effect of the limit on paragraph 58(b).
- The line item(s) of the income statement in which the above-mentioned components are included, for example, profit before tax.
- The actual return on plan assets and the actual return on any reimbursement rights recognised as an asset.

Statement of recognised income and expense
- The total amount recognised in the statement of recognised income and expense for actuarial gains and losses; and the effect of the limit in paragraph 58(b).
- The cumulative amount of actuarial gains and losses recognised in the statement of recognised income and expense.

Illustration

For an illustration of the disclosure of defined benefit plans, refer to IAS 19, Appendix B.

3. Other long-term employee benefits

3.1 Background

Other long-term employee benefits include, for example:
- long-term compensated absences such as long-service or sabbatical leave;
- jubilee or other long-service benefits;
- long-term disability benefits;
- profit sharing and bonuses payable 12 months or more after the end of the period during which the related service was rendered by employees; and
- deferred compensation payable 12 months or more after the end of the period during which the related service was rendered.

Measurement of other long-term employee benefits is not usually subject to the same degree of uncertainty as post-employment benefits. Therefore:
- Actuarial gains and losses are recognised immediately and are not subject to the 10% corridor.
- All past service costs are recognised immediately.

3.2 Recognition and measurement – other long-term employee benefits

The amount recognised as a liability for other long-term employee benefits is the net total of the following:
- the present value of the defined benefit obligation at the balance sheet date;
- minus the fair value at the balance sheet date of plan assets (if any) out of which the obligations are to be settled directly.

The net total of the following amounts should be recognised as an expense or (subject to paragraph .58) income, except to the extent that another Statement of Generally Accepted Accounting Practice requires or permits their inclusion in the cost of assets:
- current service costs*;
- interest costs*;
- the expected return on any plan asset and any reimbursement right recognised as an asset*;
- actuarial gains and losses, which shall all be recognised immediately;

- past service cost, which shall all be recognised immediately; and
- the effect of any curtailments or settlements*.

* Treatment exactly as per 2.2.2 on income statement recognition for defined benefit plans.

3.3 Disclosure – other long-term employee benefits

- No specific disclosures are required in terms of IAS 19.
- The principles relating to separately disclosable relevant items according to IAS 1 (AC 101) may apply where the size, nature and incidence of the expense from these items warrants it.
- If required by IAS 24 (AC 126), an entity has to disclose information on the long-term employee benefits in respect of key management personnel.

4. Termination benefits

4.1 Background

Termination benefits are employee benefits payable as a result of either:
- an entity's decision to terminate an employee's employment before the normal retirement date; or
- an employee's decision to accept voluntary redundancy in exchange for those benefits.

These benefits are dealt with separately from other employee benefits, as the event giving rise to them is the termination of services rather than employee services.

4.2 Recognition

An entity shall recognise termination benefits as a liability and an expense when the entity is demonstrably committed to either:
- terminate the employment of an employee before his normal retirement date; or
- provide termination benefits following an offer made by the entity to encourage voluntary redundancy.

For an entity to be demonstrably committed to a termination, the entity should have a detailed formal plan for the termination, identifying at least:
- the location, function, and approximate number of employees who will be compensated for terminating their services;
- the termination benefits for each job classification or function; and
- the time when the plan will be implemented.

4.3 Measurement

If termination benefits fall due more than 12 months after the balance sheet date, the amount of these benefits should be discounted.

In the case of an offer made to encourage voluntary redundancy, the entity should measure these benefits based on the number of employees expected to accept the offer.

4.4 Disclosure

- No specific disclosures are required by this standard, but requirements of other standards may result in disclosure.
- A contingent liability may arise where there is uncertainty about the number of employees that will accept an offer of termination benefits. The following disclosure may result from IAS 37 (AC 130):
  - a brief description of the nature of the contingent liability;
  - uncertainties surrounding the issue;
  - estimate of financial effect thereof; but
  - no disclosure if the possibility of a loss is remote.
- Termination benefits may give rise to a separately disclosable item in terms of IAS 1 (AC 101) if the size, nature or incidence of the expense warrants it.
- Where key management personnel receive termination benefits, IAS 24 (AC 126) requires disclosure.

IAS 20 *(AC 134)* and SIC 10 *(AC 410)*

Accounting for Government Grants and Disclosure of Government Assistance

❑ **SUMMARY**

BACKGROUND

This standard deals with the accounting and disclosure of government grants as well as the disclosure of other forms of government assistance.

Government assistance refers to:
- action by government;
- designed to provide an economic benefit specific to an entity or range of entities;
- qualifying under certain criteria.

When benefits are provided only indirectly through action affecting general trading conditions; that is, the provision of infrastructure in development areas or the imposition of trading constraints on competitors, it is not included in government assistance as defined by the standard.

Government grants refer to:
- assistance by government;
- in the form of transfers of resources to an entity;
- in return for past or future compliance with certain conditions relating to the operating activities of the entity.

Grants related to assets are government grants that have as a primary condition that an entity qualifying for them shall purchase, construct or otherwise acquire long-term assets. Grants related to income are government grants other than those related to assets.

ACCOUNTING PRACTICE

Government grants – general

Government grants, including non-monetary grants at fair value, are only recognised when there is reasonable assurance that:
- the entity will comply with the conditions attached to the grants; and
- the grants will be received.

Whether a grant is an amount received in cash or a reduction in a loan from government (a forgivable loan), the accounting treatment will remain the same.

Government grants shall be recognised as income on a rational and systematic basis, to achieve the best possible matching with the related costs that the grants are intended to compensate, over the periods when these costs are incurred. Such grants cannot be credited directly to equity.

A government grant will be recognised as income in the period in which it becomes receivable, if it becomes receivable as compensation for expenses or losses already incurred or for the purpose of giving immediate financial support to the entity with no future related costs.

Sometimes, a grant may take the form of a transfer of a non-monetary asset for use by the entity. An example would be the transfer of land or another non-monetary asset such as a building or equipment. Two alternative treatments are recommended:
- Measure the non-monetary asset at fair value and account for the non-monetary asset at that fair value and the grant as deferred income (at that fair value).
- Record both the asset and the grant at a nominal amount.

Presentation of grants related to assets

Presentation in the balance sheet of government grants related to assets, including non-monetary grants at fair value, should be as follows:
- account for the grant as deferred income; or
- deduct the grant in arriving at the carrying amount of the asset.

If the grant is raised as deferred income, it will be recognised as income on a rational and systematic basis over the useful life of the asset to counter the depreciation expense.

If the grant is deducted in arriving at the carrying amount of the asset, the grant is effectively recognised as income over the useful life of a depreciable asset by the reduced depreciation charge.

Presentation of grants related to income

These grants will be accounted for as follows:
- as a separate income item or under the heading 'other income'; or
- as a deduction from the appropriate expenses.

Both methods are acceptable for presenting grants related to income.

Repayment of government grants

A government grant that becomes repayable will be treated as a revision to an accounting estimate (see IAS 8 (AC 103) and accounted for accordingly.

Repayment of a grant related to income will be applied first against any unamortised deferred income raised in respect of the grant. To the extent the repayment of the grant exceeds the unamortised deferred income, or where no deferred income exists, the repayment will be recognised immediately as an expense.

Repayment of a grant related to assets will be accounted for by:
- increasing the carrying amount of the asset; or
- reducing by the amount repayable the deferred income balance.

Recognise immediately as an expense the cumulative additional depreciation that would have been recognised to date as an expense, if the grant never occurred.

DISCLOSURE

The following information needs to be disclosed.

Accounting policy

- The accounting policy adopted for the recognition of grants from the government.
- The presentation methods for government grants adopted in the financial statements.

Notes to the financial statements

- The nature and extent of government grants recognized in the financial statements.
- A list of other forms of government assistance from which the entity has directly benefited.
- Contingent liabilities attaching to government assistance disclosed in the financial statements, where unfulfilled conditions exist.

Government assistance

Excluded from government grants are certain forms of government assistance for which a value cannot reasonably be determined (e.g. free technical or marketing advice). In addition, transactions with government that cannot be distinguished from normal trading transactions of the entity (e.g. a government procurement policy resulting in sales for the entity) are also not government grants.

SIC 10: GOVERNMENT ASSISTANCE – NO SPECIFIC RELATION TO OPERATING ASSISTANCE

Background

Sometimes, governments may assist entities by encouraging or supporting business activities in the long term in specific regions or industry sectors. Under such circumstances the requirements that must be met to be eligible for such grants may not be specifically related to the operating activities of the entity.

Issue

The issue is whether such government assistance would be a government grant as intended by IAS 20, and whether the requirements of IAS 20 would be applicable to such a government grant.

Consensus

The government grants addressed by SIC 10 will be treated in accordance with IAS 20, even though there are no conditions specifically related to the operating activities of the entity. As indicated in IAS 20, such grants may not be credited directly to equity.

IAS 21 *(AC 112)* and SIC 7 *(AC 407)*

The Effects of Changes in Foreign Exchange Rates

❑ **SUMMARY**

Background
Accounting practice
Disclosure
SIC 7: Introduction of the Euro

Note: In this chapter it is assumed that all entities dealt with in the questions, chose to apply hedge accounting and met all the hedge criteria as set out in IAS 39.88. Ignore the time value of money on all forward contracts.

BACKGROUND

1. Scope

This standard prescribes:
- how to include foreign currency transactions in the financial statements of an entity;
- how to include foreign operations in the financial statements of an entity; and
- how to translate financial statements into a presentation currency different from the presentation currency of the entity.

2. Functional currency versus presentation currency

A clear understanding of a distinction between functional currency, foreign and presentation currency is essential, as these have direct bearing on the prescribed accounting treatment of the above-mentioned three matters.

Functional currency is the currency of the primary economic environment in which the entity operates.

Foreign currency is a currency other than the functional currency of the entity.

Presentation currency is the currency in which the financial statements are presented.

An entity may select any presentation currency, but a functional currency cannot be selected and an entity will have to use a specific currency as its functional currency provided certain criteria are met.

To identify the functional currency of an entity, the following factors are considered:
- the currency in which sales prices for goods and services are mainly determined (this is usually the currency in which sales prices for its goods and services are denominated and settled);
- the currency of the country whose competitive forces and regulations influence the sales prices of goods and services; and
- the currency in which the costs of providing goods or services, labour and material are determined (i.e. the currency in which these costs are denominated and paid).

The following factors may also provide evidence of an entity's functional currency:
- the currency in which financing activities are generating funds (i.e. the currency in which debt and equity instruments are issued); and
- the currency in which receipts from operating activities are usually retained.

If the functional currency of a foreign operation, and whether its functional currency is the same as that of the reporting entity (the reporting entity in this case is the entity that has the foreign operation as its subsidiary, branch associate or joint venture) could not be determined with reference to the factors listed above, the following additional factors should be considered:
- Are the activities of the foreign operation carried out as an extension of the reporting entity, or is it carried out with a significant degree of autonomy? For example, the activities are carried out as an extention when the foreign operation only sells goods imported from the reporting entity and then returns the proceeds to the reporting entity. An example of autonomous activities is when the foreign operation generates cash and other monetary items, income, incurs expenses and arranges borrowings, mainly in its own local currency without assistance from the reporting entity.
- Whether the transactions of the foreign operation with the reporting entity are a high or a low proportion of the foreign operation's activities.
- Whether cash flows of the reporting entity are directly affected by the cash flows from the activities of the foreign operation and whether the cash flows are readily available for remittance to the reporting entity.
- Whether the activities of the foreign operation will generate sufficient cash flows to service existing and normally expected debt obligations without the reporting entity having to make funds available to the foreign operation.

Unless there is a change in the underlying transactions, events and conditions that warrants a change in functional currency, it is not changed once determined.

If the functional currency is that of a hyperinflationary economy, IAS 29 (AC 124) has to be used to restate the financial statements of the entity.

3. Summary of approach required by IAS 21

- In preparing financial statements, each entity (whether a stand-alone entity, a parent entity or a foreign operation (i.e. a subsidiary or branch) determines its functional currency using the principles discussed in 2 above.
- The entity translates foreign currency items into its functional currency and reports the effects of such translation in accordance with 1 below.
- Various types of entity, whether members of a group or not, may have investments in associates or joint ventures and they could also have branches. The results and financial position of each individual entity included in the reporting entity (for instance consolidated) need to be translated into the same currency in which the reporting entity's financial statements are presented.
- The presentation currency of a reporting entity can be any currency (or currencies). Any individual entity whose results and financial position are included within the reporting entity and whose functional currency differs from the presentation currency of the reporting entity are translated in accordance with 1 below.
- A stand-alone entity preparing financial statements or an entity preparing separate financial statements in accordance with IAS 27 (AC 132) has a free choice to present its financial statements in any currency (or currencies). If the presentation currency chosen by the entity differs from its functional currency, its results and financial position should be translated into the presentation currency in accordance with 1 below.

ACCOUNTING PRACTICE

1. Financial statements of foreign operations

The method of translating the financial statements of foreign operations is determined by whether the functional currency of the foreign operation is the same as that of the reporting entity or different.

Taking into account the considerations in respect of establishing the functional currency of an entity as discussed in 2:
- an autonomous foreign operation will have a functional currency different from that of its parent; and
- a foreign operation that is an extension of the reporting entity will have the same functional currency as that of its parent.

1.1 Autonomous foreign operations

An autonomous foreign operation is an operation whose activities are not an integral part of those of the reporting entity. The closing rate method (par .38 – .50) is used for the translation of the financial statements. This method preserves as far as possible the results and the interrelationships of amounts appearing in the balance sheet and income statement, after the translation has been performed.

The translation rules are as follows:
- All assets and liabilities (monetary and non-monetary) at each balance sheet presented (also comparatives) are translated at the closing rate.
- Income statement items:
  - actual rates on transaction dates or at an appropriate weighted average exchange rate for the period;
  - common items at actual rates; and
  - depreciation at the average rate.
- Equity at acquisition is translated at the exchange rate on the date of acquisition.
- Individual components of equity are translated at historical rates. However, the total of equity in the foreign currency is translated at the applicable closing rate of each period to be in line with all assets and liabilities translated at the closing rate, because E = A - L.
- Special rules apply to foreign operations in countries with hyperinflation, and these are dealt with in IAS 29 (AC 124).
- Goodwill and fair value adjustments of assets and liabilities at acquisition of a foreign operation are seen as assets and liabilities of the foreign operation and such assets are translated at closing rate.

Exchange gains and losses are treated as follows:
- Exchange differences resulting from the translation of the financial statements of the foreign operation are taken directly to the 'foreign currency translation reserve' (non-distributable reserve) included in equity.
- Exchange differences resulting from the translation of an intragroup monetary item (which is considered to be a permanent part of equity) are taken to the income statement in the financial statements of the company itself, but is transferred to the foreign currency translation reserve (FCTR) on consolidation.
- Where a net investment in a foreign operation is naturally hedged by means of a foreign currency loan, the exchange differences are treated as cash flow hedges (see section 10 in chapter IAS 39 (AC 133)).
- Upon sale, or abandonment of all or part of an investment in a foreign operation, the applicable share of the foreign currency translation reserve (FCTR) is recognised in profit or loss. (It is not a reserve transfer in the statement of changes in equity.)

1.2 Foreign operations being an extension of the business of the reporting entity

A foreign operation that is an extension of the operations of the reporting entity carries on business as if it was an integral part of the reporting entity's operations.

The functional currency of such a foreign operation (an extension) will be the same as the functional currency of the reporting entity. Consequently all transactions and events are translated at transaction date using the normal translation rules discussed under 2 below and no further translation will be necessary. Changes in exchange rates will immediately have an effect on the reporting entity's cash flow from operations and will be similar to that which would occur if the reporting entity had conducted the operation itself.

If a foreign operation keeps its records in a currency different from the functional currency of its parent, the 'temporal method' – the translation method described in par .20 – .26 – is used for the translation of the financial statements. This method incorporates the individual items of the foreign financial statements into those of the reporting entity in a manner that achieves the same effect as if all transactions of the foreign operation had been entered into by the reporting entity itself. (This method will only be applied in exceptional cases where the foreign operation has not used the same functional currency as that of the reporting entity for practical reasons.)

The translation rules under this method are as follows:
- All monetary items are translated at the closing rate.
- Non-monetary items recorded at historical cost are translated at historical rates.
- Non-monetary items that were held by the foreign operation before the investment in such operation by the reporting entity are translated at the historical rate at the date of acquisition.
- Non-monetary items measured at fair values in the foreign financial statements are translated at the exchange rates that existed on the dates their fair values were determined. This rule also applies when the net realisable value of inventory is determined – the rate used is therefore usually the closing rate.
- Components of equity are translated at historical exchange rates.
- Income statement items (excluding depreciation) are translated at the exchange rates applicable on transaction date or at any appropriate weighted average exchange rate for the period.
- Depreciation is translated at the same historical exchange rate that is used to translate the asset.

Exchange gains and losses are treated as follows:
- The differences arising on translation of a foreign operation that is an extension of the reporting entity are taken to the income statement like normal exchange differences.

2. Foreign currency transactions

Uncovered transactions (No forward exchange contract)
- The foreign transaction is accounted for at the spot exchange rate between the functional currency and foreign currency ruling at transaction date (normally when risks and rewards are transferred). For practical reasons an approximate rate at transaction date or an average rate for a period may be used.
- Where a transaction is not settled in the same accounting period as that in which it occurred, the resultant monetary items are translated at the closing rate ruling at balance sheet date.
- Exchange differences on settlement of monetary items are recognised in income.
- Exchange differences arising from the translation of monetary items at balance sheet date are recognised in income.
- Non-monetary items measured at historical cost are translated at the spot rate on the transaction date.

- Non-monetary items measured at fair values are translated at the spot rate on the date the fair value was determined.
- Exchange differences arising from an intragroup monetary item that in substance forms part of an entity's net investment in a foreign entity (considered to be permanent equity capital) are included in profit or loss of the separate financial statements of the reporting entity or the individual financial statements of the foreign operation. On consolidation these amounts are transferred to the foreign currency translation reserve. On disposal the cumulative foreign currency translation reserve is recognised in the income statement when the gain or loss on disposal is recognised.
- Exchange differences arising from a foreign liability that serves as a hedge of an entity's net investment in a foreign entity is accounted for as a cash flow hedge in terms of IAS 39 (AC 133):
  - the effective portion of the hedge is taken directly to equity through the statement of changes in equity; and
  - the ineffective portion is recognised in the income statement.

On disposal of the foreign operation the effective portion of the hedge (currently included in equity) will be recognised in the income statement.

Hedged transactions (Forward exchange contract)

IAS 21 provides no guidance on the accounting for hedged transactions. However, IAS 39 (AC 133), which deals with the measurement and recognition of financial instruments, covers various aspects of hedge accounting.

Formal hedging for accounting purposes implies that certain derivative financial instruments (forward exchange contracts under IAS 21) are designed as hedging instruments so that changes in their fair values are wholly or partially offset against the changes in fair values of the underlying foreign exchange transactions. These underlying transactions are called hedged items. Hedged items could include:
- recognised foreign exchange denominated assets and liabilities;
- uncommitted but highly probable anticipated future transactions (also called forecasted transactions); and
- a firm commitment.

Informal hedging can also take place in practice depending on the nature of foreign currency transactions, but in this chapter the focus is placed on formal hedging for foreign currency risk in the form of forward exchange contracts.

Although hedge accounting can only be adopted when all the conditions in IAS 39 (AC 133) .88 have been met, it is assumed for purposes of this chapter that all these conditions have been met. Consequently, the focus is on the accounting treatment of hedged transactions and the related hedging instruments and hedged items, rather than whether or not the hedging criteria have been met.

For hedge accounting, please refer to section 10 in the chapter on IAS 39 (AC 133). The hedging instruments mentioned there will be FECs.

3. Changes in functional currency

- Once the functional currency is determined, it can be changed only if there is a change to underlying transactions, events and conditions that lead to the specific functional currency being determined in the first place. For example, a change in an entity's functional currency may be necessary if there was a change in the currency that mainly influences the sales prices of goods and services.
- When there is a change in an entity's functional currency, the entity shall apply the translation procedures applicable to the new functional currency prospectively from the date of the change.
- In other words, from the date of the change the entity translates all items into the new functional currency using the exchange rate at that date. The amounts for non-monetary items translated as such, are treated at their historical cost.
- Exchange differences recognised in equity as a foreign currency translation reserve, arising from the translation of a foreign operation, are not recognised in profit or loss (income statement) until the foreign operation is disposed of.

DISCLOSURE

- For purposes of disclosure, references to functional currency apply, in the case of a group, to the functional currency of the parent.

Income statement

- Disclose the amount of exchange differences recognised in profit or loss except for those arising on financial instruments measured at fair value through profit or loss in accordance with IAS 39 (AC 133).

Statement of changes in equity

- Disclose the net exchange differences classified in a separate component of equity (foreign currency translation reserve), resulting from the translation of the financial statements of a foreign operation.
- Present a reconciliation of the amount at the beginning and end of the period of such exchange differences.

Notes

- When the functional currency of either the reporting entity or a significant foreign operation changes:
  - State the fact.
  - Disclose the reason for the change in functional currency.
- When the presentation currency of an entity is different from the functional currency:
  - State the fact.
  - Disclose the functional currency.
  - Disclose the reason for using a different presentation currency.
- When financial statements or other financial information are displayed in a currency that is not the functional currency or presentation currency of the reporting entity and the requirements as stated above have not been met, the entity has to:
  - clearly identify the information as supplementary information that does not comply with IFRS;
  - disclose the currency in which the supplementary information is presented; and
  - disclose the functional currency of the entity as well as the translation method used for determining the supplementary information.

SIC 7: INTRODUCTION OF THE EURO

1. Issue

The issue is how to apply IAS 21 to the changeover from the national currencies of participating Member States of the European Union to the Euro (the changeover).

2. Consensus

IAS 21 should be strictly applied to the changeover. In particular, this means the following:
- Foreign currency monetary assets and liabilities resulting from transactions should still be translated into the functional currency at closing date. Any resultant exchange differences should be recognised in the income statement immediately, except for exchange gains or losses from cash flow hedges, which should be taken to equity as deferred hedging differences. The latter will appear in the statement of changes in equity.
- Cumulative exchange differences relating to the translation of the financial statements of foreign operations should still be classified as equity and should only be taken to profit or loss when a foreign operation is disposed of.
- Exchange differences should not be capitalised to the carrying amounts of related assets if it resulted from the translation of liabilities denominated in participating currencies.

IAS 23 *(AC 114)*

Borrowing Costs

❑ **SUMMARY**

Background
Accounting practice
Disclosure
Schematic presentation

Note: In terms of the 2007 revision of IAS 23 (AC 114), all borrowing costs on qualifying assets shall now be capitalised. The option not to capitalise therefore falls away. However, this summary still allows entities not to capitalise borrowing cost on qualifying assets, as the questions still contain the option.

BACKGROUND

Borrowing costs are interest and other costs incurred by an entity in connection with the borrowing of funds. It includes the following:
- interest incurred on bank overdrafts, borrowed short-term and long-term funds;
- foreign currency gains and losses on borrowings, which are regarded as an adjustment to the financing costs of foreign borrowed funds;
- amortisation of discounts or premiums on borrowings;
- amortisation of related costs incurred in connection with the arrangement of borrowings; and
- finance costs in respect of finance leases.

The standard requires the immediate recognition of borrowing costs in the period in which they are incurred, but allows the option that borrowing costs directly attributable to the acquisition, construction or production of a qualifying asset may be capitalised.

Such borrowing costs are only capitalised in terms of the Framework when it is probable that future economic benefits will flow to the entity as a result of the borrowing costs and the borrowing costs can be measured reliably. All other borrowing costs are recognised as an expense in the period in which they are incurred.

Qualifying assets are assets that necessarily require a substantial period of time to bring them to intended use or saleable condition. They include the following:
- inventories that take a substantial period of time to get to a saleable condition; and
- other assets such as manufacturing plants, power generation facilities and investment properties.

Consequently, other investments and inventories that are routinely manufactured or produced in large quantities over a short period of time and on a repetitive basis are not qualifying assets.

The following arguments are raised for the capitalisation of borrowing costs:
- Capitalised borrowing costs form part of the acquisition costs, which reflect the total investment in the asset more accurately. Borrowing costs in essence do not differ from other costs that are normally capitalised and that form part of the cost price of the asset.
- The capitalisation of borrowing costs complies with the matching concept in so far as it is a cost incurred in respect of the acquisition of an asset that will benefit future periods and it is debited against the revenue of the periods that benefited.
- Capitalisation results in greater comparability between the cost price of assets that were paid for during the construction stage and those that were purchased (where the price normally includes borrowing costs).

The following arguments are raised against the capitalisation of borrowing costs:
- Borrowing costs are incurred to finance all the operations. Any attempt to link borrowing costs to a specific asset is inevitably arbitrary.
- Capitalisation of borrowing costs may result in the same type of asset having different carrying amounts, depending on the entity's method of financing.
- Treating borrowing costs as an expense against revenue will result in the financial statements providing comparable results from period to period, and therefore provide a better indication of the future cash flows of the entity.

ACCOUNTING PRACTICE

Borrowing costs – benchmark treatment

Recognise borrowing costs as an expense in the period in which they are incurred.

Capitalisation of borrowing costs – allowed alternative treatment

Capitalisation of borrowing costs must commence when all of the following criteria are met:
- expenditure on an asset have been incurred;
- borrowing costs have been incurred; and
- activities are in progress which are necessary to prepare the asset for its intended sale or use.

Capitalisation should cease in the following cases:
- where the asset is materially ready for its intended use or sale;
- when active development is suspended for extended periods; and
- where construction is completed in sections and the completed part can be used independently; for example, a business park where the first phase is completed and available for rental while the other phases are still under construction (capitalisation will cease on completed section).

Capitalisation should continue in the following cases:
- where all of the components need to be completed before any part of the asset can be sold or used; for example, plant;
- for brief interruptions in activities;
- during periods when substantial technical and administrative work is being carried out; and
- for delays that are inherent in the asset's manufacturing process; for example, wines, which need long periods to reach maturity.
- Even when the accumulated cost of an asset or the expected total cost, inclusive of capitalised interest, exceeds the net realisable value or recoverable amount, capitalisation should not cease. However, the excess by which the capitalised value exceeds the recoverable amount, should be written off in terms of IAS 36 (AC 128) to reduce the carrying amount of the asset to its recoverable amount.

Capitalisation amount

The amount that may be capitalised, is those borrowing costs that could have been avoided during the period if the expenditure on the qualifying asset had not been made.

If funds are specifically borrowed for the purpose of obtaining a particular qualifying asset, the amount of borrowing costs qualifying for capitalisation on that asset is the actual borrowing costs incurred on that loan during the period, less any benefit derived from the temporary investment of those borrowings.

If funds are borrowed generally and used for the purpose of obtaining a qualifying asset, the amount of borrowing costs qualifying for capitalisation should be determined by the application of a capitalisation rate to the expenditure on that particular asset. The capitalisation rate is the weighted average borrowing costs applicable to all the borrowings of the entity that are outstanding during the period, excluding those borrowings made specifically for the purpose of obtaining a qualifying asset. The amount of borrowing costs actually incurred during a period may not be exceeded by the amount of borrowing costs capitalised during the same period.

Change in accounting policy

If an entity changes its policy to that of capitalising borrowing costs, the change in accounting policy should be applied retrospectively in terms of IAS 8 (AC 103). However, owing to the practical problems associated with the retrospective application, it is anticipated that the only borrowing costs that should be capitalised retrospectively are those incurred in respect of assets that were incomplete at the date that the new policy came into effect. If it is practically impossible to restate the comparative amounts, then the new policy can be applied prospectively.

DISCLOSURE

Accounting policy

- Disclose the entity's policy in respect of borrowing costs. Does the entity capitalise borrowing costs or not?

Notes to the financial statements

- Disclose the borrowing costs capitalised during the period.
- Show the capitalisation rate used to calculate capitalised borrowing costs.

SCHEMATIC PRESENTATION

Capitalisation of borrowing costs

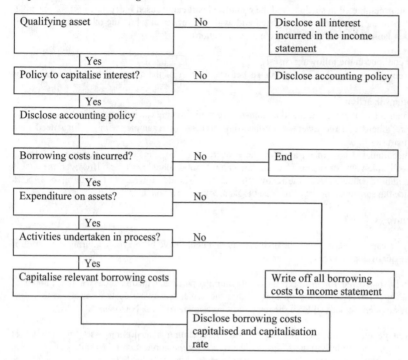

IAS 24 *(AC 126)*

Related Party Disclosures

❑ **SUMMARY**

Background
Disclosure

BACKGROUND

The objective of this standard is to ensure that an entity's financial statements contain disclosures that are necessary to draw attention to the possibility that the financial position and profit or loss of the entity may have been impacted on by the existence of related parties and by entering into transactions and having outstanding balances with such parties.

This standard shall be utilised to:
- identify related party relationships and transactions;
- identify outstanding balances between an entity and its related parties;
- identify the circumstances where disclosure of the first two items is required; and
- determine the disclosures to be provided about those items.

This standard dictates disclosure of transactions with related parties and outstanding balances in the separate financial statements of a parent, venturer or investor presented in accordance with IAS 27 (AC 132)

Owing to their highly technical nature the definitions below are virtually quoted from the standard.

A party is a related party of an entity if directly, or indirectly through one or more intermediaries, the party:[*]
- controls, is controlled by, or is under common control with, the entity (this includes parents, subsidiaries and fellow subsidiaries);
- has an interest in the entity that gives it significant influence over the entity;
- has joint control over the entity;
- is an associate of the entity;
- is a joint venture in which the entity is a venturer;
- is a member of the key management personnel of the entity or its parent;[#]
- is a close member of the family of an individual referred to in (*) or (#);[@]
- is an entity that is controlled, jointly controlled or significantly influenced by, or for which significant voting power in such entity resides with, directly or indirectly, any individual referred to in (#) and (@);[$]
- is a post-employment benefit plan for the benefit of employees of the entity, or of any entity that is a related party of the entity.

A related party transaction is a transfer or resources, services or obligations between related parties, regardless of whether a price is charged.

Close members of the family of an individual are those family members who may be expected to influence, or be influenced by, that individual in their dealings with the entity. They may include:
- the individual's domestic partner and children;
- children of the individual's domestic partner; and
- dependants of the individual or the individual's domestic partner.

Compensation includes:
- short-term employee benefits;
- post-employment benefits such as pensions, other retirement benefits, post-employment life insurance and post-employment medical care;
- other long-term employee benefits;
- termination benefits; and
- share-based payment.

Control and joint control are defined in IAS 27 (AC132) and IAS 31 (AC119) respectively.

Significant influence is defined in IAS 28(AC110).

Key management personnel are those persons having authority and responsibility for planning, directing and controlling the activities of the entity, directly or indirectly, including any director (whether executive or otherwise) of that entity.

When considering each possible related party relationship, the substance of the relationship and not merely the legal form should be borne in mind.

In the context of this standard, the following would not necessarily be related parties:
- two entities simply because they have a common director or other member of key management personnel, notwithstanding (#) and ($) in the definition of 'related party' as set out earlier;
- two venturers simply because they have joint control over a joint venture;
- providers of finance;
- trade unions;
- public utilities;
- government departments and agencies, purely based on their normal dealings with the entity; and
- a customer, supplier, franchisor, distributor or general agent with whom an entity enters into a significant volume of business, merely by way of the resulting economic dependence.

DISCLOSURE

- Relationships between parents and subsidiaries shall be disclosed irrespective of whether there have been transactions between those related parties.
- The name of the entity's parent and, if different, the ultimate controlling party, shall be disclosed.
- If neither the entity's parent nor the ultimate controlling party produces financial statements available for public use, the name of the next most senior parent that does prepare financial statements for public use shall be disclosed.
- An entity shall disclose the compensation of key management personnel in total and for each of the following categories[#]:
  - short-term employee benefits;
  - post-employment benefits;
  - other long-term benefits;
  - termination benefits; and
  - share-based payments.
- If transactions with related parties have taken place, an entity shall disclose:
  - the nature of the related party relationship; and
  - information about the transactions and outstanding balances that would be essential for an understanding of the potential effect of the related party relationship on the financial statements.
- The above disclosure requirements are in addition to the requirements for the disclosure of key management personnel compensation (see (#) above). At a minimum, disclosures shall include:
  - the amount of the transactions;
  - the amount of outstanding balances and in respect of those:
    - their terms and conditions, including whether they are secured;
    - the nature of the consideration to be provided in settlement; and
    - details of any guarantees given or received;
  - allowance accounts for credit losses related to the amount of outstanding balances; and
  - bad or doubtful debs expenses recognised during the period due from related parties.
- The disclosures required by the immediately preceding paragraph shall be made separately for each of the following categories of related parties:
  - the parent;
  - entities with joint control or significant influence over the entity;
  - subsidiaries;
  - associates;
  - joint ventures in which the entity is a venturer;
  - key management personnel of the entity or its parent, and
  - other related parties.

The following are examples of transactions that should be disclosed if entered into with a related party:
- purchases or sales of goods (finished or unfinished);
- purchases or sales of property and other assets;
- rendering or receiving of services;
- leases;
- transfers of research and development;
- transfers under licence agreements;
- transfers under finance arrangements (including loans and equity contributions in cash or in kind);

- provision or guarantees or collateral; and
- settlement of liabilities on behalf of the entity or by the entity on behalf of another party.

If items are similar in nature, they may be disclosed in aggregate. However, if separate disclosure is necessary for an understanding of the effects of related party transactions on the financial statements of the entity, they may not be aggregated.

Companies Act, 1973 (as amended)

- Details of loans made and security provided by a subsidiary to its parent and fellow subsidiaries (Sec. 37 and Schedule 4, par. 37).
- Details of a material interest that an interested director or officer of a company holds in a proposed contract (Sec. 237).
- Details of loans made and security provided for benefit of directors and managers (Sec. 38(2), 295, 296 and Schedule 4, par. 25).
- Directors' remuneration (Sec. 297).
- Indebtedness to companies in the group (Schedule 4, par. 18).
- Interests in subsidiaries, consisting of shares and amounts owing by subsidiaries (Schedule 4, par. 23).
- Indebtedness by parent and fellow subsidiaries (Schedule 4, par. 24).
- Aggregate amount of income from subsidiaries (Schedule 4, par. 42(b)).
- Interest of parent in its subsidiaries' profit or loss after tax (Schedule 4, par. 71).

IAS 27 *(AC 132)* and SIC 12 *(AC 412)*

Consolidated Financial Statements and Separate Financial Statements

❑ **SUMMARY**

BACKGROUND

This standard shall be applied in the preparation and presentation of consolidated financial statements for a group of entities (subsidiaries) under the control of a parent.

The standard also addresses the accounting treatment of investments in subsidiaries, jointly controlled entities and associates in a parent's separate financial statements.

The standard does not deal with methods of accounting for business combinations and their effects on consolidation, including goodwill.

The terms discussed hereafter are used in IAS 27 with the meanings specified. These definitions are basically quoted from the standard as they are highly technical and changing associated wording could change the meaning of the definitions:

- **Control** (for purposes of this statement) is the power to govern the financial and operating policies of an entity so as to obtain benefits from its activities.
- A **subsidiary** is an entity (including an unincorporated entity such as a partnership) controlled by another entity (the parent).
- A **parent** is an entity that has one or more subsidiaries.
- A **group** is a parent together with all its subsidiaries.
- **Consolidated financial statements** are the financial statements of a group presented as those of a single economic entity.
- **Minority interest** is that part of the profit or loss and net assets of a subsidiary attributable to equity interests which are not owned, directly or indirectly, by the parent. Indirect ownership would manifest via subsidiaries.
- **Separate financial statements** are the financial statements prepared by a parent investor (associate) or venturer, in which these investments are accounted for on the basis of a direct equity interest rather than by incorporating results and net assets of the investees.
- The **cost method** is a method of accounting for an investment whereby the investment is shown at cost.
  - The investor recognises income from the investment only to the extent that it comes from since acquisition retained earnings.
  - Distributions in excess of since acquisition profits are regarded as a recovery of investment, being a reduction of the cost of the investment.

ACCOUNTING PRACTICE

1.   General principles

A parent, except for those described directly below, shall present consolidated financial statements.

Consolidated financial statements need not be presented by a parent if:
- the parent itself is a wholly-owned subsidiary or the parent is a partially-owned subsidiary of another entity and its owners have condoned the parent not presenting consolidated financial statements;
- the parent's debt or equity instruments are not traded on a public market;
- the parent is not in a process of arranging to have any class of its instruments traded on a public market; and
- the ultimate parent or an intermediate parent produces consolidated financial statements available for public use that comply with IFRSs (ACs).

A parent that elects not to prepare consolidated financial statements in terms of the previous paragraph, complies with 2.4.

The consolidated financial statements shall include all entities controlled by the parent including subsidiaries acquired with a view to disposal and that meet the criteria to be classified as held for sale. However, such subsidiaries will be accounted for in terms of IFRS 5 (AC 142).

Control is generally presumed to exist when the parent owns, directly or indirectly through subsidiaries, more than half of the voting power of an entity, unless the contrary can be demonstrated.

Control also exists when the parent owns one half or less of the voting power when there is:

- power over more than one half of the voting rights owing to an agreement with other investors;
- power to govern the operating and financial policies of the entity in terms of a statute or an agreement;
- power to appoint or remove the majority of the members of the board of directors or other equivalent governing body and that body controls the entity; or
- power to cast the majority of votes at meetings of the board of directors or other equivalent governing body and that body controls the entity.
- If potential voting rights such as share warrants, share call options and convertible instruments exist, and these have the potential to give the entity voting power or reduce the voting power of other parties in respect of financial or operating policies, they should be considered when assessing control, provided they are currently exercisable.

2. Consolidation procedures – general

In preparing consolidated financial statements the following procedures are executed:
- The financial statements of the parent and its subsidiaries are combined on a line-by-line basis by adding together like items of assets, liabilities, equity, income and expenses.
- To ensure that the consolidated financial statements present the financial information about the group as that of a single economic entity, the following steps are taken:
  - The carrying amount of the parent's investment in each subsidiary and the parent's portion of equity in each subsidiary are eliminated (see IFRS 3 (AC 140) for detail including the treatment of goodwill).
  - Minority interests included in the profit or loss of consolidated subsidiaries for the reporting period are identified.
  - Minority interests in the net assets of consolidated subsidiaries are identified and presented in the consolidated balance sheet separately from the parent's shareholders' equity. Minority interests in the net assets comprise two components:
    - the amount at the date of the original combination calculated in accordance with IFRS 3 (AC 140) ('at acquisition equity'); and
    - the minorities' share of movements in equity since the date of acquisition ('since acquisition equity').
- When potential voting rights exist, the proportions of profit or loss and changes in equity allocated to the parent and its minorities are determined based on existing ownership.
- Taxes payable by either the parent or its subsidiaries on distribution to the parent of the profits retained in these entities are accounted for in accordance with IAS 12 (AC 102).
- Intragroup balances and intragroup transactions and resulting unrealised profits shall be eliminated in full.
- Unrealised losses resulting from intragroup transactions shall also be eliminated, unless the cost cannot be recovered.
- Temporary differences that arise from the elimination of unrealised profits and losses from intragroup transactions shall be dealt with in terms of IAS 12 (AC 102).
- The financial statements of the parent and its subsidiaries used in preparation of the consolidated financial statements shall be drawn up to the same date.
- When the reporting dates of the parent and its subsidiaries are different, the subsidiary will prepare financial statements to the same date as that of the parent's year end, unless it is impracticable. These statements shall be used for consolidation purposes.
- When the financial statements used in consolidation are drawn up at different reporting dates (same reporting dates impracticable), adjustments must be made for the effects of significant transactions or other events that occur between the date of the subsidiary's financial statements and the date of the parent's financial statements. The difference in reporting dates is limited to three months.
- Consolidated financial statements shall be prepared using uniform accounting policies for like items in similar circumstances.
- If a member of a group uses accounting policies different from those adopted in the consolidated financial statements, appropriate adjustments are made to its financial statements when these are used to prepare consolidated financial statements. This is, however, not a change in accounting policy per IAS 8 (AC 103), but merely a case of adjusting the figures of the subsidiary for purposes of the consolidation.
- The results (income and expenses) of the operations of a subsidiary are included in the consolidated financial statements as from the date of acquisition, which is the date on which the buyer gains control of the entity. Under these circumstances certain disclosures are required.

- The results (income and expenses) of the operations of a subsidiary disposed of are included in the consolidated income statement until the date of disposal, which is the date on which the parent ceases to have control over the entity.
- The difference between the proceeds from disposal of the subsidiary and the carrying amount of its assets less liabilities, is recognised in the consolidated income statement as the gain/loss on disposal of the subsidiary. As in the case of an acquisition, certain disclosures are required in the case of a disposal.
- An investment in an entity shall be accounted for as an investment in terms of IAS 39 (AC 133) in the consolidated financial statements, from the date on which it ceases to fall within the definition of a subsidiary, provided it does not become an associate or jointly controlled entity. This would require different treatments in terms of the relevant statements (IAS 28 (AC 110) and IAS 31 (AC119)).
- The carrying amount of the investment in the subsidiary at the date on which it ceases to be a subsidiary is deemed to be the cost on initial measurement of a financial asset, in accordance with IAS 39 (AC 133).
- Minority interests shall be presented in the consolidated balance sheet separately from the parent's shareholders' equity, but still as part of total equity (see specimen financial statements in chapter on IAS 1 (AC 101)).
- Minority interests in the profit or loss of the group shall be presented separately on the face of the income statement (see specimen financial statements in the chapter on IAS 1 (AC 101)).

3. Consolidation procedures specific to insolvent subsidiaries

- Under certain circumstances, the losses attributable to a minority in a consolidated subsidiary may exceed the minority interest in the equity of that subsidiary.
- The excess of such losses over the minority interest, as well as any further losses, are charged to the majority, except to the extent that the minority has a binding obligation to, and is able to, make good the losses.
- If the subsidiary subsequently makes profits, the majority is allocated all such profits up to the point where the minority's share of losses previously absorbed by the majority has been recovered.
- If a subsidiary has cumulative preferred shares in issue, which are held outside the group, the parent always computes its share of profits and losses after taking into account the subsidiary's or quasi-subsidiary's preferred dividends. This is the case regardless of whether the dividends have been declared or not.

4. Accounting for investments in subsidiaries, jointly controlled entities and associates in a parent's separate financial statements

- If separate financial statements are prepared by a company, investments in subsidiaries, jointly controlled entities and associates, provided they are not classified as held for sale in terms of IFRS 5 (AC 142), shall be accounted for at either:
  - cost; or
  - in accordance with IAS 39 (AC 133).
- The same accounting method shall be applied for each category of investment.
- Such investments that are classified as held for sale shall be accounted for in terms of IFRS 5 (AC 142).
- Investments in subsidiaries, jointly controlled entities and associates that are accounted for in terms of IAS 39 (AC 133) in the consolidated financial statements, are accounted for in the same way in the investor's separate financial statements.

DISCLOSURE

The following disclosures shall be made in consolidated financial statements:
- the nature of the relationship between the parent and a subsidiary when the parent does not own, either directly or indirectly through subsidiaries, more than 50% of the voting power;
- should it be the case, the reasons why the ownership, directly or indirectly through subsidiaries, of more than half of the voting or potential voting power of an investee does not constitute control;
- should it be the case, the reporting date of the financial statements of a subsidiary when such financial statements are used to prepare consolidated financial statements and are prepared as of a reporting date or for a period that is different from that of the parent, and the reason for using a different reporting date or period; and
- the nature and extent of any significant restrictions that would inhibit the subsidiaries to transfer funds to the parent in the form of cash dividends or to repay loans or advances.

When separate financial statements are prepared for a parent that in terms of 2.1 above, elects not to prepare consolidated financial statements, those separate financial statements shall disclose:
- the fact that the financial statements are separate financial statements;
- that the exemption from consolidation has been used;
- the name and country of incorporation or residence of the entity whose consolidated financial statements that comply with International Financial Reporting Standards (ACs) have been produced for public use;
- the address where those consolidated financial statements are obtainable;
- a list of significant investments in subsidiaries, jointly controlled entities and associates, including:
  - the name;
  - country of incorporation or residence;
  - proportion of ownership interest; and
  - if different, proportion of voting power held; and
- a description of the method used to account for the investments listed under the previous bullet paragraph.

When a parent, venturer or investor in an associate (other than a parent that elected not to prepare consolidated financial statements) prepares separate financial statements, the following must be disclosed in those statements:
- the fact that the statements are separate financial statements;
- the reasons why those statements are prepared if not required by law;
- a list of significant investments in subsidiaries, jointly controlled entities and associates, including:
  - the name of the entity;
  - country of incorporation or residence;
  - proportion of ownership interest held by the preparer of the separate financial statements; and
  - if different from percentage of ownership interest, the percentage of voting power held; and
- a description of the method used to account for the list of investments required under the immediately preceding paragraph (i.e. cost or under IAS 39 (AC 133)).

The parent, venturer and investor in an associate shall also identify the consolidated or other financial statements to which the separate financial statements relate.

SIC 12: CONSOLIDATION – SPECIAL PURPOSE ENTITIES

1. Background

Sometimes, an entity may be created to accomplish a narrow and well-defined objective. Examples of such reasons for creation are:
- to effect a lease;
- to conduct research and development activities; or
- to secure financial assets.

Such a special purpose entity (SPE) may take the form of any of the following entities:
- a corporation;
- a trust;
- a partnership; or
- an unincorporated entity.

The creator entity will often make such legal arrangements that the decision-making powers of the governing board, trustee or management are strictly limited to what the sponsor allows. For instance, these arrangements may specify that the policy guiding the ongoing activities of the SPE cannot be modified, unless the sponsor or creator authorises the change. In substance, then, the SPE is controlled by its creator or sponsor, even though the sponsor may own little or none of the SPE's equity.

IAS 27 requires the consolidation of entities controlled by the reporting entity, but does not provide explicit guidance in connection with SPEs.

This interpretation does not apply to post-employment benefit plans or equity compensation plans.

2. Issue

The issue is under what circumstances an entity shall consolidate an SPE.

3. Consensus

- A SPE shall be consolidated where the substance of the relationship between an entity and an SPE is such that the SPE is controlled by that entity.
- When looking at an SPE, control may arise through the predetermination of the activities of an SPE, even though the entity may own one half or less of the voting power of the SPE as described in IAS 27.13.
- The application of the concept of control requires, in each case, judgement in the context of all relevant factors.
- In addition to the circumstances described in IAS 27.13, which would indicate control, the following facts shall be considered when dealing with an SPE and would lead to consolidation:
    - In substance, the activities of the SPE are conducted on behalf of the entity in the context of its specific business needs, and consequently it obtains the benefits from the SPE.
    - In substance, the entity has the decision-making powers to secure the majority of the benefits of the SPE.
    - In substance, the entity has the right to obtain the majority of the benefits of the SPE and consequently, may be exposed to the risks associated with the activities of the SPE.
    - In substance, the entity retains the majority of the residual or ownership risks related to the SPE and its assets so as to obtain benefits from its assets.

IAS 28 *(AC 110)*

Investments in Associates

❑ **SUMMARY**

Background
Accounting practice
Disclosure

BACKGROUND

The equity method is directed at the accounting by the investor for investments in associates to provide users of financial statements with information concerning the investor's interest in the earnings and in the underlying assets and liabilities of the investor. The **equity method** is a method of accounting whereby the investment is initially recorded at cost and adjusted thereafter for the post-acquisition change in the investor's share of the net assets of the investee. Profit or loss of the investor includes the investor's share of profit or loss of the investee.

An **associate** is an entity:
- which is incorporated or unincorporated;
- which is not a subsidiary of the investor; nor
- a joint venture of the investor;
- over which the investor has the ability to exercise significant influence, which is evidenced by:
  - holding directly or indirectly (e.g. through subsidiaries) 20% or more of the voting power unless no significant influence is demonstrated;
  - representation on the board of directors or governing body;
  - participation in policy-making processes;
  - material transactions between the investor and the investee;
  - interchange of managerial personnel; or
  - provision of essential technical information.

ACCOUNTING PRACTICE

1. Basic accounting principles

The investment is initially accounted for at cost, which would include an amount for goodwill or excess at acquisition (old negative goodwill). The standard indicates that the carrying amount of the investment for recognition of losses should include, apart from the investment in the associate under the equity method, any other long-term interests that in substance form part of the investor's net investment in the associate (for example, long-term loans, receivables and preference shares for which repayment is not planned).

The carrying amount of the investment is increased or decreased with the investor's share of the following profits or losses of the investee after the date of acquisition:
- share of profits/losses after tax, minority interest and preference dividend;
- excess at acquisition (old negative goodwill) written off; and
- share of prior year adjustments.

(In the recognition of equity losses, the carrying amount (as explained and adjusted earlier) is reduced to nil. Additional losses are provided for to the extent that the investor has given guarantees.)

Distributions received from an associate; for example, dividends, reduce the carrying amount of the investment.

Other post-acquisition adjustments to the carrying amount of the investment would include:
- Share of revaluation surplus of property, plant and equipment.
- share of fair value adjustments of investments taken directly to equity;
- share of foreign exchange translation differences;
- share of adjustments arising on business combinations; and
- share of retained equity profits and losses of the associate relating to each purchase of equity prior to the date on which the investee became an associate.

2. General principles

An investment in an associate shall be accounted for in the consolidated financial statements under the equity method, apart from when:
- the investment is classified as held for sale in terms of IFRS 5 (AC 142);
- the parent need not provide consolidated financial statements for subsidiaries; and therefore need not equity account associates; or
- IAS 28.13(c) applies.

Investments held under the first exception in terms of IFRS 5 (AC 142) shall be accounted for in terms of IFRS 5 (AC 142) and the other investments either at cost or in terms of IAS 39 (AC 133) at fair value.

A long-term investment in an associate that is included in the separate financial statements of an investor shall either be:
- carried at cost; or
- accounted for as an available-for-sale financial asset in terms of IAS 39 (AC 133).

An investor shall commence accounting for an investment in an associate under the equity method from the date on which it falls within the definition of an associate.

The investor shall discontinue the application of the equity method if it ceases to have significant influence over an associate but retains, either in whole or in part, its investment.

The carrying amount at that date shall be regarded as the cost thereafter and such an investment shall be accounted for in terms of IAS 39 (AC 133) – that is, carried at fair value.

Many of the procedures utilised in the application of the equity method are similar to the consolidation procedures used in accounting for subsidiaries and jointly controlled entities, such as:
- Eliminating unrealised profits/losses arising from transactions between the investor and the investee. (Refer to Appendix A at the end of this summary.)
- Identifying goodwill as being the difference between the cost of the investment and the investor's share of the fair values of the net identifiable assets. Goodwill is, however, carried on the balance sheet as part of the investment in the associate.
- Goodwill is not amortised, but is tested for impairment.
- Recognising negative goodwill (excess of fair value of identifiable net assets over cost) immediately in the income statement, and thereby increasing the carrying amount of the investment.
- Adjustments for depreciation of depreciable assets, based on their fair values at acquisition.
- Adjustments for the effect of crossholdings.
- Using uniform accounting policies.

The most recent available financial statements of the associate shall be used in applying the equity method. They are usually drawn up to the same date as the financial statements of the investor, unless it is impracticable. When the reporting dates are different, adjustments are then made for the effects of any significant events or transactions that occur between the different reporting dates of the investor and that of the associate. The maximum difference allowed is three months.

If an associate uses accounting policies different from those adopted by the investor, appropriate adjustments are made (to align the associate's accounting policies with that of the parent/investor) before applying the equity method.

The investor computes its share of profits or losses after adjusting for the cumulative preference dividends, whether or not the dividends have been declared.

3. Impairment

An entity should apply the principles in IAS39 (AC133) .59 to determine whether there is an indication that an investment in an associate may be impaired. If an investment in an associate is determined to be impaired, an entity applies IAS 36 (AC 128) (recoverable amount higher of value in use and fair value less costs to sell) to the whole of the investment. Since goodwill forms part of the investment in the associate, goodwill is not tested for impairment separately in terms of IAS 36 (AC 128).

In determining the value in use of the investment for impairment testing, an entity estimates:
- its share of the present value of estimated future cash flows expected to be generated by the associate as a whole (including cash flows from operations of the associate and proceeds from the ultimate disposal of the investment); or
- the present value of estimated future cash flows expected to arise from dividends to be received from the investment and its ultimate disposal of the investment.

Provided appropriate discount rates are selected, the two approaches will render approximately the same amount.

The investor shall assess the recoverable amount of an investment in an associate for each individual associate. However, if an individual associate does not generate cash inflows from continuing use that are largely independent from other assets of the reporting entity, it will form part of a cash-generating unit.

4. Income taxes

Income taxes should be treated in accordance with IAS 12 (AC 102). (Refer to the chapter on IAS 12 (AC 102)).

DISCLOSURE

The following disclosures shall be made:

1. Income statement

- Attributable share of the associate's equity profit/loss for the year.
- Investor's share of any discontinued operations of associates shall be separately disclosed.
- Attributable share in prior year adjustments of the investee.
- Gains/losses on sale of interest in an associate or other dilutions.

2. Balance sheet

- Investments in associates are shown as a separate item (non-current asset), including:
  - carrying amount of each investment; and
  - gross amount of loans made to associates.
- Gross amount of loans received from associates (under liabilities).

3. Statement of changes in equity

- Disclose separately in the statement of changes in equity the investor's share of changes recognised directly in equity.

4. Notes

- The methods used to account for:
  - associates, including the fact if associates are not accounted for using the equity method; and
  - goodwill and negative goodwill (excess).
- Summarised financial information with regard to assets, liabilities and revenues and profit or loss (presented individually or in aggregate) for associates accounted for under the equity method and those not accounted for under the equity method.
- Nature and extent of any significant restrictions on ability of associate to transfer funds such as cash dividends or repayment of loans and advances.
- Reasons why the presumption that an investor does not have significant influence is set aside if an investor directly or indirectly holds less than 20% of the voting rights in the associate.
- The reasons why the presumption that an investor has significant influence is set aside if the investor holds, directly or indirectly, more than 20% of the voting rights in the associate.
- The reporting date of an associate where it is different from that of the investor, as well as reason why a different date was used.
- Fair value of investments in listed associates.
- The investor's share of contingencies arising from its involvement with associates.
- Those contingencies that arise because the investor is severally liable for all liabilities of the associate.
- Unrecognised amounts of an investor's share of losses of an associate for the period and cumulatively.

APPENDIX A: ELIMINATION OF UNREALISED PROFITS AND LOSSES ON TRANSACTIONS WITH ASSOCIATES

1. Background

The statement on accounting for investments in associates requires that procedures similar to those performed on consolidation be carried out in the case of associates. However, it does not give clear guidance on the elimination of unrealised profits or losses resulting from transactions between the investor (or its consolidated subsidiaries) and the associate (downstream transactions) or transactions between the associate and the investor (upstream transactions).

2. Issue

The issue is to what extent an investor should eliminate unrealised profits or losses resulting from transactions between the investor (and its consolidated subsidiaries) and associates when using the equity method.

3. Consensus

When an associate is equity accounted, unrealised profits and losses resulting from both upstream and downstream transactions between an investor (or its consolidated subsidiaries) and associates, should be eliminated to the extent of the investor's interest in the associate.

Unrealised losses should not be eliminated to the extent that the transaction provides evidence of an impairment of the asset transferred.

APPENDIX B: CONSOLIDATION AND EQUITY METHOD – POTENTIAL VOTING RIGHTS AND ALLOCATION OF OWNERSHIP INTERESTS

1. Background

An entity may own instruments such as share warrants, share call options, debt or equity instruments that are convertible into ordinary shares, or other similar instruments that have the potential (should they be exercised or converted) to increase the voting power in another entity (potential voting rights).

2. Issues

The issues are:
- When assessing whether an entity controls (IAS 27 (AC 132)) – Consolidated financial statements and accounting for investments in subsidiaries) or significantly influences (IAS 28 (AC 110)) another entity:
  - whether the existence and effect of potential voting rights should be considered, in addition to normal considerations per IAS 28 (AC 110) and IAS 27 (AC 132); and if so,
  - whether any other facts or circumstances relating to the potential voting rights should be assessed.
- Whether the percentage interest held by a parent or investor should be determined based on present ownership (without potential voting rights) or ownership after potential voting rights were exercised or converted.
- What is the appropriate accounting treatment for potential voting rights until they are exercised or expire?

3. Consensus

- The existence and effect of potential voting rights that are presently/currently exercisable or convertible should be considered, in addition to the normal factors to be considered when assessing whether control or significant influence over another entity exists.
- All potential voting rights should be considered, as well as potential voting rights held by other entities.
- All facts and circumstances that may impact on potential voting rights under consideration (see above) should be examined, except for the intention of management and financial capability to exercise or convert. Facts that should be considered include terms of exercise of potential voting rights and possible linked transactions.
- The percentage interest allocated to the parent and minorities when consolidating, or investor when equity accounting, should be determined based solely on present ownership interest.

- When applying the consolidation and equity method of accounting, instruments containing potential voting rights should be included as part of the investment in the subsidiary or associate respectively, only when the proportion of ownership interests is allocated by taking into account the eventual exercise of those potential voting rights discussed in the paragraph above. In all other circumstances the instruments containing potential voting rights are accounted for under IAS 39 (AC 133) (Financial instruments: recognition and measurement).

IAS 29 *(AC 124)*

Financial Reporting in Hyperinflationary Economies

❑ **SUMMARY**

Background
Accounting practice
Disclosure

BACKGROUND

The normal rules used to identify the functional currency of an entity, as discussed in the chapter on IAS 21 (AC 112), shall also be applied here to determine the functional currency of an entity operating in a hyperinflationary economy.

If the functional currency of the entity is the currency of a hyperinflationary economy, the financial statements of the entity are restated in terms of IAS 29, as discussed below.

This standard is applied to entities whose functional currency is the currency of a hyperinflationary economy and is enforced on both the primary and consolidated financial statements. In a hyperinflationary economy, financial reporting in the local currency without restatement is not useful because of the fact that money loses its purchasing power at a tremendous rate.

Characteristics of a **hyperinflationary economy** include:
- The general population prefers to keep its wealth in non-monetary assets or in a relatively stable foreign currency such as US $.
- Prices are normally quoted in a stable foreign currency.
- Credit transactions take place at prices that compensate for the expected loss of purchasing power during the period up to settlement.
- Interest, wages and prices are linked to price indices.
- The cumulative inflation rate over three years is more or less 100% (or more).

The financial statements of an entity whose functional currency is the currency of a hyperinflationary economy – whether they are based on a historical cost approach or a current cost approach – shall be restated in terms of the measuring unit current at the balance sheet date.

ACCOUNTING PRACTICE

1. Restatement of financial statements

This standard applies to the financial statements of any entity operating in a hyperinflationary economy, from the beginning of the reporting period in which hyperinflation is first identified in the country whose functional currency it uses.

The following principles shall be applied for the restatement of the primary and consolidated financial statements:
- A reliable general price index that reflects changes in general purchasing power shall be used. Where it is not available, a relatively stable foreign currency shall be used to calculate an index to be used.
- The current year's financial statements are restated in the measuring unit current at the balance sheet date.
- Comparatives are also restated in the measuring unit at the balance sheet date.
- When an economy ceases to be hyperinflationary, restatement is discontinued. The carrying amounts at the end of the previous reporting period serve as the basis for future reporting.
- The gain or loss on the net monetary position of the entity operating in a hyperinflationary economy shall be included in profit or loss and disclosed separately.

2. Presentation of restated financial statements

The restated financial statements in terms of IAS 29 replace the normal financial statements and do not serve as a supplement thereto. Separate presentation of the normal financial statements is discouraged.

3. Rules of restatement for historical cost financial statements

3.1 Balance sheet items

- Monetary items of the affected entity are money held and items to be received or paid in money.
- Monetary items are not restated, as they are already expressed in the measuring unit current at the balance sheet date.
- Index linked assets and liabilities are restated in accordance with the index agreement.

- Non-monetary items are restated in terms of the current measuring unit by applying the changes in the index to:
  - historical cost less depreciation since date of acquisition or the first period of restatement in terms of IAS 29, where detailed records of acquisition dates are not available;
  - the cost of purchase of inventory of finished goods from the date of purchase and from the date of conversion for work-in-progress;
  - fair values on date of revaluation; and
  - cost price at payment date if the payment for the asset is deferred without incurring an interest charge.
- Non-monetary assets are not restated if shown at net realisable value, fair value or recoverable amount at balance sheet date.
- At the beginning of the first period of the application of IAS 29, the components of owners' equity, except for retained earnings and any revaluation surplus, are restated from the dates the components were contributed. Any revaluation surplus that arose in previous periods is eliminated. The restated amount for retained earnings is the balancing figure.
- At the end of the first period and subsequent periods thereafter the components of owners' equity are restated from the date of contribution.
- The movements in owners' equity are included in equity, and disclosed in terms of IAS 1 (AC 101).

3.2 Income statement items

- The amounts in the income statement are restated by applying the change in a reliable general price index from the dates when the items of income and expenses were initially recorded in the financial statements.
- It is inappropriate to capitalise that part of borrowing costs that compensates for inflation during a period, because the capital expenditure financed by borrowings is already adjusted for the effect of inflation. This part of borrowing costs is thus recognised as an expense.

3.3 Gains and losses from restatements

- A gain or loss on the net monetary position is included in profit.

4. Group statements

When a foreign subsidiary of a parent company reports in a hyperinflationary economy, the financial statements of such a subsidiary shall firstly be restated by applying an index in accordance with IAS 29 and then translated at the closing rate.

5. Current cost financial statements

5.1 Balance sheet

- Items stated at current cost shall not be restated, as they are already expressed in terms of the measuring unit current at the balance sheet date.
- Other items would be restated applying the rules set out in 3.1.

5.2 Income statement items

The current cost income statement (before restatement) generally reports costs current at the time when the underlying transactions or events occurred. Consequently, all amounts need to be restated at balance sheet date by applying a general price index.

5.3 Gain or loss on net monetary position

Apply the same rules as under 3.3.

6. Taxes

Restatement of financial statements may give rise to temporary differences. These differences are accounted for in terms of IAS 12 (AC 102).

7. Cash flow statement

All items in the cash flow statement are expressed in the measuring unit current at balance sheet date.

DISCLOSURE

The financial statements shall disclose the following in respect of a company operating in a hyperinflationary environment:
- the fact that the current financial statements have been restated;
- the fact that the comparative amounts have been restated;
- whether the financial statements subject to restatement are based on a historical cost approach or a current cost approach;
- the identity of the price index used for restatement;
- the level of the price index used for restatement at balance sheet date;
- the movement in price index used during the current and previous financial years;
- the gain or loss on the net monetary position, which is included in profit or loss; and
- the movements in owners' equity for the period (if applicable in terms of IAS 1 (AC 101).

IAS 31 *(AC 119)* and SIC 13 *(AC 413)*

Interests in Joint Ventures

❑ **SUMMARY**

Background
Accounting practice
Disclosure
SIC 13: Jointly controlled entities – non-monetary contributions by venturers

BACKGROUND

This standard addresses the accounting for joint ventures and reporting of the assets, liabilities, income, expenses and cash flows of joint ventures in the financial statements of venturers and investors, regardless of the structures or forms under which the joint venture activities take place (substance over form).

It does not apply to venture capital organisations; or mutual funds, unit trusts and similar entities that are accounted for in terms of IAS 39 (AC 133).

A venturer with an interest in a jointly controlled entity is exempt from proportionate consolidation or equity accounting when it meets the conditions set out in IAS 31.2(a) to (c).

A joint venture is:
- one of the following economic operations:
  - jointly controlled operation;
  - jointly controlled asset; or
  - jointly controlled entity;
- resulting from a contractual arrangement;
- between two or more parties (venturers);
- which will exercise joint control over the economic activity.

Joint control is:
- contractually agreed sharing of control;
- over an economic activity;
- existing only when strategic financial and operating decisions relating to the activity require unanimous consent of the parties sharing control.

Joint control (in the case of a joint venture) is distinguished from significant influence (in the case of an associate) by the existence of a contractual agreement.

ACCOUNTING PRACTICE

1. Jointly controlled operations

- The operation of the joint venture does not take place in a separate entity. Transactions flow through each venturer's own records.
- Each venturer uses its own property, plant and equipment, carries its own inventories, incurs its own liabilities and raises its own finance.
- Each venturer carries its own expenses, irrespective of the profit sharing. The contractual arrangement does sometimes provide that certain expenses will be shared jointly in a certain ratio.
- The joint venture agreement usually provides a means by which revenue from the sale of the joint product is shared among the venturers.
- The proportionate consolidation method is not applied. Transactions will be recognised in the venturer's own financial statements as follows:
  - own assets and liabilities in respect of the joint venture;
  - own expenses incurred in respect of the joint venture;
  - income from sales/services by the joint venturer; and
  - expenses incurred jointly in respect of the joint venture which are shared in a certain ratio.

(Cash flows resulting from the above transactions are hence also reflected in the accounting records.)

Separate financial records and financial statements are therefore not required for this type of joint venture. Despite this, management accounts are sometimes prepared to measure the performance of the joint venture.

2. Jointly controlled assets

- An entity that is separate from the venturers themselves is not established. A separate bank account is sometimes opened in the name of the joint venture. Expenses are carried by venturers in their respective profit-sharing ratios.

- The venturer can also incur its own expenses, which are not recoverable from the other venturers.
- The proportionate consolidation method is not applied. Each venturer recognises transactions in its own financial statements as follows:
  - its share of the jointly controlled assets, classified according to the nature of the assets (this is not shown as an investment);
  - any liabilities which were incurred by the venturer on its own;
  - its share of any liabilities incurred jointly with other venturers in relation to the joint venture;
  - any income from the sale or use of its share of the output (production) of the joint venture;
  - its share of any expenses which have been incurred by the joint venture; and
  - its own expenses incurred in respect of the joint venture.

(Cash flows resulting from the above transactions are hence also reflected in the accounting records.)

Separate financial records and financial statements are therefore not required for this type of joint venture either. Despite this, management accounts are sometimes prepared to measure the performance of the joint venture.

3. Jointly controlled entities

- The joint venture is conducted through a separate operating entity, for example, a partnership, close corporation or company.
- The entity keeps its own records and incurs its own transactions, and even enters into transactions with other entities. Financial statements are also prepared by the entity in accordance with the legal requirements and Statements of GAAP applicable to the specific entity.
- The contributions of venturers in the joint venture are recognised in their own statements as investments. (See SIC 13 at the end of this summary.)

3.1 Consolidated financial statements of the venturer

- Venturers report on the jointly controlled entity by applying one of the two recognised proportionate consolidation methods in the consolidated financial statements as follows:
  - Consolidated balance sheet – includes a share of the jointly controlled entity's assets and liabilities on a line-by-line basis by combining them with the venturer's items, or the venturer can report its share of the relevant assets and liabilities as separate line items.
  - Consolidated income statement – includes a share of the income and expenses of the jointly controlled entity on a line-by-line basis by combining them with the venturer's items, or the venturer can report its share of the relevant income and expenses as separate line items.
  - Consolidated cash flow statement – includes a share of the cash flows of the jointly controlled entity on a line-by-line basis by combining them with the venturer's items, or the venturer can report its share of the relevant cash flow items as separate line items.
- The interests in jointly controlled entities are included in the consolidated financial statements of the venturer, even if the venturer has no subsidiaries, unless the exceptions in IAS 31.2 apply.
- Most of the procedures applied in the proportionate consolidation method are similar to those used for subsidiaries in group statements (see IAS 27 (AC 132)).
- Set-offs of applicable debits and credits are allowed only if there is a legal right in this regard and if they would reflect the intention in respect of the anticipated transaction.
- Adjust the financial statements of the jointly controlled entity if the accounting policy differs from that of the venturer, to ensure the accounting policies of the two entities are in alignment.
- An investment in a jointly controlled entity is proportionately consolidated from the date on which it complies with the definition of a jointly controlled entity.
- Recognise in group statements any goodwill or excess at acquisition (negative goodwill) on the acquisition of an interest in a jointly controlled entity (difference between the cost of acquisition and the venturer's share of the fairly valued net assets).
- Discontinue the application of the proportionate consolidation method when the venturer no longer has joint control of the jointly controlled entity; for example, on disposal of its share.
- Should a jointly controlled entity have issued cumulative preference shares and these are held by minority shareholders, the venturer should make appropriate adjustments in the consolidated financial statements for such preference dividends, whether they have been declared or not.
- Transactions between the jointly controlled entity and the venturer are accounted for as follows:
  - Assets transferred/sold by the venturer to the jointly controlled entity.

- Recognise any portion of a gain or loss attributable to other venturers. (See SIC 13 at the end of this summary.)
  - Recognise the full loss owing to a reduction in the net realisable value of current assets or an impairment loss.
- Assets purchased by the venturer from the jointly controlled entity:
  - Recognise venturer's share of the profit/loss only when the asset is resold to an external party.
  - Recognise losses immediately when a reduction in the net realisable value of current assets takes place or when an impairment loss occurs.

In both of the above cases, the substance of the transactions should be investigated. A transfer of significant risks and rewards of ownership should have taken place.

- Loans to jointly controlled entities and interest received on them are accounted for in the group statements by the elimination of the venturer's share.
- Management fee received from the jointly controlled entity is accounted for according to the standard on revenue (IAS 18 (AC 111)).
- Use the latest available financial statements of the jointly controlled entity for purposes of the proportionate consolidation. When balance sheet dates differ, the jointly controlled entity sometimes prepares financial statements on the same balance sheet date as that of the venturer. When this proves impractical, the balance sheet dates may differ, but reporting periods should have the same length and the difference between the reporting dates should not be greater than three months (See IAS 27 (AC 132)).
- When balance sheet dates differ, adjustments must be made for material events or transactions that take place between these two dates.
- The equity method may also be used as an alternative method of reporting on interests in jointly controlled entities in the consolidated financial statements. (This method is not recommended.)
- The application of the equity method should be discontinued when the venturer no longer exercises joint control or no longer has significant influence over the jointly controlled entity.
- When a venturer holds an interest in a jointly controlled entity but does not have joint control, it should report its interest as an investment at fair value in terms of IAS 39 (AC 133).
- When a venturer holds an interest in a jointly controlled entity but does not have joint control, but has significant influence, it should equity account the investment in the jointly controlled entity. (See IAS 28 (AC 110)).
- An interest in a jointly controlled entity is consolidated from the date on which the jointly controlled entity becomes a subsidiary.
- When a venturer is a wholly owned subsidiary of a South African company, consolidated statements are not required.

3.2 Separate financial statements of the investor (Refer to IAS 27 (AC 132))

- When preparing separate financial statements, investments in jointly controlled entities that are not classified as held for sale (See IFRS 5 (AC 142)) should be accounted for at either:
  - cost; or
  - fair value in terms of IAS 39 (AC 133).
  - The same accounting treatment will be applied to each category of investment.
- Investments in jointly controlled entities classified as held for sale (see IFRS 5 (AC 142)) need to be accounted for in terms of IFRS 5 (AC 142).
- Investments in jointly controlled entities that are accounted for in terms of IAS 39 (AC 133) in the consolidated financial statements, need to be accounted for in the same way in the venturer's (investor's) own financial statements.

DISCLOSURE

Accounting policy

The venturer discloses the method used to recognise its interests in jointly controlled entities; that is, proportionate consolidation or equity accounting.

Notes to the financial statements

The following disclosure requirements are applicable to all three types of joint venture:
- Disclose the total amount and nature of each of the following contingent liabilities in terms of IAS 37 (AC 130) (unless the probability of loss is remote):
  - any contingent liabilities as a result of the venturer's interests in joint ventures;
  - the venturer's share in each of the contingent liabilities which have arisen jointly with other venturers;
  - the venturer's share of the contingent liabilities of the joint ventures themselves for which it is contingently liable; and
  - those contingent liabilities that arise because the venturer is contingently liable for the liabilities of the other venturers of a joint venture.
- Disclose the total amount of the following capital commitments:
  - any capital commitments of the venturer in relation to its interests in joint ventures;
  - the venturer's share in the capital commitments that have been incurred jointly with other venturers; and
  - the venturer's share of the capital commitments of the joint venturers themselves for which it is contingently liable.
- Disclose the following information in respect of each signifant joint venture:
  - name;
  - a description of the interest in the joint venture; and
  - the proportion of ownership of jointly controlled entities.

The following disclosure requirements apply only to jointly controlled entities in the consolidated financial statements of the venturer:
- A venturer reporting on its interest in a jointly controlled entity according to the line-by-line basis or the equity method discloses in total the amounts (which are significant with regard to the venturer's share in the jointly controlled entity) of:
  - current assets;
  - non-current assets;
  - current liabilities;
  - non-current liabilities;
  - income; and
  - expenses.

SIC 13: JOINTLY CONTROLLED ENTITIES – NON-MONETARY CONTRIBUTIONS BY VENTURERS

1. Background

In IAS 31.48 it is stated that, when a venturer contributes or sells assets to a joint venture, the substance of the transaction should be reflected when any portion of a gain or loss from the transaction is recognised.

Contributions to a jointly controlled entity are transfers of assets by venturers in exchange for an equity interest in the jointly controlled entity.

As no explicit guidance is given in IAS 31 on the recognition of gains and losses resulting from contributions of non-monetary assets to jointly controlled entities, SIC 13 serves as an interpretation of the matter.

2. Issues

The issues are the following:
2.1 When should the appropriate portion of gains or losses resulting from the contribution of a non-monetary asset to a jointly controlled entity in exchange for an equity interest therein be recognised in the income statement of the venturer?
2.2 How should any consideration received, in addition to the equity interest from the jointly controlled entity, be accounted for by the venturer?
2.3 How should any unrealised gain or loss on such a transaction be presented in the consolidated financial statements of the venturer?

3. Consensus

3.1 A venturer should recognise in the income statement for the period, a gain or loss attributable to the equity interests of other venturers, except when:

- the contributed non-monetary asset's significant risks and rewards of ownership have not been transferred to the jointly controlled entity;
- reliable measurement of the gain or loss on the non-monetary contribution is not possible; or
- the non-monetary asset(s) contributed lacks commercial substance as described in IAS 16 (AC 123).

If any of the above exceptions apply, the gain or loss under discussion would be considered unrealised and would not be recognised in the income statement, unless any consideration other than an equity interest was also received from the joint venture.

3.2 If a venturer receives monetary or non-monetary assets dissimilar to those it contributed (in addition to any equity interest in the jointly controlled entity), an appropriate portion of the gain or loss on the transaction should be recognised in the income statement of the venturer.

3.3 Eliminate unrealised gains or losses on non-monetary assets contributed to jointly controlled entities, against the underlying assets under the proportionate consolidation method, and against the investment in the jointly controlled entity if the equity method is used.

Such unrealised gains or losses should not be presented as deferred gains or losses in the venturer's consolidated balance sheet.

IAS 32 *(AC 125)*

Financial Instruments: Presentation

❑ **SUMMARY**

Background
Accounting presentation
Disclosure

BACKGROUND

The statement prescribes certain requirements for presentation of on-balance-sheet financial instruments.

This statement shall be applied in presenting information about all types of financial instrument, both recognised and unrecognised. The following financial instruments are excluded:

- interests in subsidiaries;
- interests in associates;
- interests in joint ventures;
- employers' rights and obligations under employee benefit plans, to which IAS 19 (AC 116) applies;
- contracts for contingent consideration in a business combination in terms of IFRS 3 (AC 140) – this only relates to the acquirer;
- obligations arising under insurance contracts; and
- financial instruments, contracts and obligations under share-based payment transactions in terms of IFRS 2 (AC 139).

The following terms (quoted largely from the standard) are critical to an understanding of the statement.

A **financial instrument** is a contract (not necessarily in writing) that gives rise to both a financial asset of one entity and a financial liability or equity instrument of another entity. It includes both primary instruments (e.g. debtors, creditors and equity) and derivative instruments (e.g. options, swaps and futures).

A **financial asset** is any asset that is:

- cash (e.g. deposit at a bank);
- a contractual right to receive cash or another financial asset from another entity (e.g. a debtor);
- a contractual right to exchange financial instruments with another entity under conditions that are potentially favourable (e.g. FEC on a creditor where Rand deteriorates);
- any equity instrument of another entity (e.g. investment in shares); or
- a contract that will or may be settled in the entity's own equity instruments and is:
  - a non-derivative for which the entity is or may be obliged to receive a variable number of entity's own equity instruments; or
  - a derivative that will or may be settled other than by the exchange of a fixed amount of cash or a another financial asset for a fixed number of the entity's own equity instruments.

Physical assets such as inventories and patents are not financial assets. They create an opportunity to generate an inflow of cash (future economic benefits – see the Framework), but do not give rise to a present right to receive cash or other financial assets.

Similarly, contractual rights and obligations that do not involve the transfer of a financial asset, such as a commodities futures contract settled through physical delivery, do not fall in the definition of a financial instrument. Cash settled commodities futures contracts, however, would qualify as financial assets/liabilities as it involves the transfer of cash.

Financial liability is any liability that is:

- a contractual obligation to:
  - deliver cash (e.g. creditors and loans payable) or another financial asset (e.g. loan repayable in government stocks) to another entity; or
  - exchange financial instruments with another entity under conditions that are potentially unfavourable (FEC for debtor and Rand improves); or
- a contract that will or may be settled in an entity's own equity instruments and is:
  - a non-derivative for which the entity is or may be obliged to deliver a variable number of the entity's own equity instruments; or
  - a derivative that will or may be settled other than by the exchange of a fixed amount of cash or another financial asset for a fixed number of the entity's own equity instruments.

Liabilities imposed by statutory requirements such as income taxes are not financial liabilities, since they are not contractual in nature.

An **equity instrument** is any contract that evidences a residual interest in the assets of an entity after deducting all its liabilities. Note that an obligation of the reporting entity to issue an equity instrument is not a financial liability, since it results in an increase in equity and cannot result in a loss to the entity.

ACCOUNTING PRESENTATION

1. Liabilities and equity

Where a financial instrument is issued, the issuer of the financial instrument shall classify the instrument, or even its component parts, as a liability or as equity based on:
- the substance of the contractual arrangement on initial recognition; and
- the definitions of a financial liability, financial asset and an equity instrument.

1.1 No contractual obligation to deliver cash or another financial asset

When differentiating a financial liability from an equity instrument, the existence of a contractual obligation of one party to the financial instrument (the issuer) to deliver cash or another financial asset to the holder (other party), or to exchange financial assets or liabilities with the holder under conditions that are potentially unfavourable to the issuer, is critical.

The substance, rather than the legal form, governs the classification of such a financial instrument. This has the effect that some items that would previously have been recognised as equity on the balance sheet now constitute debt. For example:

A preference share redeemable in cash at the option of the holder, or redeemable on a predetermined date, creates an obligation on the part of the issuer to deliver cash in respect of the capital amount to the holder – thus meeting the definition of a financial liability.

Whether dividends on such an instrument are mandatory or discretionary will impact further on the classification thereof – mandatory dividends indicate a liability classification and discretionary dividends an equity classification.

In the case of a redeemable preference share where the issuer has an option to redeem the share, the share would not be a financial liability, because the issuer does not have a present obligation to transfer financial assets.

1.2 Settlement in an entity's own equity instruments

A contract is not an equity instrument solely because it may result in the receipt or delivery of an entity's own equity instruments.

An entity may have a contractual right or obligation to receive or deliver a number of its own shares or other equity instruments that varies so that the fair value of the entity's own equity instruments to be received or delivered, equals the amount of the contractual right or obligation. In the case of an obligation this will be a financial liability.

A contract that will be settled by an entity delivering (or receiving) a fixed number of its own equity instruments in exchange for a fixed amount of cash or another financial asset, is an equity instrument.

A contract that will be settled by the entity delivering or receiving a fixed number of its own equity instruments in exchange for a variable amount of cash or another financial asset is a financial asset or liability.

1.3 Contingent settlement provisions

There may be instances where a financial instrument requires an entity to deliver cash or another financial instrument, or otherwise to settle it in such a way that it would be a financial liability, when uncertain future events occur or do not occur (or on the outcome of uncertain circumstances) that are beyond the control of both the issuer or holder of the instrument. Examples of these occurrences are: a change in the stock market index, interest rates, and future revenues.

Since the issuer of such an instrument does not have the unconditional right to avoid settling the instrument, the financial instrument is a financial liability. Under certain circumstances, such an instrument will not be a financial liability, these being:
- part of the contingent settlement provision is not genuine; or
- settlement can only be required in the event of liquidation of the issuer.

1.4 Settlement options

When a derivative financial instrument gives one party a choice over how it is settled, it would be a financial asset or liability unless all of the settlement alternatives would result in it being an equity instrument.

2. Compound financial instruments

In the case of a non-derivative financial instrument, the issuer thereof shall evaluate the terms of this financial instrument to determine whether it contains both a liability and equity component. Once identified, such components shall be recognised separately when initially accounting for the financial instrument.

An example of such an instrument is debt bearing a specified rate of interest and redeemable in cash on a predetermined date, but providing that the holder of the debt may convert the debt into equity instruments of the issuer at a specified or determinable date.

The issuer of a financial instrument that contains both a liability and equity element shall therefore classify the instrument's component parts separately. Once so classified, the classification is not changed when economic or other circumstances change. The amounts to be used in the split are determined as follows:
- Establish the fair value of the liability component (techniques such as discounted cash flow analysis at prevalent market rates can be used) and the total proceeds on issue of the compound instrument.
- By deducting the liability component from the proceeds, the balance of the total issue price of the instrument is assigned to the equity component.

No gain or loss arises from the initial recognition and presentation of the components as separate elements.

3. Interest, dividends, losses and gains

Distributions (dividends) to holders of a financial instrument, classified as an equity instrument, shall be debited by the issuer directly to equity, net of any related income tax benefit.

Transaction costs of an equity transaction issuing or acquiring own equity instruments, shall be accounted for as a deduction from equity, net of any related income tax benefit.

Transaction costs related to the issue of a compound financial instrument are allocated to the liability and equity components in proportion to allocation of the proceeds.

The classification of the financial instrument (equity or liability) would determine whether the items mentioned above would be included as income or expense, or credited or charged directly to equity.

Dividends (for example mandatory dividends) on shares (redeemable preference shares) classified as liabilities would thus be classified as an expense in the same way as interest payments on a loan. A further implication is that such dividends would thus need to be accrued over time, similarly to interest.

Gains and losses (presumably premiums and discounts) on redemptions or refinancing of instruments classified as liabilities are reported in the income statement, while the gains and losses on instruments classified as equity of the issuer are reported as movements in equity.

4. Treasury shares

In the case where an entity buys back its own equity instruments, those instruments (called treasury shares) shall be deducted from equity. Note the following:
- No gain or loss shall be recognised in profit or loss on the purchase, sale, issue or cancellation of such own equity instruments.

- These treasury shares may be acquired and held by the entity or other members of the group.
- Any consideration paid or received is recognised directly in equity.

5. Offsetting of a financial asset and a financial liability

An entity shall offset a financial asset and a financial liability and report the net amount in the balance sheet when:
- it has a legally enforceable right to set off the recognised amounts; and
- it intends either to settle on a net basis, or to realise the asset and settle the liability simultaneously.

If the conditions mentioned above are met, the liability would be deducted from the value of the asset, and only the net asset or liability would be shown in the balance sheet. Such a presentation would reflect more appropriately the amounts and timing of the expected future cash flows, as well as the risks to which those cash flows are exposed.

Evidence of the intention of the entity with respect to settlement would comprise management representations and an absence of circumstances (such as past actions in similar circumstances) that conflict with such representations, and may indicate that the entity is able to or expects to settle on a net basis or simultaneously.

Offsetting is usually not allowed when:
- grouping of financial instruments are used to simulate the features of a single financial instrument (synthetic instruments);
- financial assets and financial liabilities arise from financial instruments that have the same primary risk exposure (for example, assets and liabilities within a portfolio of forward contracts or other derivative instruments) but involve different counterparts; or
- financial or other assets are pledged as collateral for non-recourse financial liabilities.

DISCLOSURE

Disclosure is addressed as IFRS 7 (AC 144) and no longer forms part of the financial accounting syllabus for QE1 of SAICA.

IAS 33 *(AC 104)* and Circular 8/2007

Earnings, Headline Earnings and Dividend per Share

❑ **SUMMARY**

Background
Measurement
Restatement
Presentation
Disclosure

BACKGROUND

The objective of IAS 33 and Circular 08/2007 is to ensure meaningful determination and presentation of:
- basic earnings per share;
- headline earnings per share; and
- diluted earnings per share.

The first two figures above assist users to assess a company's current performance and to compare it with its performance in prior periods. It also assists users in making comparisons between different entities in the same period. Diluted earnings per share assists users to assess the sensitivity of earnings per share to future changes in the capital structure.

The standard shall be applied to entities whose ordinary shares or potential ordinary shares are publicly traded or are in the process of being issued in public securities markets. Other entities whose shares are not publicly traded, but who wish to disclose earnings per share information shall do so in accordance with this standard.

When both separate and consolidated financial statements are presented, the disclosure requirements apply only to the consolidated information.

MEASUREMENT

1. Basic earnings per share (BEPS)

Divide the profit/loss attributable to ordinary shareholders of the parent entity and, if presented, profit or loss from continuing operations, by the weighted average number of ordinary shares outstanding during the period. The profit figure is the numerator and the number of shares the denominator.

Basic earnings

Earnings comprise the amounts attributable to ordinary equity holders of the parent entity in respect of:
- profit or loss from continuing operations attributable to the parent; and
- profit or loss attributable to the parent.

The above two amounts shall be adjusted for the after-tax amounts of preference dividends, differences arising on the settlement of preference shares, and other similar effects of preference shares classified as equity.

The after-tax deduction of preference dividends is, in the case of:
- cumulative preference dividends, the after-tax preference dividend for only the current period, irrespective of whether it was declared; and
- non-cumulative preference dividends, the after-tax amount of only those dividends declared for the current period.

Where a loss is incurred for a period, the same calculation is done as for earnings per share.

Number of shares

The weighted average number of ordinary shares outstanding during the period is calculated, based on the following principles:
- The number of ordinary shares outstanding at the beginning of the period is adjusted by those bought back or issued during the year multiplied by a time-weighting factor.
- The time-weighting factor is the number of days outstanding as a proportion of the total number of days in the period.
- Generally, shares are included in the calculation from the date that consideration is receivable (generally the date of issue).
- Ordinary shares issued as part of the cost of a business combination are included in the weighted average number of shares from the acquisition date, as profits or losses of the acquiree are only included in the parent's income statement from that date.
- Ordinary shares that are to be issued upon the conversion of a mandatorily convertible instrument are included from the contract date.

- Continently issuable shares are considered outstanding, and are included in the computation of BEPS from the date when all necessary conditions have been satisfied.
- Adjust number of shares of current and all previous periods presented for changes in shares without a corresponding change in resources; for example, bonus issues and share splits. Note that the number of shares is not weighted for these events. Examples:
  - capitalisation or bonus issue or bonus element in a rights issue; and
  - share splits and reverse share splits.
- If these changes (such as bonus issues and share splits) occur after the balance sheet date, but before the financial statements are authorised for issue, the BEPS, DEPS and DPS numbers for the current and prior periods will be based on this new number.
- If a rights issue includes a bonus element, the number of ordinary shares for all years prior to the issue shall be adjusted by the following factor:

$$\frac{\text{Fair value per share immediately prior to the exercise of rights}}{\text{Theoretical ex-rights fair value per share}}$$

The theoretical ex-rights fair value per share is calculated by taking the market value of all shares immediately before the exercising of the rights and adding it to the proceeds of the rights issue and dividing the total by the number of outstanding shares after the rights issue. Where the rights are to be publicly traded separately from the shares before exercise date, take the last cum right value of the shares as fair value for purposes of this calculation.

2. Diluted earnings per share (DEPS)

The profit or loss attributable to ordinary shareholders of the parent and, if presented, the profit or loss from continuing operations attributable to those equity holders and the weighted average number of shares are adjusted for the effects of all dilutive potential ordinary shares.

Diluted earnings

The basic earnings are adjusted for after tax effects of the following items associated with dilutive potential ordinary shares:
- Dividends for the period.
- Interest for the period.
- Other changes in income or expense that would result from a conversion of those shares. The conversion of some potential ordinary shares may lead to consequential changes in other income or expenses; for example the savings on interest related to these shares may lead to an increase in the expense relating to a non-discretionary employee profit sharing plan.

These adjustments are necessary as, after the potential ordinary shares have been converted to ordinary shares, the relevant items will no longer be incurred.

Number of shares – diluted

- Use the weighted average number of shares for BEPS plus the weighted number of shares to be issued on conversion of all dilutive potential ordinary shares into ordinary shares.
- Dilutive potential ordinary shares are deemed to have been converted into ordinary shares at the beginning of the period or, if these potential shares were issued during the current year, the date of their issue.
- Dilutive potential ordinary shares are determined independently for each period presented. This will have the result that the number of dilutive potential ordinary shares included in the year-to-date period is not a weighted average of the dilutive potential ordinary shares included in each interim period.
- Potential ordinary shares (POS) are weighted for the period that they are outstanding:
  - POS that are cancelled or allowed to lapse during the period, will be included in the calculation of DEPS from the beginning of the year until the date of cancellation.
  - POS that are converted into ordinary shares during the period, are included in the DEPS calculation from the beginning of the period till date of conversion (i.e. the period outstanding). From date of conversion the resulting ordinary shares are included in both basic and diluted EPS.

- The number of dilutive potential shares to be issued is determined from the terms of the rights of these shares. The computation assumes the most advantageous rate of conversion or exercise price from the view of the holder of the shares; that is, worst case scenario for the entity.
- Dilutive potential ordinary shares issued by a subsidiary, associate or joint venture are included in the DEPS calculation of the reporting entity if they have a dilutive effect on the consolidated earnings per share of the reporting entity.

Dilutive potential ordinary shares

- These shares are treated as dilutive only when their conversion to ordinary shares would decrease earnings per share or increase loss per share from continuing operations.
- Profit or loss from continuing operations is used as 'the control number' to establish if the potential ordinary shares are dilutive or anti-dilutive.
- Each issue or series of potential ordinary shares is considered separately rather than in aggregate and in sequence from the most dilutive to the least dilutive.
- Refer to IAS 33 Illustrative Example 9 for an illustration.
- Several different types of dilutive potential ordinary share are discussed in IAS 33.45 – .63:
    - options, warrants and their equivalents (.45 – .48);
    - convertible instruments (.49 – .51);
    - contingently issuable shares (.52 – .57);
    - contracts that may be settled in shares or cash (.58 – .61);
    - purchased options (.62); and
    - written put options (.63).

Refer to IAS 33 for detail discussions on these matters.

3. Headline earnings per share (Circular 08/2007)

The JSE requires listed entities to disclose headline earnings per share. Headline earnings is an additional earnings number which is permitted by IAS 33. The starting point for HEPS is the earnings number used to calculate BEPS, which is then adjusted for certain separately identifiable remeasurements.

Headline earnings include:
- post-tax profit or loss of discontinued operation;
- write down or reversal of write down of inventories to net realisable value;
- changes in provisions for future losses on construction contracts;
- percentage of profits recognised on construction contracts;
- changes in deferred tax balance owing to changes in tax rates (but only if the change is reflected in the income statement);
- gain resulting from recognition of deferred tax asset;
- reassessment of recoverability of deferred tax asset;
- depreciation and amortisation;
- actuarial gains/losses recognised in the income statement;
- curtailments and settlements of defined benefit plans;
- foreign exchange gains/losses;
- adjustments relating to provisions;
- remeasurement of financial assets; and
- amounts recycled to the income statement relating to cash flow ledges.

Headline earnings exclude:
- goodwill impairment;
- excess arising upon acquisition of subsidiary;
- goodwill adjustment owing to subsequent recognition of deferred tax asset of subsidiary that existed at acquisition; the corresponding deferred tax gain is also excluded;
- post-tax gain or loss resulting from IFRS 5 (AC 142) remeasurement;
- impairment losses/reversal of impairment losses on intangible assets and PPE;
- disposal gains/losses on PPE and intangible assets;
- revaluation gains on PPE and intangible assets;

- actuarial gains and losses recognised directly in equity;
- translation of the net investment in a foreign operation;
- gains on the disposal of a subsidiary, associate or joint venture;
- gains/losses on available-for-sale assets recycled to the income statement;
- fair value adjustments on investment property.

4. Dividends per share (Per IAS 1 (AC 101))

Dividends per share is:
- the dividends recognised during the year in the financial statements;
- divided by the respective number of shares in issue;
- at the date of each declaration.

RESTATEMENT

- If the number of shares outstanding is affected as a result of a capitalisation issue, bonus issue, share split or a reverse share split, the calculation of BEPS and DEPS shall be adjusted retrospectively.
- If these changes occur after the balance sheet date but before the issue of the financial statements, the per share calculations is based on the new number of shares.
- BEPS and DEPS for all periods presented are adjusted for the effect of:
  - errors; and
  - changes in accounting policies.

PRESENTATION

- BEPS and DEPS for profit or loss from continuing operations attributable to equity holders of the parent entity and profit or loss attributable to equity holders of the parent for the period are shown with equal prominence on the face of the income statement for each class of ordinary share with different rights.
- Even basic and dilutive loss per share shall be shown.
- An entity reporting a discontinued operation shall disclose BEPS and DEPS for the discontinued operation either on the face of the income statement or in the notes.

DISCLOSURE

Notes

- Amounts used as numerators for BEPS and DEPS and a reconciliation of those amounts to the profit or loss attributable to the parent entity for the year.
- Weighted average number of ordinary shares used as the denominator in calculating BEPS and DEPS and a reconciliation of these denominators to each other.
- The above reconciliations shall include the individual effect of each class of instrument that has an impact on EPS.
- If an earnings per share figure is disclosed, in addition to BEPS and DEPS (e.g. headline earnings):
  - Use same denominator as required by this statement.
  - Disclose BEPS and DEPS for such a component with equal prominence in the notes.
  - Indicate the basis on which the numerator(s) is/(are) calculated, indicating also whether such amounts are before or after tax.
  - If a component of the income statement is used that is not reported as a line item in the income statement, provide a reconciliation between the component used and a line item that is reported in the income statement.
- Disclose instruments that could potentially dilute EPS in the future, but that were not included in DEPS because they were antidilutive for the periods presented.
- Disclose a description of ordinary share transactions or potential ordinary share transactions other than items for which retrospective adjustment is required in terms of IAS 33, that occur subsequent to the balance sheet date and that would have changed significantly the number of ordinary or potential ordinary shares, had they been issued before year end.
- If retrospective adjustments to BEPS and DEPS are required because of capitalisation issues, bonus issues, share splits and reverse share splits, the fact that per share calculations reflect such changes in the number of shares, shall be disclosed.

IAS 34 *(AC 127)* and IFRIC 10 *(AC 442)*

Interim Financial Reporting

❑ **SUMMARY**

Background
Accounting practice
Presentation
Disclosure
IFRIC 10: Interim financial reporting and impairment

BACKGROUND

Users need timely and reliable interim financial information to understand an entity's financial condition and liquidity as well as its capacity to generate earnings and cash flows. This information enhances the accuracy of information for forecasting of earnings and share prices. This standard prescribes the following for interim financial reports:
- minimum content; and
- principles for recognition and measurement.

1. Scope

All entities who are required (by law or regulatory bodies) or voluntarily elect to publish interim financial reports in terms of Statements of Generally Accepted Accounting Practice (GAAP) (covering a period shorter than a full financial year, e.g. a semester or quarter) shall comply with this standard.

2. Objective of interim financial reporting

Interim financial reports contribute towards achieving the overall objective of financial statements defined in the Framework, namely 'to provide information about the financial position, performance, and changes in financial position of an entity that is useful to a wide range of users in making economic decisions' (Framework .12).

Interim financial reports cover interim periods which are different from a financial report for an entity's full financial year and can be either a full set of financial statements or an abridged set of financial statements. The **interim period** is defined as a financial reporting period shorter than a full financial year. Nonetheless, the fundamental objectives of interim and annual financial statements are the same.

3. Statutory and regulatory requirements

The preparation and presentation of interim reports in South Africa have been regulated for a number of decades by the Companies Act, 1973 (as amended) and the JSE Listing Requirements. Both of these regulate the minimum disclosure requirements to which interim reports shall comply, and the external auditor's involvement with company interim reports. Furthermore, there is a general requirement of section 303 of the Companies Act, 1973 (as amended) that the interim report shall reflect a fair presentation of the business, results and operations of the company. However, no guidance is provided of what fair presentation implies.

4. Approaches associated with interim financial reporting

Traditionally two approaches have generally been used for identifying and measuring the revenues, expenses, gains and losses of an interim period and the assets and liabilities at the interim date. They are the following:
- The **discrete approach** (condensed financial statements and selected explanatory notes) focuses on the interim period as a discrete, stand-alone reporting period. The intention of the interim financial report is to give an update on the latest complete set of annual financial statements. The focus is therefore on new activities, events and circumstances and previously reported information is not duplicated. This is the primary approach supported by IAS 34.
- The **integral approach** focuses on the interim period as being an integral part of the entire financial year and bases measurements of interim period revenues and expenses on full year estimates. According to this view, interim financial data shall primarily be predictive and explanatory of financial data for the full current financial year. Although this is not the primary approach according to IAS 34, the standard includes a number of exceptions where the integral approach is followed. For example the calculation of the income tax expense for an interim period.

It can therefore be concluded that the two approaches are not mutually exclusive.

ACCOUNTING PRACTICE

1. Recognition and measurement principles

Recognition is the process of including in the financial statements an item that meets the definition of an element (i.e. asset, liability, revenue or expense) and satisfies the criteria for recognition.

Measurement is the process of determining the monetary amounts at which the elements of the financial statements are to be recognised and carried in the financial statements.

Refer to Appendix B to the standard for detailed guidance in this regard.

1.1 Materiality

Materiality is defined in the Framework .29.

In making the decision about how to recognise, measure, classify, or disclose an item for interim financial reporting purposes, materiality has to be assessed in relation to the interim period financial data and not the estimated annual data. When an assessment of materiality is made it will be taken into account that interim measurements may to a greater extent rely on estimates than on measurements of annual financial data.

1.2 Accounting policies

An entity has to apply the same accounting policies in its interim financial statements as in its latest annual financial statements, except for accounting policy changes made subsequent to the date of the latest annual financial statements.

1.3 Measurement

The frequency of interim reporting (e.g. half-yearly or quarterly) does not affect the measurement of an entity's annual results. Measurements for interim reporting purposes are therefore made on a year-to-date basis – the so-called discrete method.

Measurements made on a year-to-date basis may involve changes in estimates of amounts reported in prior interim periods of the same financial year. The principles for recognising assets, liabilities, income, and expenses for interim periods are the same as in annual financial statements. For example:
- The same principles that would apply to the preparation of annual financial statements shall be applied in recognising and measuring losses from inventory write downs or impairments at an interim date.
- Income tax expense is recognised in each interim period based on the best estimate of the weighted average annual income tax rate expected for the full year.
- STC on dividends raised as a liability during an interim period do not form part of the weighted average income tax rate calculation set out in the previous paragraph, but is treated separately (AC 501).

1.4 Revenues received seasonally, cyclically or occasionally

Such revenues include dividends, royalties, and government grants. If anticipation or deferral will not be appropriate at the end of the entity's financial year, these revenues should not be anticipated or deferred at the interim date. Similarly, seasonal revenues of retailers are recognised when they occur – it shall not be anticipated or deferred in order to smooth revenue recognition over the year. Examples are provided in Appendix B to the statement.

1.5 Costs incurred unevenly during the financial year

These costs will be anticipated or deferred for interim reporting purposes only if it is also appropriate to anticipate or defer these costs at the end of the financial year. To illustrate, the cost of a planned major periodic maintenance that is expected to occur late in the year is not anticipated for interim reporting purposes unless the entity has a legal or constructive obligation to effect the maintenance. The mere intention or necessity to incur expenditure related to the future is not sufficient to give rise to an obligation. Examples are provided in Appendix B to the statement.

1.6 Use of estimates

The procedures to be followed regarding measurement in an interim financial report should be designed to ensure that the resulting information is reliable and appropriate disclosure is achieved for all material financial information that is relevant to an understanding of the financial position or performance of the entity.

Measurements in both interim and annual financial reports are often based on reasonable estimates. The preparation of interim financial reports will generally require a greater use of estimation methods than would normally be the case for annual financial reports. For example, full stocktaking and valuation procedures may not be required for inventories at interim dates, although it may be done at financial year end. It may be sufficient to make estimates at interim dates based on sales margins. Examples are provided in Appendix C to the statement.

1.7 Restatement of comparatives

- A change in accounting policy should be accounted for by restating the financial statements of prior interim periods of the current financial year and the comparable interim periods of prior years in terms of IAS 8 (AC 103), if practicable.
- If retrospective application is not possible, prospective application should be applied from the earliest period possible in terms of IAS 8 (AC 103).

PRESENTATION

1. Minimum components and periods required

An interim financial report means a financial report containing either a complete set of financial statements (as per IAS 1 (AC 101) or a set of condensed financial statements (as per this statement) for an interim period. It includes, as a minimum, the following:
- condensed balance sheet (end of current interim period and comparatives at end of immediately preceding financial year);
- condensed income statement(s) (current interim period and cumulatively for current financial year to date, with comparatives for the comparable interim periods (current and year-to-date) of the immediately preceding financial year);
- condensed cash flow statement (cumulatively for the current financial year to date and comparatives for the comparable year-to-date period of the immediately preceding financial year);
- condensed changes in equity statement (cumulatively for the current financial year to date and comparatives for the comparable year-to-date period of the immediately preceding financial year); and
- selected explanatory notes.

2. Form and content

A complete set of financial statements published as interim statements will comply with IAS 1 (AC 101). A condensed set of financial statements should include, as a minimum:
- each of the headings and subtotals that were included in the most recent annual financial statements;[*]
- selected explanatory notes required by this statement;[*] and
- basic and diluted earnings per share to be presented on the face of the complete or condensed income statement, for the interim period.

[*] If their omission would make the condensed interim financial statements misleading, additional line items or notes should be included.

An entity will use the same format in its interim statement of changes in equity as it did in its most recent annual financial statement.

If the entity's most recent annual financial statements were consolidated statements, an interim financial report is prepared on a consolidated basis. This standard neither requires nor prohibits the inclusion of the parent's separate statements in the entity's interim financial report.

DISCLOSURE

1. IAS 34 requirements

1.1 Notes to the interim financial report

Selected explanatory notes are intended to provide an update since the last annual financial statements. The following should be included as a minimum on a year-to-date basis:

- statement that accounting policies and methods of computation have been applied consistently with those applied in the most recent annual financial statements or a description of the nature and effect of any subsequent changes;
- explanatory comments about seasonality or cyclicality of interim operations;
- nature and amount of items that affected assets, liabilities, equity, net income, or cash flows and that are unusual because of their nature, size, or incidence;
- changes in estimates of amounts reported in prior interim periods of the current year or amounts reported in prior years, provided the changes have a material effect on the current interim period;
- issuing, repurchasing, and repayments of debt and equity securities;
- dividends paid (aggregate or per share), disclosed separately for ordinary shares and other shares;
- segment revenue and segment results for business segments or geographical segments, whichever is the entity's primary basis of segment reporting (only if segment data is normally furnished by the entity);
- material events occurring after the interim balance sheet date;
- the effect of changes in the composition of the entity during the interim period, including business combinations, acquisition or disposal of subsidiaries and long-term investments, restructurings, and discontinuing operations;
- changes since the last annual balance sheet date in contingent liabilities or contingent assets;
- any events or transactions that are material to an understanding of the current interim period (refer to IAS 34.17 for examples in this regard); and
- the fact shall be mentioned if the interim financial report is in compliance with the requirements of the statement.

1.2 Annual financial statements

Disclose in a note to the annual financial statements, the nature and amount, if an estimate of an amount reported in an interim period is changed significantly during the final interim period of the financial year but a separate financial report is not published for that final interim period.

2. Statutory and regulatory requirements

Paragraphs 73, 74 and 76 to 79 of Schedule 4 of the Companies Act, 1973 (as amended) list certain minimum disclosure requirements. Furthermore, sections 8.55 to 8.59 of the JSE Listing Requirements require certain minimum information to be included in interim financial reports. These requirements are not reproduced here.

IFRIC 10: INTERIM FINANCIAL REPORTING AND IMPAIRMENT

Background

In terms of IAS 36 (AC 128) and IAS 39 (AC 133), one should assess for impairment:
- goodwill at every reporting date;
- investments in equity investments; and
- investments in financial assets carried at cost at every balance sheet date, and if required recognise an impairment loss at that date.

It may happen that, at a subsequent reporting date or balance sheet date, circumstances have changed, resulting in the situation where the impairment loss would not have been recognised if the assessment was done at the later date. This interpretation deals with whether those impairment losses may ever be reversed.

Issue

IAS 34 requires an entity to apply the same accounting policies used in its annual financial statements in preparing its interim financial report. In terms of IAS 36 (AC 128) .124, the impairment loss on goodwill may not be reversed. IAS 39 (AC 133) .69 and .66 respectively state that the impairment loss on an investment in an equity instrument classified as available for sale and financial assets carried at cost, may not be reversed.

Consensus

An impairment loss recognised in a previous interim period in respect of goodwill or an investment in an equity instrument or a financial asset carried at cost, may not be reversed in a subsequent period.

This consensus may not be extended by analogy to other potential areas of conflict between IAS 34 and other standards.

IAS 36 *(AC 128)*

Impairment of Assets

❏ **SUMMARY**

Background
Accounting practice
Disclosure

BACKGROUND

The standard specifies the following:
- the procedures that an entity applies to ensure that its assets are not overstated; that is, that the carrying amount of an asset does not exceed the amounts to be recovered through use or sale;
- when an entity would account for an identified impairment loss and a reversal of an impairment loss; and
- disclosure of impaired assets.

This standard covers all assets other than inventories, construction contracts, deferred tax assets, assets arising from employee benefits, investment properties measured at fair value, non-current assets held for sale, biological assets relating to agricultural activity and most financial assets. However, it does cover investments in subsidiaries, associates and joint ventures that are accounted for under the equity method or carried at cost or fair value.

ACCOUNTING PRACTICE

1. Identifying an impaired asset

The recoverable amount of an asset shall normally only be estimated if, at the reporting date, there is an indication that the asset may be impaired. The entity, in assessing whether there is an indication of impairment, shall consider as a minimum the following:

External sources of information

- More than expected decline in market value during the period.
- Significant changes in technology, the market, the economy, and legal environment with an adverse effect on the entity.
- Market interest rates or other rates of return on investments have increased during the period, which affect the discount rate used in calculating an asset's value in use and decrease the recoverable amount materially.
- The carrying amount of the net assets of the reporting entity exceeds its market capitalisation.

Internal sources of information

- Evidence is available of obsolescence or physical damage of an asset.
- Significant changes with an adverse effect on the entity have taken place during the period, or are expected to take place in the near future, to the extent to which, or manner in which, an asset is used or is expected to be used. These changes include plans to discontinue or restructure.
- Evidence is available that indicates that the economic performance of an asset is, or will be, worse than expected.

Irrespective of whether there is an indication of impairment an entity shall:
- test an intangible asset if it has an indefinite useful life or is not yet available for use, at least annually:
  - the above impairment test may be performed at any time during an annual period, provided it is performed at the same time every year;
  - different intangible assets may also be tested for impairment at different times;
  - if the intangible asset was recognised for the first time in the current year it must be tested for impairment before the end of the current year; and
- test goodwill acquired in a business combination for impairment at least annually.

2. Recoverable amount

The recoverable amount of an asset is measured at the higher of its fair value less costs to sell and its value in use:
- **Fair value less costs to sell** is the amount obtainable from the sale of an asset in an arm's length transaction between knowledgeable, willing parties, after deducting any direct incremental disposal costs.
- **Value in use** is the present value of estimated future cash flows expected to be derived from an asset or cash-generating unit.

It is not always necessary to determine both an asset's fair value less costs to sell and its value in us; for example, if either of these amounts exceed the asset's carrying amount.

If there is no reason to believe that an asset's value in use materially exceeds its fair value less costs to sell, fair value less costs to sell is taken as the recoverable amount. This will for instance be the case when an asset is held for disposal.

2.1 Fair value less costs to sell

The best evidence of fair value less costs to sell is the price in a binding sale agreement in an arm's length transaction, less disposal costs. In the absence of such an agreement, an asset's market price less disposal costs would be indicative. If there is no binding sale agreement or active market for an asset, fair value less costs to sell is based on the best information available to reflect the amount that an entity could obtain, at the balance sheet date, for the disposal of the asset in an arm's length transaction between knowledgeable, willing parties, after deducting the costs of disposal.

Costs of disposal, other than those already recognised as liabilities, are deducted when determining fair value less costs to sell. Examples of such costs would be:
- legal costs;
- stamp duty and similar transaction taxes;
- removal costs related to the asset; and
- direct incremental costs to bring the asset into condition for sale.

2.2 Value in use

Estimating the value in use of an asset involves the following steps:
- estimating the future cash inflows and outflows to be derived from continuing use of the asset and from its ultimate disposal; and
- applying the appropriate discount rate to these future cash flows.

The following rules apply to the use of cash flow projections:
- Reasonable and supportable assumptions that represent management's best estimate of the set of economic conditions that will exist over the remaining useful life of the asset, shall be used.
- The most recent financial budgets/forecasts that have been approved by management shall be used. Projections based on these budgets/forecasts shall cover a maximum period of five years, unless a longer period can be justified.
- A steady or declining growth rate is used to extrapolate the projections based on the most recent budgets/forecasts for the period beyond the period covered by the budgets/forecasts, unless an increasing rate can be justified. This growth rate shall not exceed the long-term average growth rate for the products, industries, or country or countries in which the entity operates, or for the market in which the asset is used, unless a higher rate can be justified.
- Future cash flows shall be estimated for the asset in its current condition.
- Estimates of future cash flows include:
  - projections of cash inflows and outflows from the continuing use of the asset; and
  - net cash flows expected from the disposal of the asset in an arm's length transaction at the end of its useful life (after deducting the estimated costs of disposal).
- Estimates of future cash flows exclude:
  - cash inflows or outflows expected to arise from a future restructuring to which an entity is not yet committed;
  - future capital expenditure that will improve or enhance the asset's performance;
  - cash inflows or outflows from financing activities; and
  - income tax receipts or payments.

The discount rate (or rates) shall be a pre-tax rate (or rates) that reflects current market assessments of the time value of money and the risks specific to the asset. The discount rate(s) shall not reflect risks for which future cash flow estimates have been adjusted.

3. Impairment of an individual asset

3.1 Existence of an impairment loss

An impairment loss exists whenever the carrying amount of an individual asset exceeds its recoverable amount. The carrying amount shall be reduced to recoverable amount and this reduction represents the impairment loss.

3.2 Recognition of an impairment loss

An impairment loss shall be recognised in profit or loss (the income statement) for assets carried at cost and shall be treated as a revaluation decrease for assets carried at revalued amount according to IAS 16 (AC 123). After recognition of the impairment loss, the depreciation charge for future periods is adjusted accordingly and based on the revised carrying amount.

When the amount estimated for an impairment loss is greater than the carrying amount of the asset to which it relates, an entity shall recognise a liability if it is required by another IAS (AC) statement.

4. Impairment of a cash-generating unit

4.1 Definition

A **cash-generating unit** is the smallest identifiable group of assets that generates cash inflows that are largely independent of the cash inflows from other assets or groups of assets.

If the output produced by an asset or group of assets can be traded in an active market, this asset or group of assets shall be identified as a separate cash-generating unit, even if some or all of the production of this asset or group of assets is used internally.

Cash-generating units shall be consistently identified from period to period for the same asset or types of asset, unless a change is justified.

4.2 Recoverable amount

If there is an indication that an asset may be impaired, the recoverable amount of the individual asset shall first be estimated. If it is not possible to calculate the recoverable amount for an individual asset, the recoverable amount for the asset's cash-generating unit shall be determined.

The recoverable amount of a cash-generating unit is the higher of the cash-generating unit's fair value less costs to sell and value in use. It may be necessary to consider certain recognised liabilities in order to determine the recoverable amount. This can occur if the disposal of a cash-generating unit would require the buyer to assume the liability and only a single fair value less costs to sell is available.

In order to perform a meaningful comparison between the carrying amount of the cash-generating unit and its recoverable amount, the carrying amount of the liability is deducted in determining both the cash-generating unit's value in use and its carrying amount.

4.3 Carrying amount

The carrying amount of a cash-generating unit shall be determined consistently with the way the recoverable amount is determined.

The carrying amount of a cash-generating unit:
* includes the carrying amount of only those assets that can be attributed directly, or allocated on a reasonable and consistent basis, to the cash-generating unit and that will generate the future cash inflows estimated in determining the cash-generating unit's value in use; and
* excludes the carrying amount of any recognised liability, unless the recoverable amount of the cash-generating unit cannot be determined without consideration of this liability.

4.4 Goodwill

Allocating goodwill to cash-generating units

When testing for impairment, goodwill acquired in a business combination shall, from the acquisition date, be allocated to each of the acquirer's cash-generating units, or groups of cash-generating units, that will probably benefit from the synergies of the combination, irrespective of whether other assets or liabilities of the acquiree are assigned to those units or groups of units. Each cash-generating unit or group of such units to which the goodwill is so allocated shall:

- represent the lowest level within the entity at which the goodwill is monitored for internal management purposes; and
- not be larger than an operating segment determined in accordance with IFRS 8 (AC 145).

If the initial allocation of goodwill acquired in a business combination cannot be completed before the end of the annual period in which the business combination is effected, that initial allocation shall be completed before the end of the first annual period beginning after the acquisition date.

If goodwill has been allocated to a cash-generating unit and the entity disposes of a portion of that unit, the goodwill associated with that portion shall be:

- included in the carrying amount of the portion disposed when determining the gain or loss on disposal; and
- measured on the basis of the relative values of the portion disposed of and the portion of the cash-generating unit retained, unless the entity can demonstrate that some other method better reflects the goodwill associated with the portion disposed of.

An entity may reorganise its reporting structure in a way that changes the composition of one or more cash-generating units to which goodwill has been allocated. If this happens the goodwill shall be reallocated to the units affected. (This reallocation should be performed using the relative value approach similar to that used when an entity disposes of a portion of a cash-generating unit, unless the entity can demonstrate that some other method better reflects the goodwill associated with the reorganised units).

If goodwill relates to a cash-generating unit, but could not been allocated to that unit, that unit shall be tested for impairment, only when there is an indication that the unit may be impaired. This impairment test will be performed by comparing the unit's carrying amount, excluding any goodwill, with the recoverable amount of the unit. Any impairment loss shall be recognised in accordance with paragraph 4.6.

If goodwill relates to a cash-generating unit and can be allocated to that cash-generating unit, it shall be tested for impairment annually, and whenever (even more frequently than annually) there is an indication that the unit may be impaired. This is done by comparing the carrying amount of the unit, including the allocated goodwill, with the recoverable amount of the unit.

If the recoverable amount of the unit exceeds the carrying amount of the unit, the unit and the goodwill allocated to that unit shall be regarded as not impaired.

If the carrying amount of the unit exceeds the recoverable amount of the unit, the entity shall recognise the impairment loss in accordance with paragraph 4.5.

Timing of impairment tests

- The annual impairment test for a cash-generating unit to which goodwill has been allocated may be performed at any time during an annual period, provided the test is performed at the same time every year. (A period of one year will therefore pass between the two tests.)
- Different cash-generating units may be tested for impairment at different times. However, if some or all of the goodwill allocated to a cash-generating unit was acquired in a business combination during the current annual period, that unit shall be tested for impairment before the end of the current annual period.
- If the assets constituting the cash-generating unit to which goodwill has been allocated are tested for impairment at the same time as the unit containing the goodwill, they shall be tested for impairment before the unit containing the goodwill.
- Similarly, if the cash-generating units constituting a group of cash-generating units to which goodwill has been allocated are tested for impairment at the same time as the group of units containing the goodwill, the individual units shall be tested for impairment before the group of units containing the goodwill.

4.5 Corporate assets

- Corporate assets are defined as those assets, other than goodwill, that contribute to the future cash flows of both the cash-generating unit under review and other cash-generating units.
- Corporate assets do not generate cash inflows independently from other assets or group of assets.
- Corporate assets affect impairment testing in one of two ways – the corporate asset itself might be impaired or a cash-generating unit to which the corporate asset relates, might be impaired.
- In testing a cash-generating unit for impairment, an entity shall identify all the corporate assets that relate to the cash-generating unit under review.
- If a portion of the carrying amount of a corporate asset:
  - Can be allocated on a reasonable and consistent basis to that unit, the entity shall compare the carrying amount of the unit, including the portion of the carrying amount of the corporate asset allocated to the unit, with its recoverable amount. Any impairment loss shall be recognised in accordance with paragraph 4.6.
  - Cannot be allocated on a reasonable and consistent basis to that unit, the entity shall:
    - Compare the carrying amount of the unit, excluding the corporate asset, with its recoverable amount and recognise any impairment loss in accordance with paragraph 4.6.
    - Thereafter the entity should identify the smallest group of cash-generating units that includes the cash-generating unit under review and to which a portion of the carrying amount of the corporate asset can be allocated on a reasonable and consistent basis.
    - Compare the carrying amount of that group of cash-generating units, including the portion of the carrying amount of the corporate asset allocated to that group of units, with the recoverable amount of the group of units and recognise any impairment loss in accordance with paragraph 4.6.

4.6 Recognition of an impairment loss for a cash-generating unit

If an impairment loss is identified it shall be allocated to reduce the carrying amount of the assets of the unit (group of units) in the following order:
- first, to goodwill allocated to the cash-generating unit (if any);
- then, to the other assets of the unit (group of units) on a pro rata basis based on the carrying amount of each asset in the unit (group of units).

These reductions in carrying amounts shall be treated as impairment losses on individual assets either in profit or loss (the income statement) or as a revaluation decrease.

In allocating an impairment loss, the carrying amount of an asset shall not be reduced below the highest of:
- fair value less costs to sell (if determinable);[*]
- value in use (if determinable);[*] or
- zero.[*]

The amount of the impairment loss that would otherwise, than at (*), have been allocated to the asset, shall be allocated to the other assets of the unit on a pro rata basis.

A liability shall be recognised for any remaining amount of an impairment loss for a cash-generating unit if it is required by another accounting statement.

5. Reversal of an impairment loss

5.1 Indicators of a reversal

If an impairment loss was recognised in a prior period, an entity must assess at each reporting date, if there is an indication that an impairment loss recognised for that asset in previous years may no longer exist or may have decreased. If such indication exists the entity should re-estimate the recoverable amount of that asset. The entity shall consider as a minimum the following indicators:

External sources of information

- The asset's market value has increased significantly during the period.
- Significant changes have taken place during the period, or will take place in the near future, in the technological, market, economic or legal environment in which the entity operates or in the market to which the asset is dedicated that will have a favourable effect on the entity.
- There has been a decrease in market interest rates or other rates of return on investments during the period that will affect the discount rate used in calculating the asset's value in use, and therefore increase the asset's recoverable amount materially.

Internal sources of information

- Significant changes have taken place during the period, or are expected to take place in the near future, in the extent to which, or manner in which, the asset is used or is expected to be used, that will have a favourable effect on the entity. These changes include capital expenditure that has been incurred during the period to improve or enhance an asset's performance or a commitment to restructure the operation to which the asset belongs.
- Evidence is available from internal reporting that indicates that the economic performance of the asset is, or will be, better than expected.

An impairment loss recognised for an asset (other than goodwill) in prior years shall be reversed only if there has been a change in the estimates used to determine the asset's recoverable amount since the last impairment loss was recognised. This implies that there must have been a change in either the fair value of the asset, its expected future cash flows or the discount rate. An impairment loss may not be reversed simply because the present value of the future cash flows increases over time as the date of the relevant cash flow approaches. The carrying amount of the asset shall be increased to its recoverable amount. This increase is a reversal of an impairment loss.

5.2 Individual asset reversal

- There is a limit on the amount that may be reversed when reversing an impairment loss for an individual asset.
- The reversal may not increase the carrying amount of an asset above the carrying amount that would have been determined for the asset (net of amortisation or depreciation) had no impairment loss been recognised in prior years.
- A reversal of an impairment loss shall be recognised as income for assets carried at cost and treated as a revaluation increase for assets carried at a revalued amount.
- After the reversal of an impairment loss, the depreciation charge for future periods shall be adjusted.

5.3 Cash-generating unit – reversal of impairment loss

Such a reversal shall be allocated to the assets in the unit, excluding goodwill, on a pro rata basis, based on the carrying amount of each asset in the unit.

These increases in carrying amounts shall be treated as reversals of impairment losses for individual assets.

In allocating a reversal of an impairment loss, the carrying amount of an asset shall not be increased above the lower of:
- its recoverable amount (if determinable);[*] or
- the carrying amount that would have been determined (net of amortisation or depreciation)[*] had no impairment loss been recognised for the asset in prior years.

The amount of the reversal of the impairment loss that would otherwise, than at (*), have been allocated to the asset shall be allocated to the other assets of the unit on a pro rata basis.

5.4 Goodwill – reversal of impairment loss

An impairment loss recognised for goodwill may not be reversed in any subsequent period.

DISCLOSURE

Income statement and notes thereto

The following shall be disclosed for each class of assets:
- Amount recognised in profit or loss during the period for:
  - impairment losses;[#] and
  - reversals of impairment losses.[@]
- Line item(s) of the income statement in which these impairment losses (#) and reversals (@) are included in the financial statements of the entity (not for segments).
- If an impairment loss for an individual asset (including goodwill) or a cash-generating unit is recognised or reversed and is material to the financial statements, disclose the following:
  - events and circumstances that led to the loss being recognised or reversed;
  - amount recognised or reversed; and
  - for each individual asset:
    - the nature of the asset; and
    - the reportable segment to which the asset belongs (if applicable).
- For a cash-generating unit:
  - a description of the cash-generating unit;
  - the amount of the impairment loss recognised or reversed by class of assets and by reportable segment (if applicable);
  - if the aggregation of assets for identifying the cash-generating unit has changed since the previous estimate of the cash-generating unit's recoverable amount (if any), the entity shall describe the current and former way of aggregating assets and the reasons for changing the way the cash-generating unit is identified;
  - whether the recoverable amount is the fair value less costs to sell or value in use; and
  - the basis used to determine the fair value less costs to sell or the discount rate used to determine value in use and any previous value in use.
- If impairment losses recognised (reversed) during the period are material in aggregate to the financial statements as a whole, disclose a brief description of:
  - the main classes of assets affected; and
  - the main events and circumstances that led to the losses being recognised or reversed.
- Extensive disclosure on estimates used to measure recoverable amounts of cash-generating units containing goodwill or intangible assets with indefinite useful lives are required by IAS 36 (AC 128) .134 – .135.

Statement of changes in equity

- Amount recognised directly in equity during the period for:
  - impairment losses; and
  - reversals of impairment losses.

Other notes

- An entity that reports segment information in terms of IFRS 8 (AC 145), operating segments, shall disclose the following for each reportable segment:
  - the amount of the impairment loss recognised in profit or loss or directly in equity during the period; and
  - the amount of reversals of impairment losses recognised in profit or loss and directly in equity during the period.

IAS 37 *(AC 130)* and IFRIC 5 *(AC 438)*

Provisions, Contingent Liabilities and Contingent Assets

❑ **SUMMARY**

Background
Provisions
Contingencies
Disclosure
Schematic presentation
IFRIC 5: Rights to interests arising from decommissioning, restoration and environmental rehabilitation funds

BACKGROUND

The objective of the standard is to ensure:
- proper recognition and measurement of provisions, contingent liabilities and contingent assets; and
- sufficient disclosure of information about:
  - provisions: nature, timing and amount; and
  - contingencies: nature, amount and uncertainties.

The standard applies to the accounting of all provisions and contingencies, except the following:
- those resulting from executory* contracts except where such a contract is onerous; and
- those covered by other Statements of Generally Accepted Accounting Practice. See IAS 11 (AC 109), IAS 12 (AC 102), IAS 17 (AC 105) and IAS 19 (AC 116).

* An executory contract is a contract under which neither party has performed any of its obligations or both parties have partially performed their obligations to an equal extent.

PROVISIONS

1. Definitions

A **provision** is a liability for which there is uncertainty about the amount or timing of the expenditure.

Note: Impairments of assets do not give rise to the above-mentioned provisions; for example, 'provision' for impairment of property, plant and equipment. Trade payables and accruals are defined in IAS 37 (AC 130) .11(a) and (b).

2. Recognition

Recognise a provision only when an entity has:
- a present obligation (i.e. existence of obligation is more likely than not at balance sheet date);
- legal or constructive;
- as a result of past events (an obligating event occurs when there is no realistic alternative but to settle the obligation);
- to transfer economic benefits to settle the obligation (and this outflow is probable); and
- a reliable estimate of the obligation can be made.

A legal obligation arises from the operation of law; for example, contracts, statutes or regulations. A constructive obligation arises from the facts of a particular situation; for example, business practice, custom, desire to maintain good business relations or to act in an equitable manner. Third parties therefore have a valid expectation that the entity will discharge the obligation.

3. Measurement

Amount to be recognised is the best rational estimate at balance sheet date of expenditure required to settle obligation.

Guidance for making best estimates:
- An explicit calculation is done based on outcomes and probabilities.
- The expected value for large populations is based on all possible outcomes weighted by their associated possibilities.
- The most likely outcome is used when a single obligation is being measured.
- The midpoint of range is used where there is a continuous range of outcomes.
- In some cases the evidence of experts or past experience may be useful.
- Prudence (be cautious) – risks and uncertainties are taken into account.
- Discounting to the present value is applied where the effect of the time value of money is material. Discounting is performed using a pre-tax discount rate.
- Take reasonably expected future events that may affect the amount, into account; for example, new technology and legislation. There shall be sufficient objective evidence that such events will occur.
- Gains from the expected disposal of assets are not considered when the provision is measured.

4. Other aspects

Reimbursements

- Recognise a reimbursement only when it is virtually certain that the reimbursement will be received from another party when the entity settles the obligation.
- Recognise the reimbursement as a separate asset, but not exceeding the amount of the provision.
- In the income statement the reimbursement may be deducted from the related expense.

Changes in and use of provisions

- Review regularly (at least at every balance sheet date) and adjust the amount of the provision to the current best estimate. The resulting debit or credit is taken to the income statement.
- If the obligation for which a provision was raised no longer exists – reverse the provision.
- Provisions are to be used for the original purpose only.

Future operating losses

- Provisions shall not be recognised for future operating losses because an event creating an obligation has not occurred.

Onerous contracts

- An **onerous contract** is a contract in which the unavoidable costs of meeting the obligations under the contract exceed the economic benefits expected to be received from it.
- Unavoidable costs are the least net cost of getting out of the contract. This will be the lower of the cost of fulfilling it and any compensation or penalties to be paid arising from failure to fulfil it.
- The present obligation shall be recognised and measured as a provision.
- An example of an onerous contract would be an attempt to cancel a lease contract.
- Any impairment loss that has occurred on assets dedicated to the contract shall be recognised before raising a provision for the onerous contract.

5. Restructuring

Restructuring is a programme that:
- is planned and controlled by management;
- that materially changes, either:
  - the scope of business undertaken; or
  - manner in which the business is conducted.

It is a specific application of a provision.

Examples of events that may fall under restructuring include:
- sale or termination of a line of business;
- closure of business locations in a country or region;
- relocation of a business activity from one country or region to another; and
- fundamental reorganisations that have a material effect on the nature and focus of an entity's operations.

A restructuring provision is only recognised when the general recognition criteria for provisions are met. These criteria apply to restructurings as follows:

A restructuring provision shall only be raised when the following applies (constructive obligation):
- A detailed plan must exist that identifies at least:
  - business or part of business concerned;
  - principal locations affected;
  - location of employees affected;
  - function of employees affected;
  - approximate number of employees affected;

- expenditures to be undertaken; and
- time of implementation.
- A valid expectation that the restructuring will be carried out must have been created for the individuals affected by the restructuring. This is done by commencing with the implementation of the plan or by announcing the main features of the plan to the individuals affected by it.

The restructuring provision shall include only those costs that are:
- necessarily entailed by the restructuring; and
- are related to discontinued activities only (not related to ongoing activities).

Expenditure resulting from retraining or relocating existing staff, marketing or the investing in new systems or distribution networks relates to the future conduct of business and are not restructuring liabilities.

Identifiable future operating losses up to the date of restructuring are not included in a restructuring provision, unless they relate to an onerous contract.

Gains on the expected disposal of assets are not taken into account when measuring a restructuring provision even when the sale of assets forms part of the restructuring.

In respect of the sale of an operation, no obligation arises for the sale until there is a binding sale agreement. Where the sale of an operation forms part of the restructuring, the assets of the operation are reviewed for impairment.

CONTINGENCIES – LIABILITIES AND ASSETS

1. Definition

A possible obligation or asset at balance sheet date:
- arising from past events;
- the existence of which will be confirmed on the occurrence or non-occurrence of;
- one or more uncertain future events;
- not wholly within the control of the entity.
  OR
- A present obligation that, although it arises from past events, is not recognised, since:
  - an outflow of resources embodying economic benefits to settle the obligation is not probable; or
  - the amount of the obligation cannot be measured with sufficient reliability.

2. Contingent liabilities

A contingent liability shall not be recognised as a liability, but its existence would be disclosed unless the possibility of an outflow of economic benefits is remote.

If an entity is jointly and severally liable for an obligation, a provision shall be raised for that part of the obligation for which an outflow of economic benefits of the entity is probable. The part of the obligation for which the other parties are expected to be liable, represents a contingent liability and shall not be recognised as a provision but only be disclosed.

Contingent liabilities are inherently unpredictable and shall be assessed continually to determine whether or not an outflow of economic benefits has become probable. A provision shall be recognised in the financial statements when an outflow of economic benefits relating to a previous contingent liability becomes probable, unless a reliable estimate of the amount cannot be made.

3. Contingent assets

An entity shall not recognise a contingent asset, but it is disclosed where the inflow of economic benefits is probable.

An example of a contingent asset is a claim that an entity is pursuing through legal proceedings, the outcome of which is uncertain.

Contingent assets are not recognised in financial statements as this may result in the recognition of income that may fail to realise.

Contingent assets are continually assessed to ensure fair presentation of developments in the financial statements. If an inflow of economic benefits is virtually certain, the asset and its related income is recognised in the financial statements when the inflow becomes virtually certain.

DISCLOSURE

1. Provisions

Balance sheet and notes

- Carrying amount at the beginning and end of the period.
- Details of movements for each class of provision:
  - additional provisions for the period;
  - increases in existing provisions;
  - amounts used (actually incurred);
  - unused amounts reversed,;
  - the increase during the period in the discounted amount arising from the passage of time; and
  - effect of a change in discount rate.
  - Comparative information is not required.
- Disclosure for each class of provision:
  - nature;
  - expected timing of outflows; and
  - any uncertainties about amount or timing of outflow, including major assumptions used if necessary.
  - Amount of any expected reimbursement, stating the amount of any asset raised in this regard.
- Where detailed disclosure could prejudice the entity's position, the provision is raised and the following is disclosed:
  - the general nature of dispute; and
  - the fact and reason for non-disclosure of information.

2. Contingencies

If the possibility of a contingent liability is remote, no disclosure is required.

Disclosure in notes

The following is disclosed for each class of unrecognised contingent liability:
- brief description of nature;[*]
- uncertainties surrounding the amount or timing of the outflow;
- estimate of financial effect;[*]
- the possibility of reimbursement;
- statement of fact if information on contingent liabilities is not disclosed because it is impracticable to do so;[*] and
- where disclosure could prejudice the entity's position – disclose same as for provisions.[*]

[*]   Disclose this for a contingent asset where an inflow of economic benefits is probable.

SCHEMATIC PRESENTATION

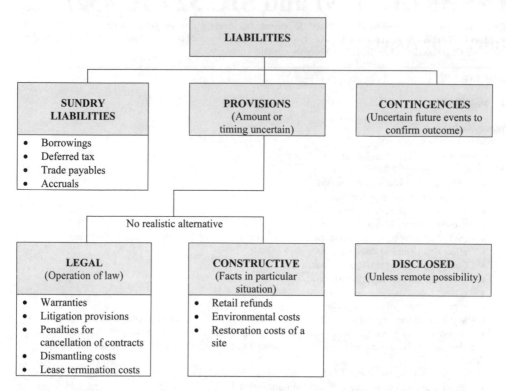

IFRIC 5: RIGHTS TO INTERESTS ARISING FROM DECOMMISSIONING, RESTORATION AND ENVIRONMENTAL REHABILITATION FUNDS

1. Background

- Entities may contribute to decommissioning funds in order to set aside assets to fund future decommissioning costs.
- These funds are administered separately and the entity's right to access the assets is restricted.

2. Issues

- The issues are how to account for the interest in such a fund, as well as how to account for the obligation to make additional contributions.

3. Consensus

- The obligation to pay decommissioning costs may not be offset against the interest in the fund.
- Regarding the interest in the fund, the entity should use equity accounting, proportionate consolidation or normal consolidation, depending on whether it has significant influence, joint control or control over the fund.
- If the entity does not have control, joint control, or significant influence over the fund, the interest in the fund is recognised as a reimbursement right.
- An obligation to make additional contributions if certain events occur, is a contingent liability. When it becomes probable that these contributions will be made, a liability is recognised.

IAS 38 *(AC 129)* and SIC 32 *(AC 432)*

Intangible Assets

❑ **SUMMARY**

BACKGROUND

This standard prescribes the accounting treatment for intangible assets (including research and development costs) and requires an entity to recognise an intangible asset if, and only if, certain criteria are met. The standard also specifies how the carrying amount of an intangible asset shall be measured and requires certain disclosure.

The following intangible assets that are covered by other standards are not covered by the standard:
- non-current intangible assets classified as held for sale;
- deferred tax assets;
- assets arising from employee benefits;
- leases;
- goodwill arising on a business combination;
- financial assets as defined; and
- intangible assets held as inventories.

The following items are covered by the standard:
- advertising;
- training;
- computer software;
- new processes;
- new systems;
- motion pictures;
- video recordings;
- plays;
- manuscripts;
- patents;
- copyrights;
- research activities;
- development activities;
- trademarks;
- brands;
- publishing titles;
- fishing licences;
- import quotas;
- franchises;
- customer relations;
- market share; and
- marketing rights.

The majority of the definitions contained in IAS 38 are similar to those contained in IAS 16 (AC 123) on property, plant and equipment. The definitions set out below are not contained in IAS 16 (AC 123).

An **intangible asset** is an identifiable, non-monetary asset without physical substance.

An intangible asset must be identifiable to distinguish it from goodwill. The identifiablility criterion is met when the intangible asset:
- is separable (the intangible asset can be sold, transferred or exchanged, either individually or with a related contract); or
- arises from a contractual or other legal right (the right does not have to be transferable or separable from the entity).

When an intangible asset is contained in or on a physical medium, an entity must use judgement to assess whether the intangible or the tangible element is the most significant, in order to determine whether the asset should be accounted for in accordance with IAS 16 (AC 123) or in accordance with IAS 38 (AC 129).

An **asset** in the above context is a resource controlled by an entity as a result of past events, and from which future economic benefits are expected to flow to the entity.

An entity can control an intangible asset when it has the power to obtain future economic benefits flowing from the underlying resource and when it has the power to restrict access of others to those benefits.

Research is original and planned investigation undertaken with the prospect of gaining new scientific or technical knowledge and understanding.

Development is the application of research findings or other knowledge to a plan or design for the production of new or substantially improved materials, devices, products, processes, systems or services prior to the commencement of commercial production or use.

Amortisation is the systematic allocation of the depreciable amount of an intangible asset over its useful life.

An active market is a market where all the following conditions exist:
- The items traded within the market are homogeneous.
- Willing buyers and sellers can normally be found at any time.
- Prices are available to the public.

ACCOUNTING PRACTICE

1. Recognition and measurement

- An item can only be recognised as an intangible asset if it meets:
  - the definition of an intangible asset; and
  - the recognition criteria:
    - it is probable that expected future economic benefits that are attributable to the asset, will flow to the entity; and
    - the cost of the asset can be measured reliably.
  - The above two criteria apply for both initial and subsequent recognition.
- An entity assesses the probability of inflow of economic benefits in the future using supportable and reasonable assumptions, being management's best estimate of the economic conditions expected over the asset's useful life.
- An intangible asset shall initially be carried at cost, being the amount of cash or cash equivalents paid, or the fair value of another consideration given to acquire an asset at the time of its acquisition or production.
- If an intangible asset is acquired separately (on its own), the cost can easily be determined.
- Cost of a separately acquired intangible asset includes import duties, non-refundable purchase taxes and directly attributable expenditure to prepare the asset for its intended use, less trade discounts and rebates.
- If payment for an intangible asset is deferred beyond normal credit terms, the normal rules on discounting for property, plant and equipment will apply.
- If an intangible asset is acquired in exchange for equity instruments of the reporting entity, the cost of the asset would be equal to the fair value of the equity instruments.
- If an intangible asset is acquired in a business combination, the cost of the asset is based on fair value at the date of acquisition. The fair value in the case of a business combination is deemed to take into account the probability criteria for recognition, automatically:
  - Best estimates of fair value:
    - being quoted market prices (current bid price) in an active market which is the most reliable measurement of fair value;
    - if current bid prices are unavailable use the prices of most recent similar transactions, provided circumstances remained unchanged; or
    - if no active market exists, consider the price the entity would have paid for the asset in an arm's length transaction at acquisition date.
- If an intangible asset is acquired by way of a government grant, the cost of the asset can be recognised at fair value (with the grant being raised at fair value), if an active market exists. Alternatively, the intangible asset can be recognised at a nominal amount, plus any attributable expenditure involved in getting the asset ready for its intended use.
- The cost of an intangible asset acquired in exchange for another asset, will be determined using the normal rules discussed under IAS 16 (AC 123) on property, plant and equipment.

2. Recognition of internally generated intangible assets

- Internally generated goodwill is never recognised as an asset.
- Internally generated brands, mastheads, publishing titles, customer lists and similar items shall not be recognised as intangible assets.
- Internally generated intangible assets (excluding internally generated goodwill) can be recognised, provided they meet the criteria for recognition:
  - They will generate future economic benefits.
  - The cost of the asset can be determined reliably.

- To assess whether internally generated intangible assets meet the recognition criteria, the generation of such an asset is classified into two stages:
  - a research phase (expense); and
  - a development phase (possible intangible asset).
- If a research and development phase cannot be distinguished, treat expenditure as if incurred during the research phase.
- No intangible asset shall be recognised from research or the research phase of an intangible asset – recognise expenditure as an expense when incurred.
- Examples of research activities are:
  - activities aimed at gaining new knowledge;
  - the search for, evaluation and final selection of applications of research findings or other knowledge;
  - the search for alternatives for materials, devices, products, processes, systems or services; and
  - the formulation, design, evaluation and final selection of possible alternatives for new or improved materials, devices, products, processes, systems or services.
- Examples of development activities are:
  - design, construction and testing of pre-production or pre-use prototypes and models;
  - the design of tools, jigs, moulds and dies involving new technology;
  - the design, construction and operation of a pilot plant; and
  - the design, construction and testing of a chosen alternative for new improved materials, devices, products, processes, systems or services.
- Development expenditure is capitalised if all the following can be demonstrated:
  - technical feasibility of completing the intangible asset so that it will be available for use or sale;
  - the intention to complete, use or sell the asset;
  - the ability to sell or use the asset;
  - how the asset will generate future economic benefits (either prove the existence of a market for the asset or its output, or if to be used internally, the usefulness of the asset);
  - resources to complete development of the asset and to use or sell it are available; and
  - the ability to measure costs of development reliably.
- Costs initially recognised as expenses may not subsequently be capitalised.
- The following do not form part of the cost of an internally generated intangible asset:
  - selling, administrative and general overheads, unless directly attributable to preparing the asset for use;
  - clearly identified inefficiencies and initial operating losses before the asset reaches its planned performance; and
  - expenditure on training staff to operate the asset.
- The following items are expensed (this is not negotiable):
  - research costs;
  - training costs;
  - pre-opening costs;*
  - establishment costs* (legal and secretarial);
  - advertising costs and promotional costs;
  - relocating or re-organising costs; and
  - pre-operating costs.*
- If a payment in respect of the above is made before delivery of goods and services, it may still be treated as an asset (prepayment).

* All part of start-up costs.

3. Measurement after recognition

An entity can use either the cost model or the revaluation model as accounting policy.

3.1 Cost model

Subsequent to initial recognition at cost, an intangible asset shall be carried at cost less accumulated amortisation and/or accumulated impairment losses.

3.2 Revaluation model

- After initial recognition, an intangible asset shall be carried at a revalued amount, being its fair value at the date of the revaluation less any subsequent accumulated amortisation and any subsequent accumulated impairment losses.
- For the purpose of revaluations under this standard, fair value shall be determined by reference to an active market – by implication then reliable measurement.
- Revaluations shall be made with sufficient regularity such that the carrying amount does not differ materially from that which would be determined using fair value at the balance sheet date.
- Intangible assets cannot be revalued if not previously recognised as an asset.
- Intangible assets can only be recognised at cost intially, therefore an intangible asset cannot be revalued 'into' the books.
- Revaluations shall apply to an entire class of intangible assets, unless there is no active market for the asset. In such a case the asset is carried at cost less accumulated amortisation and impairment losses.
- If an asset was revalued previously at fair value and fair value is no longer measurable due to the absence of an active market, the asset is carried at revalued amount at last revaluation less any subsequent accumulated amortisation and/or impairment losses. Consider impairment if an active market for the asset no longer exists.
- If a revaluation takes place, credit revaluation surplus directly. If this revaluation reverses a revaluation decrease previously recognised as an expense – recognise revaluation surplus as income to the extent of the previous decrease recognised in profit or loss (the income statement).
- If an asset's carrying amount decreased as a result of a revaluation, recognise decrease as an expense. However, a revaluation decrease shall be debited against a related revaluation surplus raised earlier, to the extent that it does not exceed the amount held in the revaluation surplus in respect of that same asset.
- The cumulative revaluation surplus included in equity in respect of an intangible asset can be transferred directly to retained earnings (not via the income statement) once the surplus is realised. Realisation takes place via disposal or retirement, or via amortisation (as the asset is used).

4. Useful life

- An entity shall assess whether an intangible asset has a finite or indefinite useful life.
- If the useful life is finite, the following shall be determined:
  - the length of the useful life; or
  - the number of production or similar units constituting that useful life.
- The useful life of an intangible asset is indefinite if, based on an analysis of all relevant factors, there is no foreseeable limit to the period over which the asset is expected to generate cash flows for the entity.
- The useful life of an intangible asset that arises from contractual or other legal rights, is limited to the period of these rights. The useful life may however be shorter than the contractual period, depending on the expected period of usage anticipated by the entity.
- If there is a renewal option attached to contractual or legal rights initially conveyed for a limited term, the useful life should include the renewal period, provided renewal can be effected at no significant cost to the entity.

5. Tangible assets with finite useful lives

5.1 Amortisation

- The depreciable amount of an intangible asset with a finite useful life shall be allocated on a systematic basis over the best estimate of the asset's useful life.
- Amortisation shall commence when an asset is available for use.
- Amortisation shall cease at the earlier of the date on which the asset (or disposal group containing it) is classified as held for sale and the date on which it is derecognised.
- The method of amortisation shall reflect the pattern of future economic benefits consumed via use of the intangible asset.
- If the pattern of benefits cannot be determined reliably, use the straight-line method.
- Recognise the amortisation charge as an expense, unless another standard allows inclusion in the carrying amount of another asset; for example, IAS 2 (AC 108) and IAS 16 (AC 123).

- The amortisation method and period must be reviewed at the end of each financial year. Any change in amortisation method and/or period is accounted for as a change in accounting estimate in profit or loss (the income statement).

5.2 Residual value

- The residual value of an intangible asset with a finite useful life shall be assumed to be zero unless:
  - there is a commitment by a third party to purchase the asset at the end of its useful life; or
  - there is an active market for the asset, and:
    - residual value can be determined by reference to that market; and
    - it is probable that such a market will exist at the end of the asset's useful life.
- The residual value of an intangible asset with a finite useful life is reviewed at each financial year end and change in useful life is accounted for as a change in accounting estimate.

6. Intangible assets with an indefinite useful life

- An intangible asset with an indefinite useful life shall not be amortised.
- However, an intangible asset with an indefinite useful life shall be tested for impairment in terms of IAS 36 (AC 128) at least annually (even if no indication of impairment); and also whenever there is an indication of impairment.
- Review at each period whether events and circumstances continue to support an indefinite useful life assessment for that asset. The change from indefinite to finite is accounted for as a change in accounting estimate.

7. Recoverable amounts

- The recoverable amount of an intangible asset shall be determined under IAS 36 (AC 128) and impairment losses recognised accordingly.
- An intangible asset that is not yet available for use, must be tested for impairment at least annually in accordance with IAS 36 (AC 128). This is irrespective of whether there are indications of impairment.

8. Retirement and disposals

- An intangible asset shall be derecognised (eliminated from the balance sheet) on disposal, or when no future economic benefits are expected from its use or disposal.
- Gains or losses arising from the derecognition of an intangible asset shall be determined as the difference between the net proceeds on disposal and the carrying amount of the asset, and shall be recognised as income or expense in profit or loss (the income statement).

DISCLOSURE

Accounting policies

For each class of intangible asset, disclose whether the useful lives are indefinite or finite. If the useful life is finite, disclose:
- amortisation rates used; and
- amortisation methods used.

Balance sheet and notes thereto

Disclose the following for each class of intangible assets, distinguishing between internally generated intangible assets and other intangible assets:
- the gross carrying amount and the accumulated amortisation (aggregated with accumulated impairment losses) at the beginning and end of the period;
- a reconciliation of the carrying amount at the beginning and end of the period showing:
  - additions, indicating separately those from internal development, those acquired separately and those acquired through business combinations;

- intangible assets classified as held for sale (or part of a disposal group) per IFRS 5 (AC 142) and other disposals;
- increases or decreases during the period resulting from revaluations and from impairment losses recognised or reversed directly in equity under the statement on impairment of assets, if any;*
- impairment losses recognised in profit or loss (the income statement) during the period under the standard on impairment of assets, if any;*
- impairment losses reversed in profit or loss (the income statement) during the period under the standard on impairment of assets, if any;*
- amortisation recognised during the period;
- net exchange differences arising on the translation of the financial statements into presentation currency and on the translation of a foreign operation into the presentation currency of the entity; and
- other changes in the carrying amount during the period.

* Disclose in addition to information required by IAS 36 (AC 128).

- Entities are encouraged to disclose the following useful information:
  - the cost and a description of fully amortised intangible assets that are still in use; and
  - a brief description of significant intangible assets controlled by the entity but not recognised as assets as they did not meet the recognition criteria in this standard or were acquired or generated before this statement was effective.
- If an intangible asset is assessed as having an indefinite useful life, disclose:
  - the carrying amount of that asset; and
  - the reasons for concluding that the asset has an indefinite useful life (in giving these reasons, the entity shall describe the factor(s) that played a significant role in determining the useful life of the asset).
- Disclose a description, the carrying amount and remaining amortisation period of any individual intangible asset that is material to the financial statements of the entity as a whole.
- For intangible assets acquired by way of government grant and initially recognised at fair value, disclose:
  - the fair value initially recognised for these assets;
  - their carrying amounts; and
  - whether they are measured after recognition under the cost model or the revaluation model.
- Disclose the existence and carrying amounts of intangible assets whose title is restricted, and the carrying amounts of intangible assets pledged as security for liabilities.
- Disclose the amount of contractual commitments for the acquisition of intangible assets.
- If intangible assets are carried at revalued amounts, the disclose the following by class of intangible assets:
  - the effective date of the revaluation;
  - the carrying amount of revalued intangible assets; and
  - the carrying amount that would have been included in the financial statements had the revalued intangible assets been carried under the cost model.
- The methods and significant assumptions applied in estimating the fair value of the assets.

Income statements and notes thereto

- Disclose the line item where amortisation is debited in profit or loss calculations for the period.
- Disclose the nature and effect of a change in accounting estimate that has a material effect in the current or future periods under IAS 8 (AC 103). Such disclosure will arise from changes in:
  - the amortisation period (useful life);
  - the amortisation method; and
  - residual values.
- Disclose the aggregate amount of research and development expenditure recognised as an expense during the period.

Statement of changes in equity

Disclose the amount of the revaluation surplus that relates to intangible assets at the end and at the beginning of the period, indicating the changes during the period and any restrictions on the distribution of the balance to shareholders.

SIC 32: INTANGIBLE ASSETS – WEBSITE COSTS

1. Background

An entity may incur internal expenditure on the development and operation of its own website for internal or external usage.

The stages of a website's development are the following:
- **Planning** – feasibility studies, defining objectives and specifications, evaluating alternatives and selecting preferences.
- **Application and infrastructure development** – obtaining a domain name, purchasing and developing hardware and operating software, installation and stress testing.
- **Graphical design development** – designing the appearance of web pages.
- **Content development** – creating, purchasing, preparing and uploading information on the site before completion of website development.

Once development is completed, the operating stage begins. The entity now maintains and enhances the applications, infrastructure, graphical design and so on of the website.

2. Issue

When accounting for the internal expenditure on development and operation of an entity's own website for both internal and external usage, the issues are:
- whether the website represents an internally generated intangible asset subject to IAS 38; and
- what the appropriate accounting treatment would be for such expenditure.

The interpretation does not apply to expenditure on purchasing, developing and operating hardware of a website. (Will be accounted for under IAS 16 (AC 123.)

IAS 38 does not apply to intangible assets held for sale in the ordinary course of business.

For leases, the following applies:
- The lessor applies this interpretation if a website is leased under an operating lease.
- The lessee applies this interpretation after initial recognition if a website is leased under a finance lease.

2. Consensus

- An entity's own internally developed website is an internally generated intangible asset subject to the requirements of IAS 38.
- Recognise such an internally generated website as an intangible asset if the asset complies with the requirements of both IAS 38.21 and IAS 38.57.
- Any internal expenditure on the development and operation of an entity's own website shall be accounted for under IAS 38. Consequently:
  - The planning stage is similar to the research phase discussed in IAS 38 and expenditure incurred at this stage is thus expensed.
  - The application and infrastructure development stage, the graphical design stage and the content development stage, to the extent that the content is developed for purposes other than to advertise and promote an entity's own products, are similar to the development stage discussed in IAS 38 and is thus capitalised as an intangible asset if it complies with the six criteria in IAS 38.57.
  - In accordance with IAS 38.71, expenditure on an intangible asset that was originally recognised as an expense in previous financial periods cannot be recognised at cost at a later stage.
  - Expenditure incurred on the content development stage, to the extent that content is developed to advertise and promote an entity's own products and services, is recognised as an expense.
  - Expenditure incurred in the operating stage (after completion of development) is recognised as an expense.
  - A website recognised as an intangible asset shall be measured after initial recognition by applying IAS 38.72 – .87.
  - The best estimate of a website's useful life would be short.

IAS 39 *(AC 133)*

Financial Instruments: Recognition and Measurement

❑ **SUMMARY**

Background
Accounting practice
Disclosure

BACKGROUND

1. Objective

The objective of this standard is to establish principles for recognising, measuring and disclosing information about financial instruments in the financial statements of business entities.

2. Scope

The standard shall be applied to all financial instruments by all entities, except:
- subsidiaries, associates and joint ventures accounted for under the appropriate statements;
- rights and obligations under leases in terms of IAS 17 (AC 105);
- employee benefit plan assets and liabilities in terms of IAS 19 (AC 116);
- rights/obligations under insurance contracts in terms of IFRS 4 (AC 141);
- equity instruments issued by the reporting entity, including options and warrants;
- financial guarantee contracts;
- contingent consideration in business combination (see IFRS 3 (AC 140)) only applied to the acquirer;
- contracts between an acquirer and a vendor in a business combination to buy/sell an acquiree at future date;
- loan commitments that cannot be settled net in cash or another financial instrument; and
- financial instruments, contracts and obligations under share-based payment transactions to which IFRS 2 (AC 139) applies.

Some of the exclusions listed above are, however, adjusted slightly to include the following:
- lease receivables (derecognition);
- derivatives embedded in insurance contracts; and
- loan commitments that the entity designated as financial liabilities at fair value through profit or loss.

3. Definitions

The definitions of the following items have already been addressed in IAS 32 (AC 125). However, the following definitions have not been discussed. Owing to the technical nature of the definitions involved, they are virtually quoted from IAS 39 (AC133):

Fair value is the amount for which an asset could be exchanged, or a liability settled, between knowledgeable, willing parties in an arm's length transaction.

A **derivative** is a financial instrument with all three the following characteristics:
- whose value changes in response to the change in a specified interest rate, security price, commodity price, foreign exchange rate, index of prices or rates, a credit rating or credit index, or similar variable (sometimes called the underlying);
- that requires no initial net investment or little initial net investment relative to other types of contract that have a similar response to changes in market conditions; and
- that is settled at a future date.

A **financial asset or liability at fair value through profit or loss** is a financial asset or liability that meets any of the following conditions:
- It is classified as held for trading. A financial asset or liability held for trading is one that was acquired or incurred principally for the purpose of generating a profit from short-term fluctuations in price or dealer's margin. A financial asset shall be classified as held for trading if, regardless of why it was acquired, it is part of a portfolio for which there is evidence of a recent actual pattern of short-term profit taking. Derivative financial assets and derivative financial liabilities are always deemed held for trading unless they are designated and effective hedging instruments.
- Upon initial recognition it is designated by the entity as fair value through profit or loss. Financial assets and liabilities in this standard may, in limited circumstances when initially recognised, be designated as a financial asset or liability at fair value through profit or loss. In addition to other limitations, investments in equity instruments that do not have a quoted market price in an active market and whose fair value cannot be reliably measured, may not be designated as such.

Held-to-maturity investments are non-derivative financial assets with fixed or determinable payments and fixed maturity that an entity has the positive intent and ability to hold to maturity, other than:

- those that an entity designates at fair value through profit or loss upon initial recognition;
- those that an entity designates as available for sale; and
- those that meet the definition of loans and receivables.

Loans and receivables are non-derivative financial assets other than:

- those that are originated with the intent to be sold immediately or in the short-term, which shall be classified as held for trading;
- those that the entity upon initial recognition designates as at fair value through profit or loss;
- those that the entity upon initial recognition designates as available for sale; and
- those for which the holder may not substantially recover all of its initial investment (other than through credit deterioration), which shall be classified as available for sale.

Available-for-sale financial assets are those non-derivative financial assets that are designated as available for sale or are not classified as:

- loans and receivables;
- held-to-maturity investments; or
- financial assets at fair value through profit or loss.

Amortised cost of a financial asset or financial liability is the amount at which the financial asset or liability was measured at initial recognition minus principal repayments, plus or minus the cumulative amortisation on the effective interest method of any difference between that initial amount and the maturity amount, and minus any write-down (directly or though the use of an allowance account) for impairment or uncollectability.

The **effective interest method** is a method of calculating the amortised cost of a financial asset or liability and of allocating the interest income or expense over the relevant period.

The **effective interest rate** is the rate that exactly discounts the expected stream of future cash payments through the expected life of the financial instrument or a shorter period (market-based repricing date) to the current net carrying amount of the financial asset or financial liability. That computation shall include all fees and points paid or received between parties to the contract that are an integral part of the effective interest rate, as well as transaction costs and all other premiums or discounts.

Transaction costs are incremental costs that are directly attributable to the acquisition or disposal of a financial asset or liability. An incremental cost is one that would not have been incurred if the entity had not acquired, issued or disposed of the financial instruments.

A **regular way purchase or sale** is a purchase or sale of a financial asset under a contract whose terms require delivery of the asset within the time frame established generally by regulation or convention in the market place concerned.

A **firm commitment** is a binding agreement for the exchange of a specified quantity of resources at a specified price on a specified future date or dates.

A **forecast transaction** is an uncommitted yet anticipated future transaction.

Derecognise means remove a financial asset or liability, or a portion of a financial asset or liability, from an entity's balance sheet.

Hedging, for accounting purposes, means designating one or more hedging instruments so that their change in fair value is an offset, in whole or in part, to the change in fair value or cash flows of a hedged item.

A **hedged item** is an asset, liability, firm commitment, or highly probable forecast transaction or net investment in a foreign operation, that:

- exposes the entity to risk of changes in fair value or changes in future cash flows; and
- for hedge accounting purposes, is designated as being hedged.

A **hedging instrument**, for hedge accounting purposes, is a designated derivative or (in limited circumstances) another designated non-derivative financial asset or liability whose fair value or cash flows are expected to offset changes in the fair value or cash flows of a designated hedged item. Under IAS 39, a non-derivative financial asset or liability may be designated as a hedging instrument for hedge accounting purposes only if it hedges the risk of changes in foreign currency exchange rates.

Hedge effectiveness is the degree to which changes in fair value or cash flows of the hedged item attributable to a hedged risk are offset changes in fair value or cash flows of the hedging instrument.

Taking the above definitions into account, the following categories of financial assets and liabilities can be distinguished:
- financial assets:
  - financial assets at fair value through profit or loss;
  - held-to-maturity investments;
  - loans and receivables; and
  - available-for-sale financial assets (strategic long-term share investments).
- financial liabilities:
  - financial liabilities at fair value through profit or loss; and
  - other (not defined as such, but all financial liabilities not at fair value through profit or loss, meaning non-trading liabilities).

It is essential that you are able to distinguish between these different types of financial asset and liability before continuing with this summary.

4.   Classification of held-to-maturity investments

For an investment to be classified as a held-to-maturity investment, the entity must have the positive intent and ability to hold the investment to maturity. An entity does not have positive intent if:
- it intends holding the asset for an undefined period;
- it stands ready to sell the asset in response to changes in market conditions; or
- the issuer can settle the asset at an amount significantly below its amortised cost.

Financial assets may not be classified as held-to-maturity investments if disposals took place in the current or preceding two years, other than if:
- the sale was close to maturity and therefore changes in the market rate of interest did not significantly affect its fair value;
- substantially all of the asset's original principal had been collected; or
- the sale was an isolated event beyond the entity's control and could not reasonably have been anticipated by the entity.

An example of a held-to-maturity investment would be a debt security with a variable interest rate, while an equity security, such as shares held, will not be a held-to-maturity investment.

ACCOUNTING PRACTICE

1.   Initial recognition of a financial asset or liability

A financial asset or liability, as defined, shall be recognised when an entity becomes a party to the contractual provisions of an instrument, other than regular way purchases of financial assets. Note the following:
- All derivatives, as defined, are recognised.
- Executory contracts are not recognised (see IAS 37 (AC 130) .3 for the definition of an executory contract).
- Use trade or settlement date for regular way purchases of financial assets.[*]
- Use trade or settlement date for regular way sales of financial assets.[*]

[*]   Once a decision on the method has been taken, it shall be applied consistently for all purchases and sales of financial assets that belong to the same category of financial assets.

The **trade date** is the date that an entity commits to purchase or sell an asset. Trade date accounting refers to the recognition and derecognition of an asset to be received and the liability to pay for it on the trade date.

The **settlement date** is the date that the asset is delivered to or by the entity. Settlement date accounting refers to the recognition or derecognition of the asset on the day on which the asset is transferred to or delivered by the entity.

2. Derecognition of financial assets and liabilities

2.1 Financial assets

A financial asset is derecognised when:
- the contractual rights to the cash flows from the asset expire (for instance a debtor has settled his account in full);
- it is transferred and the transfer qualifies for derecognition (see # below).

A financial asset is transferred if an entity either:[#]
- transfers the contractual rights to receive cash flows related to the financial asset; or
- retains the contractual rights to receive cash flows of the specific financial asset, but assumes a contractual obligation to pay over the cash flows to one or more other parties, provided the three conditions in IAS 39.19 are met.

On derecognition, the difference between the proceeds and the carrying amount of a financial asset shall be included in profit or loss. Any prior cumulative gain or loss recognised to reflect the asset at fair value in the mark-to-market reserve in equity, shall also be included in profit or loss.

Part of a financial asset

If only part of a financial asset is derecognised, remove only the part of the carrying amount relating to the portion sold and compare that to the proceeds. The resultant gain or loss and related part of the reserve on restatement to fair value (if applicable) are taken to the income statement.

2.2 Financial liabilities

- An entity shall remove a financial liability (or a part of a financial liability) from its balance sheet when it is extinguished; that is, when the obligation specified in the contract is either discharged, cancelled, or expires.
- The difference between the amount paid for the financial liability and the carrying amount of a liability (or part of a liability) extinguished or transferred to another party, shall be included in profit or loss for the period.

If an exchange takes place between an existing borrower and lender of a debt instrument with substantially different terms, it shall be accounted for as:
- an extinguishment of the original liability; and
- the recognition of a new liability (financial).

Should a substantial modification of the terms of an existing financial liability or part thereof occur, it shall be accounted for as:
- an extinguishment of the original liability; and
- the recognition of a new liability (financial).

3. Initial measurement of financial assets and liabilities

When a financial asset or financial liability is recognised for the first time, an entity shall:
- measure it at fair value; and
- include transaction costs directly attributable to its acquisition or issue in the initial measurement of the financial assets and liabilities.

However, transaction costs will not be included at initial measurement for a financial asset or liability at fair value through profit or loss.

4. Subsequent measurement of financial assets

Refer again to the four different categories of financial assets and the two categories of liabilities identified just after the definitions in this chapter, before reading further. Three possibilities are available for subsequent measurement of financial assets:

Measurement at cost

The following financial assets will be measured at cost (not amortised cost or fair value):
- any financial asset that does not have a quoted market price in an active market and whose fair value cannot be reliably measured using other techniques to determine fair value; and
- derivatives that are linked to and must be settled by delivery of such unquoted equity instruments.

Measure at amortised cost (see definition)

The following types of financial asset are carried at amortised cost using the effective interest method subsequent to initial recognition (at cost plus transaction costs):
- loans and receivables not held for trading; and
- held-to-maturity investments.

Measure at fair value (see definition)

The following financial assets are carried at fair value (without deducting any transaction costs it may incur on sale or other disposal) subsequent to initial recognition:
- derivatives (refer to definitions);
- financial assets at fair value through profit or loss;[#] and
- available-for-sale financial assets.[*]

[*] Note that the gains or losses realised when subsequently measuring the carrying amount of these assets are taken directly to a mark-to-market reserve in equity. The latter reserve will be transferred to retained earnings via the income statement on derecognition of the asset.

[#] Note that an entity shall not reclassify a financial instrument into or out of the fair value through profit or loss category while it is held or issued. Fair value adjustments will go directly to profit or loss.

5. Subsequent measurement of financial liabilities

Two possibilities exist for subsequent measurement of financial liabilities:

Measure at fair value

The following financial liabilities are carried at fair value subsequent to initial recognition:
- derivatives (except if the derivative relates to an unquoted equity instrument when it shall be measured at cost); and
- financial liabilities at fair value through profit or loss.

Measure at amortised cost

All other liabilities are carried at amortised cost using the effective interest method.

6. Fair value

Fair value was defined earlier in this summary under definitions.

For a detailed discussion on fair value issues, refer to IAS 39 (AC 133), Appendix A, paragraphs .A69 – .A82.

In summary, situations where fair value can be reliably measured are:
- where there are quoted prices in an active market;
- where there is no active market, but other acceptable valuation techniques are used; and
- where there is no active market, but equity instruments can be valued accurately.

7. Recognition of fair value gains or losses

- Gains and losses on financial assets and liabilities classified as fair value through profit or loss are included in profit or loss for the period.
- Gains and losses on available-for-sale financial assets (other than for hedges) shall be included directly in equity through the statement of changes in equity. The reserve arising on the adjustment to fair value is called a mark-to-market reserve. On disposal, this gain or loss is recognised (recycled) in profit or loss for the period.
- Interest calculated on the effective interest method (if an interest-bearing item is classified as available for sale) and dividends received (on equity instruments), both relating to available-for-sale financial assets, are recognised in profit or loss.
- For detail rules on impairment for available-for-sale financial assets, see 9 below.

8. Subsequent measurement consideration specific to held-to-maturity investments

In general, IAS 39 considers fair value rather than amortised cost to be a more appropriate measurement basis for most financial assets. Refer to 4 under Background for detail guidance on when an asset will be classified as a held-to-maturity investment based on intent and ability.

An entity may no longer classify a financial asset as a held-to-maturity investment if the entity does not have the demonstrated ability to hold such an investment to maturity. This will be the case if:
- it does not have the financial resources available to continue to finance the investment until maturity; or
- it is subject to an existing legal or other constraint that could frustrate its intention to hold the financial asset to ability.

If, owing to a change in intent or ability, it is no longer appropriate to carry a held-to-maturity investment at amortised cost, it shall be reclassified as available-for-sale and remeasured at fair value. On reclassification from amortised cost to fair value, any gain or loss is accounted for directly in equity in the mark-to-market reserve, as would normally be the case for available-for-sale financial assets.

Should it for some reason become appropriate to carry a financial asset at amortised cost rather than fair value, the following will apply:
- On reclassification from fair value to amortised cost, use fair value at date of change as new cost or amortised cost and amortise differences in carrying amounts as if these are premiums or discounts using the effective interest method. If no maturity period, any gain/loss shall remain in equity until derecognition when it will be recognised in profit or loss.

9. Impairment and uncollectibility of financial assets

- At each balance sheet date (interim dates and at year-end), financial assets shall be assessed for impairment using objective evidence in respect of impairment of financial assets (see IAS 39.59 for detail guidance on such indications of impairment).
- The disappearance of an active market for an entity's financial instruments (instruments no longer traded publicly) does not represent an indication of impairment.

The treatment of impairment and collectibility of financial assets is split into three categories:

Financial assets carried at amortised cost

- If objective evidence exists that an impairment loss on loans and receivables or held-to-maturity investments (all carried at amortised cost) has been incurred:
  - The amount of the loss is the difference between the asset's carrying amount and its recoverable amount. The recoverable amount is the present value of estimated future cash flows (excluding credit

losses not yet incurred), discounted at the financial asset's original effective interest rate (determined at initial recognition).

- The carrying amount of such asset shall be reduced to recoverable amount either directly or through an allowance account.
- The impairment loss shall be recognised in profit or loss.
- If there is a reversal of a previous impairment loss related objectively to an event occurring after the previous impairment was recognised, the previously recognised impairment loss shall be reversed in the same manner as originally accounted for.
- The reversal of the impairment loss is limited to the amount that would increase the existing carrying amount to what the amortised cost of the asset would have been at this stage, had no impairment loss been recognised earlier.
- The amount of the reversal is recognised in profit or loss.

Financial assets carried at cost

- The amount of the impairment loss for such assets where there is objective evidence of impairment, is measured as the difference between the cost-based carrying amount and the present value of estimated future cash flows from the asset, discounted at the current market rate of return for a similar financial asset.
- Impairment losses on such assets are recognised in profit or loss.
- Such impairment losses may not be reversed.

Available-for-sale financial assets

- When the fair value of an available-for-sale financial asset has declined and this loss has been recognised directly in equity, this does not necessarily mean that the asset has been impaired.
- However, if there is objective evidence that the asset is impaired, such cumulative loss (debit) in equity shall be removed from equity and recognised in profit or loss, even though the asset has not been derecognised.
- The amount of the cumulative loss removed from equity and now recognised in profit or loss, is the difference between the acquisition cost (net of principal repayment and amortisation) and current fair value, less any impairment loss in respect of that asset recognised previously in profit or loss.
- Impairment losses recognised in profit or loss for an investment in an equity instrument (available-for-sale) shall not be reversed through profit or loss.
- In the case of a debt instrument (available-for-sale) where a reversal of an impairment loss recognised an profit or loss occurs due to a specific event, the reversal will be recognised in profit or loss.

10. Hedge accounting

Refer to the definitions of hedging, a hedged item and a hedging instrument as defined under 3 under Background. Note that hedging involves an appropriate gain/loss offset between changes in the fair value of, or cash flows attributable to, a hedging instrument and hedged item. Hedge accounting (a voluntary choice of accounting model) may only be applied if the hedging criteria are met.

Hedging instruments – qualifying instruments

- Generally speaking, derivatives will be used as hedging instruments, provided the hedging criteria have been met.
- A non-derivative financial asset or liability may be designated as a hedging instrument only for a hedge of a foreign currency risk.
- For hedge accounting purposes, only instruments that involve a party external to the reporting entity can be designated as a hedging instrument. This means that a hedging instrument in group context will only qualify if the other party falls outside the group. However, instruments within the group may qualify as hedging instruments in the separate financial statements of entities within the group.

Hedged items – qualifying instruments
- A hedged item can be:
  - a recognised asset or liability;
  - an unrecognised firm commitment;

- a highly probable forecast transaction; or
- a net investment in a foreign operation.
- Loans and receivables can be hedged items with interest rate and prepayment risk, but held-to-maturity investments cannot be hedged items for this type of risk.
- Held-to-maturity investments can be hedged items in the case of foreign exchange risk and credit risk.
- Hedged items can only be designated as hedged items if they involve a party external to the entity.
- Hedged items that are intragroup items may be designated as hedged items for foreign currency risk.

Designation of non-financial items as hedged items

If the hedged item is a non-financial asset or liability, it shall be designated as a hedged item for:
- foreign currency risk; or
- in its entirety for all risks.

Hedging relationships

- Fair value hedge: a hedge of exposure in changes of fair value of a recognised asset* or liability* or an unrecognised firm commitment*, or a part of the items marked (*), that is attributable to a specific risk and could affect the income statement (profit or loss).
- Cash flow hedge: a hedge of the exposure to variability in cash flows that is:
  - attributable to a particular risk associated with a recognised asset or liability (such as interest payments in the future on variable rate debt) or a highly probable forecast transaction; and
  - that could affect profit or loss.
- Hedge of a net investment in a foreign operation: a hedge of a reporting entity's interest in the net assets of another operation.
- A hedge of a foreign currency risk of a firm commitment may be accounted for as either a fair value hedge or a cash flow hedge.

Examples of the three types of hedging relationship:
- Fair value hedges: a hedge of exposure to changes in the fair value of fixed rate debt as a result of changes in interest rates.
- Cash flow hedges: a hedge of future foreign currency risk in an unrecognised contractual commitment for a fixed amount of foreign currency.
- A hedge of a net investment in a foreign entity.

Criteria for the application of special hedge accounting

A hedging relationship qualifies for special hedge accounting if the following apply:
- At the inception of the hedge, the hedging instrument is designated as such and there is formal documentation setting out the hedge details. An example would be a forward exchange contract.
- The hedge is expected to be highly effective in leading to offsetting changes in fair value or cash flows attributable to the hedged risk.
- In the case of a cash flow hedge for a forecasted transaction, the anticipated transaction must be highly probable, and variations must ultimately affect profit or loss.
- It is possible to reliably measure the effectiveness of the hedge.
- The hedge was effective throughout the reporting periods for which the hedge was designated and is assessed on an ongoing basis.

Accounting treatment of the different types of hedge

Fair value hedges

If a fair value hedge qualifies for hedge accounting by meeting the criteria for the application of special hedge accounting (see IAS 39.88), the fair value hedge shall be accounted for as follows:
- The gain or loss arising from remeasuring the hedging instruments at fair value (for a derivative instrument) or the foreign currency component of its carrying amount for a non-derivative hedging instrument, shall be recognised in profit or loss (the income statement).

- The gain or loss on the hedged item attributable to the hedged risk, shall be used to adjust the carrying amount of the hedged item and be recognised in profit or loss:
  - This is the case if the hedged item is otherwise measured at cost.
  - If the hedged item is an available-for-sale financial asset, the gain or loss on the hedged item shall also be recognised in profit or loss even though it would normally go directly to equity.
  - The discontinuance of hedge accounting is discussed in IAS 39.91 to .94.

Cash flow hedges

If a cash flow hedge qualifies for hedge accounting because it meets the criteria for the application of special hedge accounting (see IAS 39.88):
- The portion of the gain or loss on the hedging instrument that is determined to be an effective hedge is recognised directly in equity through the changes in equity statement. It is called either a deferred hedging gain or loss.
- The ineffective portion of the gain or loss on the hedging instrument is recognised in profit or loss.
- More specifically, the separate equity component (deferred hedging gain) recognised is adjusted to the lesser of the following:
  - the cumulative gain or loss on the hedging instrument from inception of the hedge; or
  - the cumulative change in fair value (present value) of the expected future cash flows on the hedged item from inception of the hedge.
- If hedge of a forecast transaction subsequently results in the recognition of a financial asset or liability:
  - The associated gains or losses that were recognised directly in equity (deferred hedging gain or loss) as a result of this being a cash flow hedge, shall be reclassified into (transferred to) profit or loss in the same period/periods during which the hedged item will affect profit or loss (for instance when interest income or expense is recognised in the income statement).
  - If an entity expects that all (or a portion) of the loss or gain recognised directly in the deferred hedging gain reserve will not be recovered in one or more accounting periods in the future, the amount not expected to be recovered, shall be taken to profit or loss immediately.@
- If hedge of a forecast transaction subsequently results in the recognition of a non-financial asset or liability, or a forecast transaction for a non-financial asset becomes a firm commitment for which fair value hedge accounting is applied, the entity shall adopt one of the two accounting policies set out below:
  - Reclassify associated gains and losses recognised directly in equity when applying normal cash flow hedge accounting rules, into profit or loss in the same period or periods during which the asset acquired or liability assumed affects profit or loss (e.g. when depreciation or cost of sales is recognised). Also apply (@) here.
  - Remove the associated gains and losses that were recognised directly in equity when applying normal cash flow hedge accounting rules, and include them in the initial cost or other carrying amount of the asset or liability (this is called the basis adjustment).
  - Whichever accounting policy is selected, it shall be applied consistently to all hedges discussed under this heading.
- For cash flow hedges other than those for financial and non-financial assets and liabilities, amounts recognised directly in equity shall be recognised in profit or loss in the same period or periods during which the forecast transaction affects profit or loss.
- The discontinuance of cash flow hedges is discussed at length in IAS 39.101(a) – (d).

Hedge of net investment in a foreign entity
- This type of hedge is accounted for in the same way as a cash flow hedge. The effective portion of the gain or loss is recognised in equity, while the ineffective portion is included in profit and loss.
- The gain or loss recognised directly in equity (effective portion) shall be recognised in profit or loss on disposal of the foreign operation.

DISCLOSURE

Disclosure is no longer addressed in IAS 39, but has been transferred to IFRS 7 (AC 144). In addition, disclosure no longer forms part of the financial accounting syllabus for QE1 of SAICA.

IAS 40 *(AC 135)* and SIC 21 *(AC 421)*

Investment Property

❑ **SUMMARY**

Background
Accounting practice
Disclosure
SIC 21: Income taxes – recovery of revalued non-depreciable assets

BACKGROUND

The standard prescribes the accounting treatment for investment property, but does not deal with matters covered in IAS 17 (AC 105) (Leases).

Investment property is defined as property, land or buildings or part of it, held by the owner or by a lessee under a finance lease, to earn rentals and/or for capital appreciation, rather than for:

- the use of the asset in the production or supply of goods or services or for administrative purposes; or
- the sale of the asset in the ordinary course of the business.

Owner-occupied property is property held by the owner or by a lessee under a finance lease, for use in the production or supply of goods or services or for administrative purposes, for example, an office building occupied by the employees of an entity.

Fair value is the amount for which an asset could be exchanged between knowledgeable, willing parties in an arm's length transaction.

Cost is the amount of cash or cash equivalents paid or the fair value of other consideration given to acquire the asset at the time of its acquisition or construction.

Carrying amount is the amount at which the asset is presented in the balance sheet.

Judgement is needed to determine whether a property qualifies as investment property. An investment property generates cash flows largely independently of the other assets held by an entity. The following are examples of investment properties:

- land held for long-term capital appreciation;
- a building owned by an entity and leased out under one or more operating leases;
- land held for a currently undetermined future use – it is considered to be held for capital appreciation; and
- a vacant building that is held to be leased out under one or more operating leases.

Certain properties include a portion that qualifies as an investment property and another portion which qualifies as an owner-occupied property. If these portions could be sold separately or leased out separately under a finance lease, an entity accounts for the portions separately. If the portions could not be sold separately, the property will only be accounted for as an investment property if the owner-occupied portion is an insignificant portion.

A property interest that is held by a lessee under an operating lease can be classified and accounted for as an investment property, provided the property would otherwise meet the definition of an investment property (held to earn rentals). The lessee uses the fair value model to account for the asset recognised.

The classification is available on a property-by-property basis, but once this classification alternative is selected for a property interest held under an operating lease, all qualifying investment property will be carried under the fair value model.

The decision tree on the next page summarises which accounting standard applies to various kinds of property.

ACCOUNTING PRACTICE

1. Recognition

Investment property shall be recognised as an asset when:

- it is probable that the future economic benefits associated with the investment property will flow to the entity; and
- the cost of the investment property can be measured reliably.

THE APPLICATION OF ACCOUNTING STANDARDS TO VARIOUS KINDS OF PROPERTY

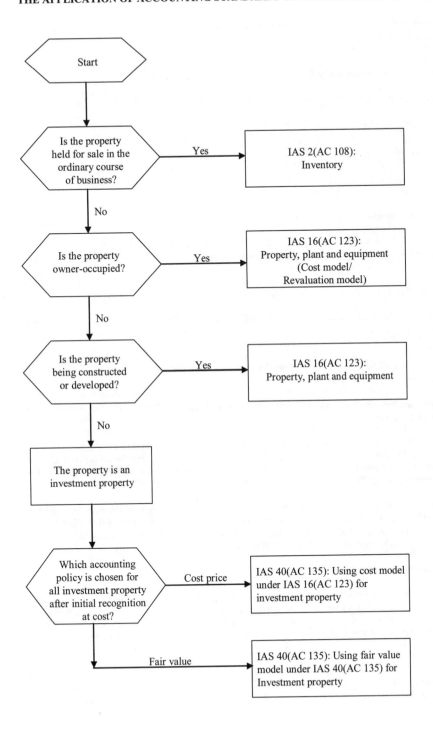

2. Measurement

2.1 Initial measurement

At cost, including transaction costs at initial measurement.

The cost of a self-constructed investment property is the cost thereof at date of completion.

If payment for the property is deferred beyond normal credit terms, the cost is the cash price equivalent.

The initial cost of a property interest held under an operating lease and classified as an investment property, shall be determined as for a finance lease in terms of IAS 17 (AC 105) at the lower of:
- the fair value of property; and
- the present value of minimum lease payments.

Exchanges of investment properties are treated the same as for PPE (see IAS 16 (AC 123)).

2.2 Subsequent measurement

Investment property shall be carried at either the fair value or at cost less accumulated depreciation and accumulated impairment losses. An entity shall select an accounting policy and shall apply that policy to all its investment properties.

2.2.1 Fair value model

Fair value is measured at the most probable price reasonably obtainable in the market at balance sheet date in an arm's length transaction between knowledgeable, willing parties. The fair value reflects market conditions at balance sheet date. Future transaction costs are excluded from the fair value.

When a property interest held by a lessee under an operating lease is classified as an investment property, the fair value model shall be applied – there is no choice.

The profit or loss arising with the fair value adjustment of investment property shall be included in profit or loss for the period in which it arises.

The best evidence of fair value is normally given by current prices on an active market for similar property in similar circumstances (location, condition and so on). In the absence of current prices on an active market, an entity considers information from a variety of sources, for example, recent prices on less active markets, recent prices on an active market for different properties after adjustment, and discounted cash flows.

In determining the fair value of investment property, double accounting for assets and liabilities must be avoided. For example, if an office building is leased on a furnished basis, the fair value of the office building generally includes the fair value of the furniture, because the rental income relates to the furnished office. The furniture shall therefore not be recognised as a separate asset in accordance with IAS 16 (AC 123).

Inability to measure fair value reliably

There is a rebuttable presumption that an entity will be able to determine the fair value of an investment property reliably on a continuing basis. If, however, in exceptional cases there is clear evidence that an entity will not be able to determine the fair value reliably, an entity is compelled to measure the investment property using the cost model. All other investment property is still measured at fair value, if that accounting policy was selected.

2.2.2 Cost model

After initial recognition investment property is measured by using the cost model in IAS 16 (AC 123) (Property, Plant and Equipment);1 that is, at cost less any accumulated depreciation and accumulated impairment losses.

3. Transfers

Transfers to or from investment property shall only be made when there is a change in the use of the property. For detail refer to IAS 40 (AC 135) .57.

4. Derecognition

The carrying amount of an investment property is derecognised on disposal or when the investment property is permanently withdrawn from use and no future economic benefits are expected from its disposal.

The gain or loss arising from the derecognition of the investment property shall be determined as the difference between the disposal proceeds and the carrying amount of the relevant asset and shall be recognised as income or expense in profit or loss for the period (the income statement).

5. Compensation from third parties

- Compensation from third parties arising from investment property that was impaired, lost or given up, shall be recognised in profit or loss when the compensation becomes receivable.
- The losses or impairment of assets, the compensation received from third parties to compensate for these losses and the acquisition of replacement assets are all separately accounted for, as they are separate economic events.

DISCLOSURE

Accounting policies

- Whether it applies the cost model or fair value model.
- If the fair value model is applied, whether and under which circumstances property interests held under operating leases are classified and disclosed as investment property.
- When classification is difficult, the criteria developed by the entity to distinguish investment property from owner-occupied property and property held for sale in the ordinary course of business.
- The methods and significant assumptions applied in determining the fair value of investment property, including a statement whether the determination of the fair value was supported by market evidence or based on other factors (disclose these factors) (can also be disclosed in the investment property balance sheet note).
- If an independent valuer was involved in determining the fair value and to what extent.
- If no independent valuation was done, state the fact (can also be disclosed in the investment property balance sheet note).

Balance sheet and notes thereto

- The following will be disclosed whether the investment property is measured at cost or at fair value:
  - the existence and amounts of restrictions on the realisability or the remittance of income and proceeds of disposals;
  - material contractual obligations to purchase, construct or develop investment property; and
  - investment property mortgaged as security.
- When investment property is measured at fair value, the following shall also be disclosed:
  - detailed reconciliation of the carrying amount at the beginning and end of the period.
  - If the fair value could not be measured reliably and the investment property was measured at cost, amounts relating to this property shall be disclosed separately from other investment property. Further additional disclosure for this property is required, as follows:
    - a description of the property;
    - an explanation why fair value cannot be determined reliably;
    - if possible, the range of estimates within which fair value will probably be; and
    - certain disclosures on disposal.
- When a valuation obtained with a view to disclosing investment property in the balance sheet is adjusted significantly for purposes of the financial statements, for instance to avoid double counting, an entity shall disclose a reconciliation between the value obtained and the adjusted valuation shown in the balance sheet. Show separately the aggregate amount of any lease obligations added back and other significant adjustments.
- When investment property is measured at cost, the following shall also be disclosed:
  - depreciation methods used – can also be disclosed in accounting policy note;
  - useful lives or depreciation rates used – can also be disclosed in accounting policy note;
  - the gross carrying amount and the accumulated depreciation at the beginning and end of the period;

- detailed reconciliation of the carrying amount at the beginning and end of the period; and
- the fair value of the investment property.

Income statement and notes thereto

- Disclose the amounts included in the income statement for:
  - rental income received;
  - direct operating expenses for investment property generating rental income; and
  - direct operating expenses for investment property not generating rental income.

SIC 21: INCOME TAXES – RECOVERY OF REVALUED NON-DEPRECIABLE ASSETS

Refer to the chapter on IAS 12 (AC 102) for a summary of this interpretation.

IFRS 1 *(AC 138)*

First-time Adoption of IFRS

Not addressed.

IFRS 2 *(AC 139)*

Share-based Payment

❑ **SUMMARY**

Background
Accounting treatment
Disclosure

1. BACKGROUND

Entities often grant shares or share options to employees or other parties, for instance suppliers (such as suppliers of professional services). Share option plans and share plans are a common phenomenon of employee remuneration, especially for directors and senior executives. Many of the Black Economic Empowerment deals also make use of shares and share options to enable previously disadvantaged individuals to become owners in an entity, irrespective of whether they are employees of the entity. There was no IFRS standard that dealt with the measurement and recognition of these transactions until IFRS 2 (AC 139) was issued. Because of the popular use of this type of transactions in many countries it was a gap in IFRS that needed to be filled.

The standard defines three types of share-based payment transaction:

- An **equity-settled share-based payment transaction** is a transaction in which the entity receives goods or services as consideration for equity instruments of the entity (i.e. shares and share options).
- A **cash-settled share-based payment transaction** is a transaction in which the entity acquires goods or services by incurring liabilities to the supplier of those goods or services for amounts that are based on the price (or value) of the entity's shares or other equity instruments of the entity.
- Transactions in which the entity receives or acquires goods or services and the terms of the arrangement provide either the entity or the supplier of the goods or services with a choice of whether the entity settles the transaction in cash or by issuing equity instruments.

2. ACCOUNTING TREATMENT

2.1 General

When an entity makes use of a share-based payment, the entity is required to reflect the effects of the share-based payment transaction in its profit or loss and on its financial position. This includes expenses associated with the share-based payment transaction with employees.

2.2 Recognition

The goods or services received or acquired in a share-based payment transaction will be recognised by the entity on the date it obtains the goods or services. If it is an equity-settled share-based payment transaction, a corresponding increase in equity needs to be recognised. If, however, it is a cash-settled share-based payment transaction, a corresponding increase in liabilities will be recognised by the entity.

If the goods or services received in a share-based payment transaction do not meet the definition of an asset, it will be recognised as expenses.

2.3 Equity-settled share-based payment transactions

For equity-settled share-based payment transactions with parties other than employees there is a rebuttable presumption in the standard that the fair value of the goods or services can be estimated reliably. Therefore, the entity will measure the goods or services received and the corresponding increase in equity directly at the fair value of the goods or services received, and will measure the transaction on the date the entity obtains the goods or the counterparty renders the services.

For equity-settled share-based payment transactions with employees, it is impossible to reliably estimate the fair value of the services the employee renders, because it is linked to a remuneration package. Therefore, the entity will measure the goods or services received and the corresponding increase in equity indirectly by reference to the fair value of the equity instruments granted and will measure the transaction on grant date (the date the entity and another party agree to a share-based payment arrangement).

Transactions measured by reference to the fair value of the equity instruments granted

Determining the fair value of equity instruments granted

An entity will use the market price of the equity instruments to measure its fair value, after taking into account the terms and conditions of the share-based payment. If the market price is not available the fair value of the equity instruments will be determined by using a valuation technique.

Vesting conditions

A grant of equity instruments may be subject to vesting conditions. Vesting conditions are those conditions that must be satisfied before the counterparty becomes entitled to receive the equity instruments. Vesting conditions include service conditions and performance conditions.

Performance conditions can either be a market condition (market price of shares) or a non-market condition (i.e. growth in profit or EPS). If the performance condition is a market condition it is taken into account when estimating the fair value of the equity instruments granted. If the performance condition is a non-market condition it is not taken into account when estimating the fair value of the equity instruments granted, but will have an effect on the vesting period itself.

After vesting date

After receiving the goods or services and raising the corresponding increase in equity the entity will not make any subsequent adjustments to total equity. The entity may however make transfers within equity.

Modifications to the terms and conditions on which equity instruments were granted including cancellations and settlements

Irrespective of any modifications to the terms and conditions on which the equity instruments were granted, an entity will as a minimum recognise the services received at the fair value at grant date. The entity will further recognise the additional effects of beneficial modifications (increase in total fair value of the share-based payment or otherwise more beneficial to the employee) over the remaining vesting period from the date of the modification until vesting date. This is also applicable to share-based payment transactions with parties other than employees.

If a grant of equity instruments is cancelled or settled by the entity during the vesting period, the entity will account for the cancellation or settlement as an acceleration of vesting. This means that the entity will recognise immediately the amount that would have been recognised over the remaining vesting period for services received. If the entity makes a payment to the employee for cancellation or settlement of the grant, that payment will be treated as a repurchase of an equity interest.

If the entity repurchases equity instruments from an employee that has already vested, such payment will be accounted for as a deduction from equity. Any excess of the payment above the fair value of the equity instruments will be expensed.

2.4 Cash-settled share-based payment transactions

The entity will measure the goods or services obtained and the liability incurred in a cash-settled share-based payment transaction at the fair value of the liability. The entity will remeasure the fair value of the liability at each reporting date and at the settlement date until the liability is settled. Any changes in the fair value of the liability will be recognised in profit or loss for the period. The cash-settled share-based payment transaction will be recognised over the vesting period if applicable.

2.5 Share-based payment transactions with cash alternatives

Entity has choice of settlement

When the terms of a share-based payment transaction provides the entity with the choice of cash or equity settlement, the entity will account for the grant as a cash-settled share-based payment transaction if the entity has incurred an obligation to settle in cash. If the entity has no obligation to settle in cash, the entity will account for the grant as an equity-settled share-based payment transaction.

The entity has a present obligation to settle in cash if:
- settlement in equity instruments has no commercial substance;
- the entity has a past practice or stated policy of settling in cash; or
- generally settles in cash on request of the counterparty.

Counterparty has choice of settlement

If the counterparty was granted the right to choose whether the entity should settle the grant in cash or by issuing equity instruments, the entity has granted a compound financial instrument that consists of a debt and an equity component. The share-based payment transaction should be accounted for in its components. To the extent the entity has incurred a liability to settle in cash, a cash-settled share-based payment transaction should be accounted for; and to the extent that no such liability has been incurred an equity-settled share-based payment transaction should be accounted for.

For transactions with parties other than employees (fair value of goods or services measured directly) the entity will measure the equity component of the compound financial instrument as the difference between the fair value of the goods or services received and the fair value of the debt component. Measurement takes place on the date the goods or services are received.

For transactions with employees, the entity will measure the fair value of the compound financial instrument as follows:
- Firstly, measure the fair value of the debt component.
- Secondly, measure the fair value of the equity component.
- The fair value of the compound financial instrument is the sum of the two components.

3. DISCLOSURE

Disclose information to enable the users of the financial statements to understand the nature and extent of the share-based payment transactions that existed during the period:
- A description, including the general terms and conditions, of each type of share-based payment transaction that existed at any time during the period.
- For each of the following groups of options the number of weighted average exercise prices of share options:
  - outstanding at the beginning op the period;
  - granted during the period;
  - forfeited during the period;
  - exercised during the period;
  - expired during the period;
  - outstanding at the end of the period; and
  - exercisable at the end of the period.
- The weighted average share price at the date of exercise for share options exercised during the period.
- The range of exercise prices and weighted average remaining contractual life for share options outstanding at the end of the period.

Disclose information that will enable the users of the financial statements to understand how the fair value of the goods or services received, or the fair value of the equity instruments granted during the period, was determined:
- If the fair value of the goods or services received was measured indirectly with reference to the fair value of the equity instruments granted:
  - for share options granted during the period, the weighted average fair value of those options at the measurement date as well as information on how that fair value was determined;
  - for other equity instruments granted during the period, the number and weighted average fair value at the measurement date as well as information as to how that fair value was measured; and
  - for share-based payment transactions that were modified during the period, an explanation of those modifications, the incremental fair value granted and information as to how the incremental fair value granted was measured.
- If the fair value of the goods or services received during the period was measured directly the entity needs to disclose how that fair value was determined.
- If the presumption was rebutted that, for share-based payment transactions with parties other than employees, the fair value of the goods or services acquired can be determined reliably, disclose that fact and give an explanation of why the presumption was rebutted.

IFRS 3 *(AC 140)*

Business Combinations

❑ **SUMMARY**

Background
Accounting treatment
Disclosure

1. BACKGROUND

The objective of this statement is to prescribe the accounting treatment of business combinations by an entity under an acquisition.

Accounting for an acquisition involves:
- the determination of the cost of the acquisition;
- the allocation of the cost of the investment over the identifiable assets, liabilities and contingent liabilities of the entity being acquired;
- accounting for the goodwill or negative goodwill (excess of net assets over cost of the business combination) arising from allocating the cost of the investment, both at acquisition and subsequently;
- the determination of the minority interest amount;
- accounting for acquisitions which occur over a period of time;
- accounting for subsequent changes in the cost of acquisition or in the identification of assets and liabilities; and
- the disclosures required.

Amongst other possibilities, a business combination may result in a parent–subsidiary relationship in which the acquirer is the parent and the acquiree is the subsidiary. In such circumstances the acquirer applies this statement in its consolidated financial statements. The parent includes its interest in the acquiree (the subsidiary) in its separate financial statements as an investment in a subsidiary (see IAS 27 (AC 132)).

A business combination which involves the purchase of the net assets (including goodwill) of another entity, instead of shares in another entity, does not result in a parent–subsidiary relationship.

IFRS 3 does not deal with:
- the separate financial statements of a parent;
- transactions among entities under common control; and
- interests in joint ventures and the financial statements of joint ventures.

Several definitions used in this standard are also encountered in IAS 27 (AC 132). Since definitions are very technical, they are virtually quoted from IFRS 3 (AC 140). Only those not specified in IAS 27 (AC 132) are set out below:
- A **business combination** is the bringing together of separate entities or businesses into one reporting entity as a result of one entity obtaining control over the net assets and operations of another entity.
- An **acquisition** is a business combination in which one of the entities (the acquirer) obtains control over the net assets and operations of another entity (the acquiree) in exchange for the transfer of assets, incurrence of a liability or issue of equity.
- **Date of acquisition** is the date on which control of the net assets and operations of the acquiree is effectively transferred to the acquirer.
- **Date of exchange** is the date on which each individual investment in shares is recognised in the financial statements of the acquirer.

2. ACCOUNTING TREATMENT

2.1 General

- A business combination is classified as an acquisition and shall be accounted for on the purchase method of accounting. The use of the purchase method results in an acquisition of an entity being accounted for similarly to the purchase of other assets.
- The application of the purchase method involves the following:
  - identifying an acquirer;
  - measuring the cost of the business combination; and
  - allocating the cost of the business combination to the assets acquired and liabilities and contingent liabilities assumed, at the date of the acquisition.

2.2 Identifying an acquirer

- An acquirer must be identified for all business combinations, and the acquirer is the entity that obtains control over the other combining entities or businesses.

2.3 Cost of a business combination

- The cost of a business combination (BC) shall be measured by the acquirer as the aggregate of:
  - the fair values of assets given, liabilities incurred or assumed and equity instruments issued by the acquirer, in exchange for control of the acquiree (all at date of exchange); plus
  - any costs that can be attributed directly to the BC.
- When a business combination involves more than one exchange transaction, the cost of the BC would be the aggregate cost of the individual transactions.
- When an acquisition is achieved in stages, accounting for the acquisition will commence as from the date of acquisition (date control is obtained), but the costs and fair value information determined at the date of each exchange transaction (date each individual investment is recognised by acquirer) will be used.
- Assets given and liabilities incurred or assumed (contingent or otherwise) are measured at their fair value at the date of the exchange transaction.
- If settlement of the purchase consideration is deferred, the cost of acquisition is the present value of the consideration and not the nominal value thereof.
- When equity instruments are issued by the acquirer as consideration for an acquisition, these securities are measured at their fair value – market price as at the date of the exchange transaction.
- Direct costs incurred in relation to the acquisition include professional fees paid to accountants, legal advisors, valuers and other consultants to effect the acquisition.
- The cost of issuing equity instruments and arranging and issuing financial liabilities are, even though they may be associated directly with the BC, not part of the cost of the BC, but forms an integral part of the equity and liability issue transactions.
- General administrative costs and other costs not directly attributable to a particular acquisition are not included in the cost of acquisition, but are recognised as an expense when incurred.

2.4 Allocation of the cost of a business combination to assets acquired, liabilities incurred and contingent liabilities assumed

- The acquirer identified in a BC shall, at acquisition date, allocate the cost of the business combination (BC) by recognising the following at their fair value at that date:
  - identifiable assets;
  - identifiable liabilities; and
  - contingent liabilities.
- An exception to the above list would be non-current assets that were classified as held for sale in terms of IFRS 5 (AC 142) even at date of acquisition. These items will be recognised at fair value less costs to sell.
- Any difference between the cost of the BC (see 2.3) and the acquirer's interest in the net fair value of identifiable assets, liabilities and contingent liabilities, shall be identified as either goodwill or negative goodwill (old term) – now called 'excess of acquirer's interest in net fair value of acquiree's identifiable assets, liabilities and contingent liabilities over cost.' For the sake of brevity the phrase in inverted commas will be called 'excess over net fair values'.
- Identifiable assets, liabilities and contingent liabilities of the acquiree will only be recognised separately at acquisition date, if they satisfy the following criteria at that date:
  - In the case of identifiable assets other than an intangible asset:
    - the associated future economic benefits will probably flow to the entity; and
    - its fair value can be determined (measured) reliably.
  - In the case of an identifiable liability other than a contingent liability:
    - an outflow of resources embodying economic benefits will be required to settle the obligation; and
    - its fair value can be determined (measured) reliably.
  - In the case of intangible assets and contingent liabilities:
    - The fair value can be determined (measured) reliably.
- In the acquirer's income statement, the acquiree's profits and losses after acquisition date will be included after adjusting these amounts for the effect of the allocated cost of identifiable items as allocated per the cost of the BC.

- The application of the purchase method commences from acquisition date; that is, the date on which the acquirer obtains control of the acquiree.
- Because the acquirer shall recognise the acquiree's identifiable assets, liabilities and contingent liabilities at their fair value at acquisition date, minority interests in the consolidated financial statements will also be based on these amounts.

2.5 Goodwill arising on acquisition

Recognition and measurement

- On date of acquisition, the purchaser shall:
  - recognise as an asset, goodwill acquired in the BC; and
  - measure goodwill at cost initially.
- The cost of goodwill is the excess of the cost price of the BC over and above the acquirer's interest in the net fair value of identifiable assets, liabilities and contingent liabilities.
- Recognition of goodwill as an asset is justified as goodwill arising on acquisition represents a payment made by the acquirer in anticipation of future economic benefits.
- Goodwill shall, after initial recognition, be carried at cost less any accumulated impairment losses.

2.6 Excess of acquirer's interest in the net fair value of acquirer's identifiable assets, liabilities and contingent liabilities over cost of the BC

- Should the acquirer's interest in the net fair value of identifiable assets, liabilities and contingent liabilities be more than the cost of the BC, the acquirer shall:
  - reconsider and check the identification and measurement of the identifiable assets, liabilities and contingent liabilities of the acquiree as well as the measurement of the cost of the BC; and
  - once reassessed and satisfied, recognise such remaining excess immediately in profit or loss.

2.7 Adjustments to the purchase consideration contingent on future events – immediately and subsequently

- If the BC agreement allows an adjustment to the purchase consideration contingent on one or more future events, the amount of the adjustment should be included in the cost of the acquisition at the date of acquisition, provided the adjustment is probable and the amount can be measured reliably.
- If a contingency affecting the amount of the purchase consideration is resolved subsequent to the date of acquisition, the cost of acquisition should be adjusted, provided payment of the amount to the acquirer is probable and a reliable estimate of the amount can be made. (For details refer to IFRS 3.32 – .35).

2.8 Initial accounting determined provisionally

For detail on this matter, see IFRS 3.61 – .64.

2.9 Taxes on income

For detail on this matter, see IFRS 3.65.

3. DISCLOSURE

- An acquirer shall disclose sufficient information to enable users of its financial statements to evaluate the nature and financial effect of BCs that were executed:
  - during the period; and
  - after the balance sheet date but before the financial statements are authorised for issue.
- The acquirer shall disclose the following information for each BC that was effected during the period:[*]
  - of the combining entities or businesses – the names and descriptions;
  - the date of acquisition;
  - the percentage of voting equity instruments acquired;
  - the cost of the BC as well as a description of the components making up that cost, including any costs directly attributable to the BC. If equity instruments are issued or issuable as part of the cost, the following must be disclosed:

- equity instruments issued or issuable – the number ; and
- the fair value of these equity instruments and the basis used for determining that fair value. Should a published price not exist for the instruments at the date of exchange, the significant assumptions used to determine fair value must be disclosed. If a published price does exist at the date of exchange but was not used when determining the cost of the BC, that fact shall be disclosed together with:
  - the reasons the published price was not used;
  - the method and significant assumptions that were used to attribute a value to the equity instruments; and
  - the aggregate amount of the difference between the value attributed to, and the published price of, the equity instruments.
- in the case of any operations the entity has decided to dispose of as a result of the combination – the details;
- in the case of each class of the acquiree's assets, liabilities and contingent liabilities, the amounts recognised at the acquisition date and, provided disclosure would not be impracticable, the carrying amounts of each of those classes, as they were determined in accordance with IRFSs (ACs), immediately before the combination. If such disclosure would be impracticable, this fact must be disclosed, as well as an explanation as to why this is the case;
- the amount of any excess (old negative goodwill) that was recognised in profit or loss immediately as well as the line item in profit or loss in which the excess is recognised;
- a description of the factors that contributed to a cost that results in the recognition of goodwill:
  - a description of each intangible asset that was not recognised separately from goodwill and an explanation of why the intangible asset's fair value could not be measured reliably; or
  - a description of the nature of any excess (old negative goodwill) recognised in profit or loss immediately;
- the amount of the acquiree's profit or loss since the acquisition date that was included in the acquirer's profit or loss for the period, provided such disclosure would not be impracticable. If such disclosure would be impracticable, this fact shall be disclosed, together with an explanation of as to why this is the case.

Everything marked * shall be disclosed in aggregate for BCs effected during the period that are not (individually) material.

- Should the initial accounting for a business combination effected during the current period be determined only provisionally (see 2.8), this fact shall also be disclosed in conjunction with an explanation as to why this is the case.
- The acquirer in a BC shall disclose the following information, provided such disclosure would not be impracticable, in respect of the income statement:[#]
  - the revenue of the combined entity for the period as though the acquisition date for all business combinations effected during the period had been the beginning of that period; and
  - the profit or loss of the combined entity for the period as though the acquisition date for all business combinations effected during the period had been the beginning of the period.

Should disclosure of this information (marked #) prove to be impracticable, this fact shall be disclosed, in conjunction with an explanation as to why this is the case.

- The acquirer shall disclose the information required by paragraph marked (*) for each business combination effected after the balance sheet date, but before the financial statements are authorised for issue, provided such disclosure would not be impracticable.If disclosure of any of that information would be impracticable, this fact shall be disclosed, in conjunction with an explanation of why this is the case.

- An acquirer must disclose information to enable users of its financial statements to evaluate the financial effects of gains, losses, corrections of errors and other adjustments recognised in the current period that relate to BCs that were effected in the current or in previous periods. Consequently, the acquirer shall disclose the following information:
  - The amount as well as an explanation of any gain or loss recognised in the current period that:
    - is related to the identifiable assets acquired or liabilities or contingent liabilities assumed in a BC effected in the current or a previous period; and
    - is of such size, nature or incidence that disclosure will be relevant to an understanding of the combined entity's financial performance.
  - If the initial accounting for a business combination effected in the immediately preceding period was determined only provisionally at the end of that period, the amounts and explanations of the adjustments to the provisional values recognised during the current period.
  - The information about corrections or errors that shall be disclosed in terms of IAS 8 (AC 103) for any of the acquiree's identifiable assets, liabilities or contingent liabilities, or changes in the values assigned to those items, that the acquirer recognises during the current period in accordance with 2.7.
- Information enabling users of financial statements to evaluate changes in the carrying amount of goodwill during the period, shall be disclosed. Consequently, the entity shall disclose a reconciliation of the carrying amount of goodwill at the beginning and end of the period, indicating separately:
  - the gross amount of accumulated impairment losses at the beginning of the period;
  - any additional goodwill recognised during the period, with the exception of goodwill included in a disposal group that, on acquisition, meets the criteria to be classified as held for sale in accordance with IFRS 5 (AC 142);
  - any adjustments resulting from the subsequent recognition of deferred tax assets during the period in accordance with 2.9;
  - any goodwill included in a disposal group classified as held for sale in accordance with IFRS 5 (AC 142) and goodwill derecognised during the period without having previously been included in a disposal group classified as held for sale;
  - any impairment losses recognised during the period in accordance with IAS 36 (AC 128);[@]
  - net exchange differences arising during the period in accordance with IAS 21 (AC 112);
  - any other changes in the carrying amount during the period; and
  - the gross amount and accumulated impairment losses at the end of the period.
- The entity shall disclose information about the recoverable amount as well as impairment of goodwill in accordance with IAS 36 (AC 128) in addition to the information required to be disclosed by the paragraph marked with (@).
- If in any situation the information required to be disclosed by this IFRS (AC) does not satisfy the main objectives set out earlier, the entity shall disclose such additional information as is necessary to meet those objectives.

IFRS 5 *(AC 142)*

Non-current Assets Held for Sale and Discontinued Operations

❑ **SUMMARY**

Non-current assets held for sale
Background
Accounting practice
Presentation and disclosure

Discontinued operations
Presentation and disclosure

BACKGROUND – NON-CURRENT ASSETS HELD FOR SALE

1. Objective

IFRS 5 specifies the accounting treatment of assets held for sale, as well as the presentation and disclosure requirements relating to discontinued operations.

2. Other

The standard deals specifically with non-current assets and disposal groups. A disposal group is a group of assets to be disposed of, by sale or otherwise, together as a group in a single transaction, as well as liabilities associated with those assets that will be transferred in the same transaction.

Two types of requirement feature in this standard, namely:
- the classification and presentation requirements; and
- and measurement requirements.

Classification and presentation requirements of this standard apply to all non-current assets and disposal groups of an entity. These requirements deal with the stage at which assets should be classified as held for sale, as well as how these assets should be presented in the financial statements.

The measurement requirements of this standard apply to all recognised non-current assets and disposal groups, except for the following assets, which are deemed to fall outside the measurement requirements of IFRS 5:
- deferred tax assets (IAS 12 (AC 102);
- assets arising from employee benefits (IAS 19 (AC 116);
- financial assets within the scope of IAS 39 (AC 133); and
- non-current assets that are accounted for in accordance with the fair value model in IAS 40 (AC 135).

The measurement requirements deal with the determination of the carrying amount of the related assets.

3. Classification of non-current assets or disposal groups as held for sale

A non-current asset (or disposal group) is classified as held for sale if its carrying amount will be recovered principally through a sale transaction, rather than through continuing use.

For this classification to be made, the following two conditions should be complied with:
- The asset (or disposal group) must be available for immediate sale in its present condition.
- Its sale must be highly probable. This will be the case if the following is true:
  - The appropriate level of management is committed to a plan to sell the asset (or disposal group), and an active programme to locate a buyer and complete the plan has been initiated.
  - In addition, the asset (or disposal group) must be actively marketed at a reasonable price (compared to its current fair value).
  - The sale should be expected to be completed within one year from the date of classification.
  - All indications should be that it is unlikely that significant changes to the plan will be made or that the plan will be withdrawn.

Non-current assets or disposal groups that are to be abandoned will not be classified as held for sale.

ACCOUNTING PRACTICE – NON-CURRENT ASSETS HELD FOR SALE

1. Measurement of a non-current asset or disposal group

- Immediately before the initial classification of an asset (or disposal group) as held for sale, the carrying amount of the asset (or all the assets and liabilities in the group) is measured in accordance with the Statements of GAAP applicable to the specific assets or liabilities.
- Immediately after classification as held for sale, the asset (or disposal group) is measured at the lower of its carrying amount and fair value less costs to sell.
- Fair value is the amount for which an asset could be exchanged, or a liability settled, between knowledgeable, willing parties in an arm's length transaction.

- Costs to sell refer to the incremental costs directly attributable to the disposal of an asset (or disposal group), excluding finance costs and income tax expense related to the disposal transaction.
- If the asset (or disposal group) is still unsold at year-end, it should again be remeasured to the lower of its carrying amount and fair value less costs to sell.
- On subsequent remeasurement of a disposal group, the carrying amounts of any assets and liabilities not within the measurement scope of IFRS 5, which are included in the disposal group, shall be remeasured in accordance with their applicable Statements of GAAP, before the fair value less costs to sell of the disposal group is remeasured.[#]

2. Recognition of impairment losses

- An impairment loss is recognised for any initial or subsequent write-down of an asset or disposal group from carrying amount to fair value less costs to sell, to the extent that it has not been recognised in accordance with the paragraph marked (#) under the previous heading.
- An impairment loss related to an individual non-current asset will reduce the carrying amount of only this asset to fair value less costs to sell and an impairment loss will be recognised.
- An impairment loss related to a disposal group will reduce the carrying amounts of only the non-current assets in the group that are within the scope of the measurement requirements of IFRS 5, in this order:
  - first against goodwill, if included in the disposal group; and
  - then against other assets in the disposal group, pro rata based on their carrying amounts.

3. Recognition of reversals of impairment losses

- If there is a subsequent increase in an asset's fair value less costs to sell, the entity should recognise a gain for any such increase, but not in excess of the cumulative impairment loss that has previously been recognised in terms of IFRS 5 or IAS 36 (AC 128) (Impairment of assets). A reversal of an impairment loss related to an individual non-current asset will therefore increase the old fair value less costs to sell to the new fair value less costs to sell, but not in excess of the cumulative impairment loss that had been recognised, either in accordance with IFRS 5 or previously in accordance with IAS 36 (AC 128).
- If there is a subsequent increase in a disposal group's fair value less costs to sell, an entity shall recognise a gain for any such increase:
  - to the extent that it has not been recognised for assets outside the measurement scope of IFRS 5; but
  - not in excess of the cumulative impairment loss that has been recognised, either in accordance with IFRS 5 or previously in accordance with IAS 36 (AC 128), on the non-current assets that are within the measurement scope of IFRS 5 (AC 142). This gain should be allocated to the non-current assets within the measurement scope of IFRS 5, excluding goodwill.

4. Other matters

- A gain or loss not yet recognised by the date of sale of a non-current asset or disposal group, shall be recognised when the asset or disposal group is sold.
- An entity shall not depreciate a non-current asset while it is classified as held for sale or while it forms part of a disposal group that is classified as held for sale.
- Interest and other expenses attributable to the liabilities of a disposal group classified as held for sale, will continue to be recognised.

PRESENTATION AND DISCLOSURE – NON-CURRENT ASSETS HELD FOR SALE

Balance sheet and notes

- Disclose a non-current asset classified as held for sale and the assets of a disposal group classified as held for sale separately from other assets in the balance sheet.
- Disclose the liabilities of a disposal group classified as held for sale separately from other liabilities.
- The assets and liabilities of a disposal group may not be offset.
- An analysis should be given, either on the face of the balance sheet or in the notes, of the major classes of assets and liabilities classified as held for sale, except when dealing with a subsidiary that was classified as held for sale at date of acquisition. (Refer to Implementation Guidance to IFRS 5, Example 13.)
- Any cumulative income or expense recognised directly in equity relating to a non-current asset (or disposal group) classified as held for sale, should be disclosed.

- Comparative amounts should not be reclassified or represented to reflect the classification in the balance sheet for the latest period presented.
- The following information should be disclosed in the period in which a non-current asset (or disposal group) has been either classified as held for sale or sold:
  - a description of the non-current asset (or disposal group);
  - a description of the facts and circumstances of the sale;
  - the expected manner and timing of the disposal;
  - the gain or loss recognised on write-off or reversal of an impairment loss and, if not separately presented on the face of the income statement, the line item in the income statement that includes that gain or loss; and
  - if applicable, the segment in which the non-current asset (or disposal group) is presented.

PRESENTATION AND DISCLOSURE – DISCONTINUED OPERATIONS

1. General

- A component of an entity comprises operations and cash flows that can be clearly distinguished, operationally and for financial reporting purposes, from the rest of the entity. In other words, a component of an entity will have been a cash-generating unit or a group of cash-generating units while being held for use.
- A discontinued operation is:
  - a component of an entity that either has been disposed of, or is classified as held for sale; and
  - represents a separate major line of business or geographical area of operations;
  - is part of a single co-ordinated plan to dispose of a separate major line of business or geographical area of operations; or
  - is a subsidiary acquired exclusively with a view to resale.

2. Detail disclosure and presentation

Income statement and notes

- Disclose a single amount on the face of the income statement comprising the total of:
  - the post-tax profit or loss of discontinued operations; and
  - the post-tax impairment losses/reversals recognised on the measurement/ disposal of the assets or disposal group(s) constituting the discontinued operation.
- An analysis of the above-mentioned single amount into:
  - the revenue, expenses and pre-tax profit or loss of discontinued operations;
  - the related income tax expense;
  - the impairment loss/reversal recognised on the measurement/disposal of the assets or disposal group(s) constituting the discontinued operation; and
  - the related income tax expense.
- The analysis may be presented in the notes or on the face of the income statement, in a section identified as relating to discontinued operations.
- Comparative amounts should be restated to reflect the above disclosures.
- Adjustments in the current period relating to amounts previously presented in discontinued operations shall be classified separately in discontinued operations in the current period. The nature and amount of such adjustments shall be disclosed.
- If an entity ceases to classify a component of an entity as held for sale, the results of operations of the component previously presented in discontinued operations shall be reclassified and included in income from continuing operations for all periods presented. It should be indicated that comparative amounts have been restated.

Cash flow statement and notes

- The net cash flows attributable to the operating, investing and financing activities of discontinued operations should be disclosed. These disclosures may be presented either in the notes or on the face of the financial statements.

IFRS 7 *(AC 144)*

Financial Instruments: Disclosure

Not addressed.